DEDICATION

This book is dedicated to those with courage to follow their dreams.
History will show their efforts have not been in vain.

TABLE OF CONTENTS

Acknowledgements ix

Chapter I Conception 1

Chapter II Pursuit 39

Chapter III Acquaintances 64

Chapter IV The Checkride 87

Chapter V The Vial 101

Chapter VI Furlough..121

Chapter VII Putting Out Fires..158

Chapter VIII The American Dream..177

Chapter IX The Glass Ceiling 183

Chapter X Air Wars 204

Chapter XI Going to See Henry..230

Chapter XII Fair Skies 241

Chapter XIII Tip of the Iceberg..261

Chapter XIV The Gauntlet...280

Chapter XV The Stalker 289

Chapter XVI Alarms 325

Chapter XVII The IOEs 353

Chapter XVIII The Final Chapter..359

Epilogue 372

Glossary..379

ACKNOWLEDGEMENTS

Thanks to my friend **Craig T'assainer** for coming up with the name of this book: **Air Affair,** which so aptly describes the contents.

I would like to acknowledge **Karen Dee Rider,** literary agent, for helping me with the tone of the book, getting started writing it, and the first one hundred pages of the initial draft. Distance precluded us from continuing and I turned to **Kate Robinson**, my editorial advisor for eight years. Her patience, encouragement, expertise and speed in perusing my many drafts was inspirational.

Linda and **Tom Russell** offered their expertise with computers. **Ruth Magadini**, writer and artist, for her suggestions, and **Kari Roberson,** WHO HAS WRITTEN MY FOREWORD for encouragement and friendship through the several times the computer processor failed, when I lost my initial drafts and I wasn't sure I could recreate them. With encouragement, I began again.

And my brave husband, **John Knight,** for his support during the difficult times, his encouragement to stick up for myself and my principles, and for his patience when I awoke him every night for ten years while getting up in the wee small hours to work on this manuscript.

CHAPTER I

CONCEPTION

Seattle's airline terminal embraces its parking structure with a bear hug. Crossing the enclosed aerial walkway, rain hammers the glass and big drops spread out distorting the view. Glad to be inside, our wheeled suitcases make bumping sounds as they pass over the floor, pulled along as if they were bodily appendages. The walkway spills us out into the middle of the ticketing area. Looking up, I expect to see the Delta Air Line's marquee which has been there since Western Airlines was acquired in 1986; a dark blue logo replaced the bright red "W," then. Instead, there is nothing but a vacant space where my airline used to be. We pause a moment taking this in, then look up and down the crowded rotunda for indications of where Delta might be. Is Delta even *here* anymore?

We can't see around the curves of the building so I ask a passing security person: "Can you tell me, please, where is Delta?"

"They've moved to the west end," she says with a tentative smile. I gaze at her lips and wonder at the mystery of their expression. She has a distant look in her eyes that makes me wonder if she remembers when Delta was a presence, here, too. We resume our quest, walking, walking, along the crowded facade and I wonder why, when there is so much space in the terminal, there isn't room to pass other travelers without touching?

Finally, we arrive in front of Delta ticketing. Squeezed between two small airlines I've never heard of, I feel my heart begin throbbing. Seattle used to be a large and vibrant base with extensive counter space, but now presents as a small booth in left field; "Delta" is written above it. Five young people work the counter in a plethora of colored contract uniforms. Suddenly, I miss the gray-haired kindness of the Delta Customer Service Representatives, and the people-oriented inquiries of the Red Coats who mixed with passengers, giving answers and directions with confident sophistication. The diagonal sign of "April 30, 2007" sprawls across the Delta crest. The significance of the sign is not lost on me: this is the day Delta emerged from bankruptcy. Absolved of its contracts, it will operate into the future unencumbered by its financial past, but there is one contract Delta will not be able to avoid. It is the most important contract of all...

We connect to Kenmore Air's floatplane for a flight to Campbell River. The water turns from gray to blue as we fly out from under the overcast and into the sunshine. The hills appear as sparkling emeralds washed by the many rain showers of early fall. I gaze out the airplane window with my husband holding my hand, and reminisce my days at Delta. *What became of all the fine people who used to work there? Aren't corporations made of people?* Breathe in, breathe out, lapsing into a reverie of hope, hoping they are doing okay, missing them, feeling the vibration of the Beaver's engine throbbing, coursing like blood through my body.

It was a premiere day, finding myself as the only female in a class of twelve new hire pilots for Western Airlines, but I'd had firsts before. Like an AC/DC sine wave, this day had its ups and downs. I looked around at my eleven classmates, dressed in handsome, varied suits, and admired their maleness. Healthy and smiling with even white teeth, they looked six feet or taller, athletically muscular and built like "V's": broad across the shoulders and narrow at the hips. Their ages ranged from twenty to their late thirties and they *looked* like pilots. Western hired Hollywood-handsome guys, advancing the popular image of what an airline pilot should look like: suave, confident, racy. A presentable female, and of their same relative age, education, and flight experience, I discovered during introductions that I'd logged twice the flight hours of my classmates who were, generally, military trained and had flown less often. At thirty-one, I'd flown professionally in General Aviation for more than twelve years.

At noon one of our instructors, Paul Hendricks, escorted us to the *Wild Hare* for lunch. I should have realized the restaurant's name might have been a portent of things to come. After a morning of Boeing 737 Aircraft Systems slide shows, peppered with full medal beaver shots and dirty jokes ostensibly to keep the boys awake, I was catching the drift, so eating in a place with peanut shells on the floor and getting served pitchers of beer by topless waitresses came as no surprise. I tried to lunch in good humor as if this was nothing new; I'd seen breasts before, though never drooped over sheets of pizza or in connection with a flying job.

What motive could the instructor have in bringing us on our much-anticipated, first day of class, to a place like this to eat? My expectations suffered and though I was embarrassed, I tried not to let my disappointment show. But the little girl inside me withered a bit and I hardly tasted my food. This was a new, rougher game, tawdry even for 1976, and it felt shocking! That my initiation was to be hazing, eventually extending over twenty years of active service, is understated.

My classmates seemed stunned by the instructors' conduct and a couple even apologized for his indiscretions, but charades conducted throughout training on my behalf had them more than a little concerned as we moved collectively from one venue to the next. Had my presence somehow compromised *their* arrival at the airline? I could see it in their faces while we conversed and whenever they looked at me. I saw it in the faces of the staff. They had the same haunted expressions I remembered seeing before, but that was back in 1961.

When the Freedom Riders drove through Marks, Mississippi, it was a hot summer day. I was visiting my Uncle Q Vance, in neighboring Vance, MS., and had come to watch the parade. I stood in a crowd of white people on one side of the street while the blacks stood on the other as the brave little procession drove slowly along the boulevard. Near the edge of the sidewalk in a front row, hot, sweaty bodies rubbed up against me as we inclined fore and aft to see. I saw the black and white faces of the Freedom Riders through the open windows of their car. They passed only feet in front of me. I leaned down for a better look: they were not smiling; their skin was ashen, the color of fear.

I stood up and looked around at the faces of the volatile but inquisitive crowd. What I saw in both black and white faces were the troubled expressions born of uncertainty. History's frame of reference that day was those few minutes indelibly etched in my mind.

Faces of my classmates at Western were just as haunting as those faces in Marks. A reflection of discomfort and anxiety, expressions wrought by enduring change, a reminder of fear of the inevitable, and like it or not, everyone was a part of it. No women were employed as pilots by United States' commercial airlines before the Women's Liberation Movement. It was a long stretch since the Civil Rights Act of 1964 until women were finally hired. I was fortunate to be among the first. Conceiving the idea of becoming a commercial airline pilot was a solitary venture. Though I had no examples to follow, it wasn't something I just pulled out of the air or saw at the movies; my early life was a preface to my career.

Awareness of a world outside my own was a new discovery. Pumping my Schwinn three miles to school while reciting multiplication tables: "Two times two is four, three times three is nine…" I chanted over and over hoping the rhythm would secure the answers in my head. I felt lucky to be riding. My mother often reminded me: "No matter what the weather, *I* walked uphill three miles to school and three miles home each day." *How it could have been uphill each way?*

Scabs covered my knees in a range of colors from dark red to purple. I seldom fell off my bike; the culprit was my roller skates. Those little metal clips attached to the soles of my shoes were forever letting go. Eventually, the sore appearance of my knees brought comments from my dad: "What man will ever marry you with knees like *that*?" His comment disturbed me because he seemed concerned for my potential as a wife. *Aren't I a little young to be worrying about something so far in the future?* I wished I could ask, discuss with him that I wasn't interested in being a wife, but I dared not seem impudent.

Chastened by parents and educators for having a precocious nature and an adventuring spirit that might compromise what was viewed as the current appeal, what lingered was angst about altering my behavior for boys who someday may or may not choose me because of something so insignificant as the appearance of my knees! I questioned the importance of women at all if visualization was all that mattered. But not to be chosen was a concern, and I decided to avoid this situation by making certain that *I* would be the one to choose.

✈

When my family sailed for Anchorage I was in the middle of third grade and viewed the world through hazel eyes and a cloud of sunny curls. Holding onto a rail of the *Thomas Jefferson,* I watched as the bay cities got smaller. We sailed out from under the Golden Gate and I ran up stairs to the top deck to get closer to the bridge. It passed some distance overhead and the sea lions barked from the pillars as we passed. We sailed on toward the Farallon Islands where the bow of the ship began rising and falling on the swells. Green and white water spilled off the sides and spray filled the air. I leaned fore and aft developing my sea legs, and wondered what extreme weather would do if this was what was considered good. I put this question aside, rode the rhythmic swells, and eagerly anticipated finding Alaska just over the far horizon.

I practiced ballet in the vacant ballroom, and spent time reading to Lassie in her large doghouse tethered to the aft portion of the upper deck. During frequent winter storms, we snuggled together and I read to her from *Black Beauty.* She had the area entirely to herself as the only dog aboard. She was not allowed below decks, and I was glad for her heavy coat that kept her warm through high seas, strong winds, and cold February temperatures.

"Next to you, Lassie, I love horses most of all," I murmured, dreaming of pony rides I'd taken. The ponies were paint or palomino, or black with flowing manes and long white tails. It was years before my parents disclosed that to avoid them they drove miles out of the way. When we happened on one, I admired them with such yearning that, exasperated, my parents would stop so I could ride. My passion for horses developed at an early age. I dreamed not of the day when I'd grow up and have children as my sister did, but of the day when I could have horses in numbers. No wonder my mother was always saying, "*Horse* is your middle name!"

I managed to remain intact on the rolling seas until I got to the part about Black Beauty again finding Ginger. I felt so sad I cried. Tears upset my stomach. Before I realized what was happening, I was seasick.

When Dad saw my red eyes and tear streaked face: "It's only a story..."

"Yes, but such a sad one."

"So sad it makes you seasick?"

"I can't help it. Once I start crying, I get sick." I'd never felt this way before. The power of words invoked impressive emotion and I began writing sketches and stories, later saving them in a hope chest given one birthday by my paternal grandmother, Ann, and intended for nuptial treasures. My feelings and stories were safely sequestered there.

Winter storms made for a rough passage across the Gulf of Alaska that week. Even some of the crew was seen hanging over the rail while our ship pitched through waves so high they broke over the bow. Green water cascaded across the porthole windows, and the only safety was in sitting down. When we sailed into Cook Inlet, water frozen to the ship's lines and adhering to the decks gave us a ghostly appearance as if we were a phantom ship from some Alfred Hitchcock story.

We stepped on shore Alaska, mooring our merchant ship in Anchorage harbor which was dug out like a bathtub for ships to remain afloat as the world's highest tidal bore, after the Moncton Bore, came and went each day. With an average flood of more than twenty feet, when the water vacated the harbor, iceberg solitaires from distant Portage Glacier proved a surreal contrast to the ocean floor.

✈

Next day, we changed to rail. En route to Fairbanks, we were treated to splendid views of Alaska's interior, winding through the mountains in and around Mt. McKinley. I wandered the nearly empty train during the twelve hour ride and found myself alone in a cargo car with piles of *Mad Magazine* stacked against the walls. I probably wasn't supposed to be there but the draw of the comics and fresh air from the open sliding doors was too much to resist. *Clickety clack clikety clack.* The deafening sound of the wind going by, the tortuous motion of the train, and *Mad Magazine's* bright, garish pictures made me woozy. There were a lot of words I hadn't seen before and I had to sound them out, but the inferences were clear. I inhaled the fresh air and felt better.

The train slowed. There, framed in the opening of the door, was a woman feeding a moose in a Ramada. The animal towered over her with antlers like a broad wooden umbrella. I was so captivated by this scene I didn't realize that suddenly the conductor was leaning over me. His hands were on his knees. "Raised him from a newborn after finding him beside his dead mother," he shouted to be heard. "Nearly starved, she took him in. Now he's grown and comes every day to be fed when he hears the train coming."

My lips smiled at this information, but inside, I felt alarmed by this presence. The conductor's body radiated heat. He leaned close to my ear and lowered his voice. I felt his hot breath against my cheek: "It lets us have a chance to enjoy their special relationship, even though there is only one animal more dangerous..."

I turned slowly toward him; my gaze focused on his mouth. Stained teeth were mostly hidden by his dark and heavy moustache. Litter stuck in the hairs and his breath was ripe with pipe smoke and something else. His eyes glittered and grew larger.

Quickly, I replaced *Mad Magazine* on a stack and scrambled for the door. Passionately, I hoped he wouldn't grab me though I could almost feel his grasp. If his mission was to scare me from the car, he'd been successful. I jumped through the door toward the next car, traversing the open space of the moving platform with a frightened leap. What if I misunderstood his intentions and they were nothing more than what happened? Leaning against the wall, I closed my eyes a moment to still my wild heart. I decided to forego mentioning this, I wasn't supposed to be exploring the train anyway, and a distortion of the event might be unfortunate for the conductor.

We were met by two army staff cars at the Fairbanks train station for the hundred-mile ride to Delta Junction and our new home. Alaska greeted us greenhorn Cheechakos with its coldest winter weather. The thermometer plunged and stayed between 48 and 55 degrees below zero for nearly two weeks after our arrival, and given no chance to venture out in the deep cold, I could hardly wait to explore. From our cabin windows I watched as snow blew around like sawdust. The air was so dry that moisture disappeared, leaving snowflakes shining and silvery. Snow piled up against the cabin walls and solidified in tall drifts. When we were finally allowed outside to play, the drifts were so crusty we could walk on top.

At the tender age of nine, I found myself living in a one-room log cabin near the settlement of Big Delta, not far from the Yukon border. There was no housing other than a bachelor officer quarters on the post where Dad lived for six months before our arrival. There were few dependents here and my family was one of the first ancillary to move to this outpost. Dad told me Big Delta was chosen as the Army's Cold Weather Test Station because it had the coldest temperatures and fastest wind speeds in North America. Situated on a high plain, the Brooks and Alaska Mountain Ranges offered year-round snowy views. Abundant trees, meadows, creeks and streams made the environment ideal for wildlife. Years before, the park service moved bison here from the lower forty-eight states. They thrived, grazing like cows, and seemed to be everywhere. We had to drive around them in our yard to park near our cabin.

We arrived to find our home in the wilderness, fourteen miles from civilization and without the amenities of running water, indoor plumbing, or a telephone. Dad was happy and full of smiles. "We're together again. It'll be a lot of fun, a new adventure!" He was pleased to have found an accommodation that made our presence possible, our family circle complete.

My mother was wide-eyed and pale, as the second front door past the long and narrow vestibule where we would hang our heavy clothes, swung open to reveal six army cots, a table, and six chairs. "Oh my, it's rather plain," she moaned. We'd been advised luxury was unnecessary on the last frontier. This was so different from our attractive home in California. Had she envisioned living in some idyllic setting? Without her lovely furniture, how could she have imagined something other than a spartan existence?

Once situated in these close quarters, I became a reluctant witness to my parents' relationship. Mine was a front row seat by proximity, with little hope of escape. I tried understanding what went on between them. In the restricted space of our cabin walls I watched them banter back and forth much as a fan watches a tennis match, my head turning left to right and back again. I found him straightforward and clear while she was mysterious and confusing. He was patient and without exasperation. I found these qualities admirable.

Over time, observing her behavior, I knew I *couldn't* be like her. I didn't *want* to be like her. She was my father's chattel, just as we were his dependent children. Why else would she act so beguiling? Had she forgotten her UC Berkeley and Oakland Art School education? She used her feminine wiles to advantage and my father regularly fell, unwitting, into her traps.

Everything she said to him seemed to have more than one meaning. If he commented on one topic, she addressed another. "You have to be adept at the double entendre if you want to have a successful marriage," she advised, presumably delivering one of her marital secrets though all it did was help me put together the bottom line: I wanted to be like my dad and not like my mom. I knew she loved him and only maneuvered for position, but if these were feminine ways, I wanted no part, and wondered, *why act differently than the person you are?*

I liked my dad and couldn't help but contrast my mother's behavior with my own. I felt open and genuine. He responded with warmth and affection, happy to have me around. Vaguely aware I was creating my own political craft, I found her watching me from the corners of her eyes as if she wasn't sure what I was doing, if I was doing anything at all. This contrast in our behavior estranged us, and I was often uncomfortable in her presence.

✈

We had propane gas for heating, powering a cooking stove, and running the refrigerator. It was strange how such a cold place necessitated having a refrigerator to keep things *from* freezing. Instead of the idyllic cache on stilts of pictofame, we used what was available: discarded army trunk lockers. *For* freezing game and berries and protecting them from the occasional raid, we hacked away at the permafrost along the base of the cabin, digging out a trench to lay-in the trunks. Below eight inches the ground never thawed.

Dad chopped logs with an axe nearly as long as I was tall. Then I chopped them into smaller ones by choking up on the handle. Careful to keep my toes clear, my classmate Tommy Fuller missed his swing and cut his left foot like a "V." He lost some of his toes and was a bloody mess when his mom found him. Nearly unconscious, she sealed the wound with a burning log from the fire and then he did lose consciousness. Because it took so long to find a doctor, his foot didn't heal right. When I saw him in school he limped and had trouble keeping his balance. He acted unhappy, sat apart from the rest of us, and frowned most of the time.

As part of my chores, each night I built a large fire outside the cabin. Sometimes I stacked the wood like a teepee and other times in the shape of a square before putting a match to the tinder. "It should take only one match to start a fire," Dad said. So I tried to start fires, even in the wind, with just one. I heated water for dishwashing and bathing my baby brothers. Dad got to shower at the BOQ on the army post. Once a week, using the same water, we bathed in a galvanized tub placed in the center of the room. With little privacy for a pubescent girl, I huddled, and hurried through my baths amid stares and teasing.

We hauled water from the Post in five-gallon jerry cans carried in the trunk of our red and black '52 Roadmaster Buick shipped from the States. The stylish car had four silver holes on each side of the hood. Dad said it was modern and had a dynaflow transmission. It was parked just outside the front door and plugged into a head bolt heater so it would start on cold mornings.

When running to the outhouse meant braving the elements, we stayed indoors and used a "honey bucket." Kept inside as contingency and perched at the side of the room, it was a large, hollow, porcelain affair resembling a throne. Dad emptied the honey bucket somewhere every day. Discovering it had nothing at all to do with honey was an amusing twist and one of the ironies of life in Alaska.

✈

Joking that political misfits were sent to an outpost called Fort Huachuca, Dad loved to tease a friend saying that someday he would find himself there. "Let's play a joke, have some fun," friend said before a welcoming party for the new post commander. Friend, who loved a practical joke, rigged up a speaker down the hole of our outhouse. He waited until the colonel's wife was assumed comfortably seated, then announced with all gathered at the window to see: "Could you hold it a moment please, Madam? We're down here painting." We all laughed.

In a heartbeat the outhouse door flew open and the colonel's wife jumped out. Her trousers hung on one leg and she stabbed her foot at the hole of the other as she began running. She tripped and somersaulted and the joke became a spectacle more explicit than friend anticipated. The broad moon of her bottom going round contrasted with the carpet of green moss. It was terribly embarrassing for me to witness, and I was only a bystander. I felt sorry for the colonel's wife. Laughter silenced as she looked up to see us gathered at the window. Her face smudged, her expression began with surprise and quickly transformed through embarrassment to anger. She and the colonel didn't stay long at the party. To our dismay, Dad reported that friend was being transferred to Fort Huachuca, another climatic extreme in the southern Arizona desert.

✈

My pretty, dark-haired mother developed a bad condition: skin peeled off her hands in thick layers, leaving them raw. They were painful to use, and as the oldest of her four children, chores involving water fell to me. I knew the dishes were waiting as I climbed down the ladder of the army personnel carrier that took my little sister and me to and from school.

"I'm sorry you have to help so much."

"It's OK, I don't mind." I knew the work had to be done. I looked out the windows at the mountains and sky, and dreamed of other things. There just had to be more to life than washing dishes, changing diapers, and ironing. If this was what I had to look forward to as a woman, life hardly seemed worth living.

When I spoke to her, my eyes dropped to her sore and sometimes bleeding hands. I wondered if her frustration was manifest there. Blue veins showed through translucent skin. She was scaly like a fish. It would have been better if she wore gloves, then we wouldn't be reminded of how much she didn't want to be in Alaska. My heart seized every time she said: "My mother would roll over in her grave if she could see the way we're living now! Why, our family came to America on the *Ark and the Dove*, descended from Lord Baltimore and William the Conqueror."

Oh, not this again.

"We shouldn't be living in such primitive conditions!"

I thought we were living well on the last frontier, having a great adventure, building character. I wished she didn't confide these things to me. Did she mistake my willing nature for naïveté? It would have been a conflict if she gave it any thought because my grades were good and I was a year ahead in school.

✈

On Saturdays, Dad heated up oil and spark plugs for the generator and ran the hundred yards to an underground shack with the smoking pan. If it wasn't too cold, the generator started. Some days he spent half a day cranking. Occasionally his efforts were futile. It was just too cold. But when it started, we had electricity. Above the dinner table, a single light socket had an outlet for a cord. Powered, I helped with ironing for the week.

During the winter, it was dark most of our waking hours. The sun made a shallow arc low on the horizon for a ten a.m. sunrise and a two p.m. sunset. There weren't many hours for outdoor activity because it was dark so much of the time. But I was an outdoors girl and explored in the dim light with Lassie at my side. After cutting wood and building a fire it was time to come inside. When supper dishes were done, I did homework by kerosene lantern.

Lessons were taught in a Territorial school, first through the twelfth grades in one room. Some might have thought this arrangement awkward, but there were only a few students in each class. I thought this arrangement advantageous, and listened carefully to the older kids' lessons. Alaska teachers were versatile, teaching all subjects. My favorite was Alaska History. It titillated me to learn about the early days when it was Russia's domain. It seemed strange we were studying about the Russians in a favorable way when I knew Dad's job was developing and testing weapons to use against them. I didn't tell him that my teacher, Miss Patruska, was of Russian descent as I feared it might bring trouble. Because this was happening in Alaska must be the reason they called it the *Cold War*.

Television hadn't come to Alaska, though to some people it seemed nearly as important as statehood. To pass time we played Scrabble and Chess. I sent away for books about faraway places: *Bomba the Jungle Boy, Gunga Din, Marco Polo*. Wistfully, I turned each page, longed to travel someday, and see how other people were.

Fourteen miles away at the Post, Dad was in charge of research and development of missiles and rockets. He wore a special type of clothing he called *arctic gear*. He and his troops spent time lying around in rivers in thermal suits and driving through the wilderness in enclosed all-terrain vehicles called Weasels and Otters. When they weren't threading their way through dense fir and pine forests, they roared across meadows, bouncing off grass tussocks stacked like peat moss. When they fired Honest John Rockets at the range miles away, the noise echoed through valleys and mountain passes sounding like avalanches.

Mountaineers came to climb the vertical faces of the Alaska and Brooks Ranges. I visualized climbing the rugged peaks we saw from our cabin windows. I heard about a bush pilot named Don Sheldon. His expertise extended to include glacier flying. He staged or rescued parties of climbers by using glaciers as landing fields. Wadded newspapers soaked in kerosene lighted marked runways at night as he flew in and out around the clock. Independent climbing expeditions and the army's mountain climbing school employed his services to ascend peaks of nearby statuesque mountains Fremont and Deborah before attempting Mount McKinley.

The Athabascan Indians call McKinley *Denali*. Most mountaineers considered Denali only practice for Everest and K-2; perhaps climbing a lesser mountain deceived them. But weather, arctic weather, posed the greatest threat to climbing and was, time after time, revealed as the culprit when things went wrong. Whole expeditions were lost. In 1952, a report transmitted over the crystal radio Dad and I built portrayed the drama of a Japanese climbing expedition. Composed of thirteen women, to my horror, the expedition was lost on the high slopes of Denali in a violent spring storm. Sometimes the wind roared like a freight train around the peaks at more than a hundred miles per hour. To measure howling cold air, part of nature's bounty and moving at such ferocity seemed incredible. These lost women joined others entombed in snowfields and icy crevasses. One day their bodies might appear at the foot of a glacier pushed out onto a plain of silt, but it wouldn't be anytime soon.

Excitement expressed in local news fliers reported first, the discovery of a Wooly Mammoth, then an ancient Ice Man found preserved in nearby glaciers. These accounts were stimulating. What other wonders lay captive beneath the ice? I wrote *Face in the Ice*, a youthful speculation of these accounts written by flashlight under the bedcovers, and read to my fourth grade classmates at recess. They hadn't heard or ever imagined such things, and listened, wide-eyed.

The way hoar frost formed after a cold snap was exquisite. Icy fingers decorated the reds of willow bushes growing in creeks along the Alaska Highway. In recognition of the joint construction effort between Alaska and Canada during the Second World War, the highway was previously called the *AlCan* and extended from the northern U.S. border through Canada to Alaska. It went through our region of Big Delta, passed in front of our house, and terminated another hundred miles further north in Fairbanks. Delta Junction was the settlement of some 75 people at the intersection of the Alaska and Richardson Highways.

Ice crystals locked to willow branches shone in the sunshine and threw dots of color on the snow along the Richardson Highway, where food and supplies were trucked 350 miles northeast from Anchorage through the interior of Alaska. Peripheral to winter, a transport of food could be frozen and thawed, frozen and thawed, sitting on loading docks only to be frozen again. Fresh foods arrived often inedible, and scurvy was common as diets lacked Vitamin C. To avoid this health problem, we planted a garden during the short summer. The rich black soil in the Land of the Midnight Sun produced heads of lettuce the size of basketballs and string beans a foot long nearly overnight!

Eating wild berries was another source of Vitamin C, and gathering berries became a favorite outing. When school recessed for summer and days were long, we went strawberry hunting along creeks. Often there was a sudden cold breeze sweeping down from the mountains, making me wish I'd worn the exquisite fur parka, one of a set that Dad surprised my sister and me with for Christmas. They had black and white rabbit skins arranged in an attractive pattern and edged in caribou. The sewn-in tags at the inside of the collars said, "Made by Eskimos in Pt. Barrow and *chewed* into shape." I read this tag every time I put on the jacket and was sure they meant to have sewn it on their moccasins. With hoods outlined by a wolf ruff and a gray satin lining, they were warm and functional, soft and beautiful. In warm weather they were stored in our winter closet. Though the card had said "From Santa," I suspected Dad found them on one of his trips north to Pt. Barrow.

One day while hunting for berries, my sister and I wore our gaily-colored light parkas. Like spring flowers, we were easy to see. Unzipped and hanging off our shoulders, we endured their flapping, knowing we might need them during cool afternoon breezes. We found raspberries, blackberries, and strawberries growing in patches nearby and in the fall there were so many cranberries that they made a red and green carpet under our feet.

My favorites were blueberries. They were enormous, as big as small mushrooms, and oh! so pungent, but in a sweet way. They grew on bushes in something called a *draw*. To an artist, a draw might look like creases sketched to define hillsides. We spent hours picking and eating, eating and picking. It was hard to keep our buckets full. After awhile, we were full and tired, and lay down in the tall grasses to nap in the sunshine.

As the sun moved across the sky and the day grew long, the temperature became slightly cooler and we awoke to resume our picking. Hearing a twig crack, I turned from a laden bush to suddenly face a grizzly bear. He was maybe forty feet away and just as surprised to see me as I was to see him. I nudged my sister and pointed in the bear's direction.

> "We must be downwind. He can't seem to smell us. Maybe he isn't sure what we are..." When she saw him, she started sniffing and crying softly: "I didn't want to come today..."

"I'm sorry," I said, trying to comfort her. I felt like doing anything but crying. I was scared, but as the big sister, I felt responsible. That bear was so big... I felt so small. Lassie started barking as the bear rose to his full two-legged height. Statuesque, he towered above the blueberry bushes. His dark eyes pierced the distance; he never moved his focus from us. Saliva hung in strings from his snout. His mouth opened, revealing large yellow teeth. We watched, gripped by this presence. I took my sister's cold little hand.

He tilted his head back and sniffed the air several times. I decided to make the first aggressive move. With a loud scream I threw our jackets and buckets full of berries in his direction and took off running dragging my sister by the hand. For many yards her five-year-old feet never touched the ground. Lassie kept barking as we ran for our lives.

I was afraid to look back because I knew that bear was right behind us. I could feel his breath and hear his great weight pounding the ground. *Ka thump. Ka thump.* We ran and ran. *How close is he? I'm a fast runner but a bear is a very fast runner. Why hasn't he caught us?* Out of breath and bewildered, I ventured a look over my shoulder. He had dropped to all fours and was, for some fortunate reason, loping away up a hill in the opposite direction. After this encounter I was never at ease picking blueberries. I felt threatened every moment

I spent in a draw. I always looked over my shoulder for *that* bear. Is it any wonder blueberries taste so bittersweet?

✈

I was the oldest child with my sister and two brothers to follow, and naturally in command, but an unfortunate rift developed between my sister and me. Before this fateful day, she was sweet and dear to me as any strawberry blonde sister could be. Her soft pink skin sunburned easily and when this happened, her freckles turned chartreuse. Her baby teeth exuded charm when she smiled. We were such a contrast, my dark hair to her fair. Though we were different as night and day, our names were similar, mine *Bliss* and hers *Gay*.

One Saturday, we three oldest children were dropped off at a ski hill just outside the Post while Mother went to the grocery store with our baby brother, Doug. He was too little - a babe in arms - to go sledding with us that frosty morning. I pulled the sled up the long hill with my siblings on it. Occasionally, I asked Gay to get off and walk as I was out of breath and steamy hot in my parka, even though it was an average twenty-five below zero day.

"It's strange there aren't any other skiers. Not even buffalo grazing at the bottom. The hill's deserted," I commented as we trekked. "Oh, well, no big wooly bodies to steer around." I laughed at the image. There weren't any rope tows or ski lifts. If you wanted to get to the top, you walked. That day, because the powder was fresh and deep, it was slow going, making the hill seem more like a mountain. Nearly an hour later, we arrived on top.

The view was endless, with clouds topping the Alaska Mountain range in gray continuity. Tall firs, their branches laden with snow from the night before, clustered on hillsides. We three sat astride to ride: Gay in front, me in the middle, and Greg in back. I steered better with the sled balanced this way.

Looking down the long hill, the panorama offered a variety of routes: wide runs clear of trees, narrow trails with lots of trees, and twisting, turning ways to go. Our Saturdays were like this whenever Mother went to the grocery store. We pushed off with our feet and got started downhill by bumping up and down with our bottoms. Soon the sled moved easily through the powder. *Shuusssh.*

Down we went through a stand of trees. The trunks stood close together but the branches were far above the ground. I steered, trying to stay on the narrow trail. *Bummmfff!* We slowed in the deep powder because Gay got her foot stuck in the forward slot of the "T" steerage and it dragged just enough to hinder our forward motion.

"Get your foot back up on the sled or we'll get stuck!"

"There isn't room on this sled for all of us!" As she struggled to pull her size four boot out of a size three slot, she stuck her other leg out straight to the side. Free, we accelerated, steering this way and that through the trees, and then... *Smaaaaccck!* Her straight leg struck the trunk of a thick tree. The sled stopped abruptly and we all rolled off into the snow. I checked Greg. He wasn't hurt, just disappointed the ride stopped. Then I looked at Gay. She lay still in the snow, her round little girl face patterned in pain, her cheeks very red.

"Are you hurt?"

"My leg..." she whimpered.

"See if you can stand on it." I helped her to her feet. She tried to put weight on her leg to take a step. Her face lost all color. "Ohhhhh," she moaned and fell backward, collapsing into the snow.

"Oh, you really aren't pretending." I hoped she was because if she wasn't we had a problem. Though I'd thought she might be pretending, in my heart I knew she wasn't. All the color left her face. Her leg was either sprained or broken, and I caused it. I felt terrible.

"Gosh, you've really hurt your leg. Here, stretch out on the sled, lean against Greg, and I'll pull you the rest of the way down the hill."

After a bit, I took off my parka and put it over her legs, hoping it might keep her warm. Our little procession slid this way and that down the trail toward the base of the hill.

"Too heavy, you're too heavy," Greg said to Gay, who was considerably larger than he. "Off. Get off," he said, pushing her aside.

"Oh, great, here, I'll piggyback you. Get on." His little three year frame climbed on my back and we continued down the hill. The snow was too deep for him to walk, and I was anxious about my sister. I hurried to reach the bottom of the hill. Gay was not moving or saying much. I wondered how far it was to the infirmary on the Post...

Suddenly, out of the trees with a "*whoooosssh*" came - of all people - my fourth grade teacher. She had a man with her. He must be her date.

"Hello, Miss Patruska," I said, looking up at her face and trying, uncomfortably to smile. I needed to ask for a favor. *Ohhh, boy, now she'll make me clean erasers for a week after class but I have to take that risk and ask for a ride in her car.*

"Hello, Bliss." She looked at us and her gaze settled on Gay: "What's wrong with your little sister?"

"We were sledding and she hit her leg on a tree." We looked at Gay lying on the sled. She was pale and not talking. I'd only known her to be pink and talking. Both kneeled to take a closer look. We were quiet, waiting for an adult conclusion. To allay any doubt as to how tired I was, I asked: "How far is it to the infirmary?"

Her date, the lieutenant - I knew he was a lieutenant because Dad taught me to tell rank and this man had a single gold bar on the front flap of his arctic hat - said: "It's about three miles to the infirmary. How about we give your sister a ride?"

"That would be good. You can get her there faster in a car than I can on the sled. I'm afraid her leg is hurt and now she's gotten cold."

"Where are your parents?"

"Dad is out on maneuvers and our mother left us here to sled while she's grocery shopping."

The pair skied on down the hill to get the car. I continued walking downhill with Greg on my back. It would've been easier to ride the sled but there wasn't any room; she wasn't able to sit up because of the pain. I pulled the sled over to the car. It had only a front seat - no back seat. My heart tightened a little knowing that only Gay would ride.

They loaded my sister between them and supported her leg on the dashboard. Greg and I stood by the sled. As they drove away, the car suddenly stopped and the driver door opened. The lieutenant held out my parka. "Here, you might need this." Then he slammed the door shut and drove away spinning his tires on the ice. I kept looking after them, expecting them to roll down a window and announce they'd be back for us, but they didn't. Greg and I would walk. Or, I would walk pulling the sled and Greg would ride. The car got smaller and began to look like a beetle crawling along a silver ribbon floating over a black and white meadow.

The road was deserted and icy. The sled slid easily, but traction was difficult. I had to move my feet quickly to keep from falling. After shuffling along in silence - it was so quiet the only sound was my snowsuit pants brushing back and forth, back and forth - we passed a sign: "Infirmary: 3 miles."

"If this road wasn't so flat this would be easier," I said with some exasperation. "Maybe we'll find Mommy coming the other way," I tried to hearten myself. There was no comment from Greg; he was quiet, as usual.

Quite some time later while Greg nodded in sleep, the infirmary came into view at the other end of the road. A car came towards us. It was the dark beetle and the lieutenant was driving. When he recognized our procession he rolled down his window and stuck his head out. As he began talking his face disappeared in a cloud of steam. "Hop in. I'll drive you the rest of the way." Then he got out and tied our sled to the rear bumper.

It was warm inside the car. I appreciated the ride and told him so, even though it was short and our walk had been long. "Your sister's leg has multiple fractures," he explained as we pulled up to the front door of the infirmary. "We called your mother at the grocery store. She should be here soon."

Multiple fractures, I guess that means her leg is broken in more than one place. She will never forgive me for making her stand on it. I felt awful.

After her accident, the medical attention, ambulances to Fairbanks, hospital stays, missed school, casts put on and then taken off by large, rotating saws that might've cut her but didn't, she changed. Because of my inability to protect her, her sweetness and sensitivity were compromised by life's harshness. She became a whirling fancy, and gave pause to even my lively brothers who stayed out of her way and quietly labeled her *Auntie Hurricane.*

Dad spent his spare time hunting and fishing to stock our freezers. He often asked if I'd like to come along and I loved the adventure. "It's good to learn about surviving in the wilderness," he'd say, "Living by one's wits." He taught me how to tie flies, track animals, and shoot birds. I was getting better with a bow and arrow, and could quickly throw a knife at a tree from ten feet and usually made it stick. I learned to gut a Caribou by watching. It wasn't much different than cleaning rabbits except the innards were bigger. Laying them out on the snow - the blood a dark blotch and a stark contrast to pure white - we identified each organ.

At first we used shotguns, but the twelve gauge had such a big kick, it knocked me backwards, so Dad had me use the smaller twenty gauge. Of all the game we ate, and game was what we ate, my favorite was a crafty little bird called a Ptarmigan. "Spelled with a silent 'pee' as in swimming, Dad teased. Ptarmigan were plump and sumptuous and mostly dark meat. Cleverly disguised to blend with foliage in summer colors of brown and russet, they'd turn to winter white with the change of season.

When we cleaned the birds, finding all the bb shot was important as Dad had broken a molar and there were no dentists. "We should be shooting .22's. First, we'll scare them into the air, it's only fair, then with a single shot, we'll shoot their heads off." Though our marksmanship measurably improved, Ptarmigan, with their tiny little heads, became a delicacy.

Sometimes we flew into the wilderness with bush pilots who landed in front of our cabin. Other times, we hiked or skied, our guns carried in slings across our backs. We used a version of the Eskimo sled called an *Akio*, an oval saucer pulled with a bridle. The army didn't use whalebone for the sled as the Eskimos did; it used fiberglass for the structure and rope for the bridle.

One December day, we checked out a Weasel from the motor pool and went moose hunting. Designed as a personnel transport, it looked like a Snowcat and carried three passengers and a driver but didn't have a gun. Provisioned for a few extra arctic nights in the event we got stuck somewhere, we left an itinerary with the Military Police, and departed.

Dad let me drive once we were out of sight of the post. It couldn't have been more fun! The vehicle had handles for steering that moved back and forth instead of a wheel. The Weasel went anywhere, straight up or down. We zoomed across wet meadows, through forests, up, onto, and over trees. After we passed, they'd spring back upright again.

Hunting season ended New Year's Eve. It was early December, and we were twenty miles southwest of the post following moose prints through fresh powder. Accidentally, I drove over a downed tree at just the angle to wedge the trunk into the Weasel's tread. With a loud snapping sound, it flew off and landed in the trees. Now, we weren't going anywhere! We climbed out to assess the situation. Walking was out of the question, with snow waist deep for Dad and he was tall. At ten years old, I barely came up to his shirt pocket.

Immobile and resigned, we made camp. Pitching our arctic sleeping bags of double goose-down into the snow, we used one side of the Weasel to support a lean-to of canvas tarpaulins. We looked for dry wood under the snow-laden boughs of trees. We started a fire in the clearing opposite the open end of our lean-to and once it was roaring we added green branches, as it was so hot it would burn *anything*.

Tired from the exertion of setting up camp, we climbed into our sleeping bags with our clothes on and ate a dinner of Mom's stew, kept warm in a large thermos. It was dark early as it always is when Alaska tips away from the sun during the winter zenith. "Everything looks better in the morning," Dad said. "I'll keep watch on the fire to make sure it burns through the night."

The moon was a silver disc in a violet sky; stars brightened, a contrast in illumination. The Northern Lights pulsated the atmosphere into golden waves near the horizon. I could hear wolves calling to each other but they seemed a long way off. They sounded as if they were relaying messages rather than howling. Hands under my head, I scanned the heavens. Nothing appeared to move across the sky. The Big Dipper floated just above the horizon with its eight stars. Warm in my sleeping bag, I drifted away with the vague realization that the wolf calls seemed to be getting louder. Were they moving just beyond the perimeter of our campfire at the edge of my sleep? Through the night, I awakened now and again when I heard the fire crackling as Dad added wood to the embers. I checked the position of the Big Dipper: dreamlike, it waltzed in slow revolution around the North Star.

Next morning I opened my eyes to bright sunshine and ice fog hanging low in the trees, a clue to how cold it was. Moisture frozen into ice crystals, the particles sparkled with color and danced in the air. There was no noise; everything was still except for the crackling of new logs added to the fire.

"Gooood morning!" Dad greeted me when he saw I was awake. "It's a beeeautiiful day in Alaska... though it's pretty cold." He rubbed his hands together inside his gloves. When the fire was burning well and the heat radiated off my cheeks, I crawled out of my sleeping bag, still in yesterday's clothes. The intensity of the cold hit me! It was *cold,* so cold that my eyeballs immediately felt icy and dull as if they were too big for their sockets. Why, it was easier to turn my head than to move my eyes!

"How cold is it?" Impressed by how the low temperature felt, I quickly bundled into my parka and gloves. Being a scientific type, Dad had not only a thermometer inserted in a silver tube and clipped to his breast pocket, but a compass around his neck. So we would know elevation, he also anchored an altimeter to the Weasel's dashboard.

"Let's see how cold it is," he said, unscrewing the top of the tube and pulling the thermometer out of its case. He adjusted the instrument by turning it slightly this way and that to get a better look at the mercury. He either couldn't see the numbers or didn't believe what he read. He took off his glasses. Holding them between his teeth by a wand and peering at the numbers for what seemed a long time, I waited expectantly under the scarf tied across my face as a barrier to the cold, hoping for a record temperature.

"Wow! Seventy-eight below zero. Coldest temperature I've ever experienced."

This said something as Dad was always out in the cold, testing.

"Me, too," I added, and wondered how cold too cold was. My bulbous lips made talking difficult. A mental flash of my frozen body in snow gear passed before my eyes. No wonder it was easier to turn our heads than to move our eyes. In spite of our heavy arctic clothing my joints ached with the news. Extremities like fingers, toes and nose suddenly felt colder. The time spent out of my gloves would be no more than seconds. "Making breakfast won't be easy in these big gloves."

"We'll give 'er a try in a few minutes after the fire burns down to coals." We waded into the snow in opposite directions, disappearing into the trees for privacy to attend our morning constitutionals. I didn't want to expose my bare skin to these elements, but I'd waited all night and couldn't wait any longer. The cold air hit my bottom with a *whack*! After only a few seconds my cheeks were numb. As I gazed around, I noticed large paw prints everywhere in the snow.

We met again at the fire with the same conclusions. It was *really* cold and wolves had circled us all night, a discovery that made me shiver. "The snow is beaten down in a trail all the way around our camp, Dad."

"I know," he replied thoughtfully, and warmed his outstretched hands over the fire alongside mine. "There may be a half dozen or more. It's hard to tell because there're so many tracks."

"They're probably pretty hungry. With such deep snow it must be hard to find things to eat." For a moment, a tiny moment, I felt sorry for the wolves, though quickly relented when I visualized getting eaten.

"Arctic hares live under the snow. Somehow the wolves must be able to smell them." Dad climbed into the Weasel to retrieve our food storage boxes, handing them out to me. I arranged them in the snow. "A good roaring fire will keep them away," he said, smiling optimistically in my direction. He always had an optimistic smile. "And I left them a tall yellow stem to mark our territory," he chuckled.

I remember I smiled though I wasn't quite sure what he meant. Had he tried to scare the wolves some way? When he saw my questioning look he sat down and began telling a story about "yellow stems." I was vaguely aware of their presence though hadn't given them much thought.

They bordered a path through woods from the barracks to the Enlisted Men's Club on the Post. When we wanted to go to the movies we parked in the barracks parking lot and walked two hundred yards because the theater was in heavy trees and the barracks stood in a clearing. Children going to matinees were let out of cars to walk, unescorted, along the path. I'd seen the yellow stems protruding through the snow along the periphery of the path. They seemed to multiply through the winter. They were never mentioned before and I'd seen them nowhere else.

I recalled that walking towards the theater there were not so many stems on the right side of the path. Those that were there, leaned fore, but walking away from the theater they flourished, and leaned aft. Admittedly, not knowing what they were left me with questions. Could they be some discolored arctic icicles? They had weird shapes: some were curly and others were straight. Some were long and skinny, and others were short and thick.

Most weekends my family attended an evening movie, and if the landscape was bathed in moonlight, the yellow stems shined like gold and looked surreal. Were they an aberration of the arctic night? Sticking out of the snow at differing angles, no one spoke of the obvious. I assumed they were something taboo since they were never mentioned, but exactly how they got there and what they were remained a mystery until Dad's story.

"When the new post commander walked on the path through the area," Dad began, "he inquired of his executive officer: 'What are these tall yellow stems sticking up through the snow, some kind of arctic flower?'

The executive officer replied with a snort: 'No, sir, colonel, these yellow stems are beer stems.' When the colonel didn't answer, he continued: 'There's a contest among the men to see who can...' But he didn't finish his story when he saw the colonel's expression. The executive officer abruptly realized the new commander was not amused. The colonel paused a moment to gaze at the tarnished icicles. He stood looking at a particularly large one. 'The barracks are this way, sir, the exec pointed in one direction, and the NCO Club and movies are that way,' he said, pointing in the other. 'There isn't much for the men to do...' He was hesitant to be part of removing fun from a place that didn't have much.

The colonel stopped again and regarded the crop. 'To go to the movie theater a person has to walk along this path?'

'Yes, sir, there's no other way. Cars can't get any closer.'

The colonel kind of gasped. Maybe he envisioned taking his wife to the movies and having to explain the yellow stems. His expression changed to anger: 'Order dispatch of a platoon, to knock down these disgusting things and clean this area up immediately!'

'Yes, sir, right away, sir.'

'And put up a sign forbidding this activity!'

'Er, what should the sign say, sir?'

The colonel looked down and shuffled his feet. 'You think of something, major.' The sign posed a problem, but the real quandary was what to use to knock down the three and four foot tall forest of yellow stems.

'What should we use to dispatch them, sir, rifles, bayonets?'

'I don't care if you use tanks! Just get rid of them and don't continue this practice. We have families and guests walking to the movies along this path. This behavior will not be tolerated!'"

When he finished telling the story, Dad looked over at me with a sheepish smile and an embarrassed look that made his dark blue eyes darker. I'm not sure he thought he should have told me this story, but it was too late.

Our silence was awkward. Could this be typical behavior expected of men? I posed a question, though it was not really the one I had in mind: "What did they use to knock 'em down, Dad?" I spoke in a soft voice.

"They finally settled on baseball bats."

"But how'd they stop the contest?"

"The army built a row of outhouses, put 'em alongside the path with signs posted at intervals."

"Is that what all those outhouses are for! What do the signs say, Dad? I can't remember."

"Please use facilities." We were smiling then, our tension relieved, but I wondered what replaced this activity? Finding out about those yellow stems made me feel strange, and somehow, older, as if a good part of me had gone away. I wondered, why would men do such a thing, because they can?

Discovering hungry wolves had been circling all night, Dad was trying to distract and amuse me with this story, injecting a little humor into our situation. He must have thought I felt vulnerable, stranded, hoping to be rescued. I made a special effort to let him know that I didn't feel this way at all. This was a great adventure and we were enjoying it together. To let him know how I felt, I smiled and smiled.

We cooked breakfast. After the sausage was nearly done and it was time to add the eggs, I had to be quick to get them into the frying pan before they froze. I was too young to drink coffee, but that day I felt its warmth go all the way to my toes. We ate propped up against the side of the Weasel. Not too much else we could do other than visit. Dad assured me that a helicopter would come looking for us when our return time passed. The snow was too deep to walk around in and the temperature kept us close to the fire. Occasionally, we heard a wolf call and another answer. Each time this happened we stopped talking.

Dad told me stories about camping as an Eagle Scout and how he worked summers as a lumberjack in Wisconsin, where his parents' families settled after immigrating. He was pleased to be invited by the Swedish embassy as the only living heir in the dedication of John W. Hanson's home in Port Tobacco, Maryland. John Hanson was President of the First Continental Congress, before the thirteen states were ratified. I recalled seeing his statue above the entry door on Capital Hill in Washington, D.C.

I suppose growing up lumberjacking was why Dad effortlessly cut our wood, swinging the axe in a rhythmic motion as if he were listening to a song. He confided to me something he said he never told his mother: while she thought he only dug ditches for the Oakland Water Company to supplement his scholarship at UC Berkeley where he majored in electrical engineering, the pay was better working as a hard hat diver welding the San Francisco - Oakland Bay Bridge. He liked swimming under water and with his large barrel chest he could stay under longer than anyone I knew. He told me: "It's valuable to make sure your pump man's your friend, because your life may depend on him continuing to turn that wheel!"

We had nothing to do but pass time. It felt good talking with him because we were usually in a hurry, going our separate ways. Each night of this adventure I sang Girl Scout songs for him by the fire. He told me his favorite was "You Are My Sunshine," and I sang it more often than the rest...

Two chilly days and freezing nights later, Dad's army helicopter came *bup bup bup* looking for us. It hovered above us for the rescue from a place where, among the trees at night, I saw many oval-shaped eyes reflecting our firelight.

Climbing the swinging ladder below the helicopter was tough. My arctic clothes were bulky and got in the way. The downwash of the rotor blades blasted me as I reached up rung by rung for a crewmember's outstretched hand. Finally inside, I was stiff and cold. My fingers were frozen and hard to bend. I could see a white spot of frostbite on my nose by crossing my eyes - my face scarf must have blown aside during the ascent. Carefully, I removed my glove exposing too-pink fingers, and placed one over the spot on my nose. There was little that hurt more than thawing frostbite, it was like eating too-cold ice cream and the brain pain that follows is momentarily debilitating. The pain brought tears to my eyes, but I didn't cry. I brushed my dark eyebrow, ostensibly to smooth the hair but really to clear away a tear, and the hairs came off on my fingers. I gazed at them a bit and envisioned how strange I'd look with only one brow. What would the kids at school say?

Dad looked at me after he'd settled inside the helicopter. He noticed what my face was missing. "Here, now, we can't have you looking so bedraggled," he said, moving closer. He smoothed the other brow away with his thumb. I smiled at the prospect of seeing my bald face framed by dark lashes and hair, but soon forgot about it, focusing on sights outside the aircraft window.

The air was smooth and the trip in the big Sikorsky lasted only minutes. We were moving so fast we passed birds, which left me smiling. This wasn't the first time I'd noticed flying. It impressed me before. Sometimes it took ardent persuasion to convince my parents how important it was for me to go along with members of the local

Aero Club. Each pilot was gracious letting me try the controls, knowing how I loved to fly. I was happiest then, and knew that in the air was where I wanted to be, seeing big things little and feeling bigger inside.

Was it because of being above the trees instead of down in them? This vantage point was so different from the customary one. In affording a greater view, could it also be a higher one? Moving through the air at speed, the distance between our camp and home was covered so rapidly that reality nearly seemed altered. We were close to being in two places at the same time...

We landed safely at our cabin and as the helicopter engine wound down toward idle we jumped to Earth, receiving warm, relieved hugs. With my arms around my mother, I turned to the pilot who looked from outer space in his padded flight suit with the helmet chinstrap dangling, first thanking him, then asking, "How did you find us?"

"It was easy to spot your campfire smoke from a long way away, air's so clear, and there aren't many campers in December," he grinned. I smiled at him and looked up at my mother, hoping she was glad for our return and proud we'd weathered the experience. She held me at arm's length and studied my naked face. "Something's changed about you. Something's different." Then she looked over my head. Dad must've gestured and a look of recognition passed between them. She looked where my eyebrows used to be and hugged me tight. Dad told me later he would go for the Weasel at Break-up: when the ice started melting and the dog poop thawed.

✈

The Episcopal Bishop of Alaska was a flying bishop. He'd turned to the church, but did I hear him say that he was a U.S. pilot shot down in Germany? Amidst Homer and Jethro's *Squaws Along the Yukon* playing in the background, "*There's a salmon scented girl, who has set my head awhirl,*" he related a story to my parents about several years spent in a Prisoner of War camp. While I listened intently from my bed - "*and she lives up in the Yukon far away*" - I wondered if this experience had caused him to choose a spiritual life.

One night, he asked Dad if he'd serve as Deacon in the Episcopal Church. The next time we saw the bishop, he flew into our homestead with a daughter my age, landing on the Alaska Highway in front of our house. He taxied his new Cessna 180, a gift from his parishioners, into our yard. One time the plane was on skis, another time on amphibs, and yet another time on balloon tires.

One time, the bishop delayed take-off, waiting for the weather to clear. When it was time to go, the temperature dipped with the storm's passage and it was so cold the plane wouldn't start. Like the generator, draining the oil and removing the spark plugs to heat them in a frying pan became necessary. It sounded funny to hear the bishop say: "When these things get hot, stay out of the way 'cause I'm goin' to run like hell for the plane to try and start it!"

At Tok Junction, there was a caribou migration of some one million animals each year. Native Americans shared celebration of the migration with food cooked over fire pits and we ate caribou stew served out of new garbage cans. One time, and one time only, I ate bear stew with a tribe. The meat had such a strong flavor that it brought to mind the old story of the boot pulled off a missionary who was about to be eaten. Because the boot tasted so bad, the missionary was spared. How bad that bear stew tasted, boiled even, made me wonder what on earth that bear could have eaten to have such a strong flavor, a low flying aircraft?

It seemed our missions were to compete with the Catholic Church. Snuggled together in the small airplane cabin, the bishop, Dad the deacon, the bishop's daughter and I took off for an Athabascan Indian village near Tok Junction. Athabascans call themselves *Medzeyh te hut 'Aane,* People of the Caribou. Landing in the turbulent and swift Tanana River, we floated backwards at idle power to a beach on an island in the middle of the river. White caps whisked the water and the current was strong. We had to jump off the pontoon to reach the island without getting wet. Then we climbed into a long riverboat with a big motor for the ride through rapids downstream to the village. I couldn't decide which was more exciting: landing on the rough surface in the strong wind and nearly dipping a wing into the water at the wild moment of touchdown, or, trying to keep the boat from capsizing as we navigated the surf.

Our bishop ministered to the white man's perceived spiritual needs of the Native Americans, and my dad, ever the engineer, to their practical ones - clean water and sewage treatment. However reluctant they were to accept the white man's ways spiritually, they were grateful for our concerns, always gracious, and loved us children. We joined them in celebration and jumped in the blanket toss. Made of animal skins sewn together, the blanket became a trampoline.

Besides the children, I met a 111-year-old woman whose reputation among the tribes was legendary. When there was no food, she hunted, returning with enough for the village. Her husband and many of her children died long ago. Esteemed, her posture was straight and her movements, agile. She wore dresses made from caribou skins. Her gaze was distant; her face, a carving of her life. She was matriarch of the tribe and an example of natural superiority in women unknown to me until then. Her stories riveted me to the stool in front of her fire: caribou hunts, spiritual revelation, totems, the meaning of dreams, and the devastation of disease that came with the white man.

✈

These experiences are kept close to my heart, though at the time my heart was breaking. Dad was transferred to duty in downtown New

York City. New York City! I was absolutely crestfallen hearing of his new assignment.

"Wouldn't you rather stay in Alaska and homestead, Dad?" I offered a hopeful alternative. "You've said many times how much you'd like to live life on the Last Frontier..."

"You mean quit the army?" This forfeiture seemed inconceivable, even to me. "Your mother's so happy about our move to New York... we'll be close to her brother, Virgil, in Westchester..."

I didn't have the heart to continue pressing for my own desires. Dad would be on the cutting edge, taking command of a new guided missile battalion. It would guard the entrance to New York harbor and points north along the Hudson River toward West Point. He enjoyed teaching and would teach something called nuclear physics in the evenings.

I tried to be happy for him. Somehow it helped to soothe my longings for Alaska knowing he would be advancing his career, but I was *so* disappointed. City buildings would replace the wilderness; solitude of the kind I had grown to love would not be found in New York with its millions of people. No more hunting or fishing trips, or flights with bush pilots. I would probably not attend the University of Alaska...

I looked out my school windows at the Manhattan skyline and longed for the mountains and trees of Alaska. I resolved never to forget how to tie a fly or shoot the head off a ptarmigan in flight. I thought about tracking game through silent forests during snowfall and dreamed about flying above the wilderness. I yearned to go back more than my hurting heart could bear and the intensity kept me separate me from the other children.

My sister and I were the only two gentiles at P.S. 114, Queens. "Small chance a moose or lynx would walk by outside our classroom windows being that we are four stories in the air," I wrote in an autobiographical sketch for my seventh grade teacher. "The view isn't pretty: no mountains and not one tree in the schoolyard, only dusty old brick buildings."

Dear Mrs. Spiers admonished me. "You are privileged to have a view of the most famous skyline in the world: downtown Manhattan." But the significance was lost on homesick, twelve-year old me...

✈

CHAPTER II

PURSUIT

During the Second World War, women pilots helped the war effort by flying for the United States as WASPs (Women Air Service Pilots). They held commissions as officers in the U.S. Army Air Corps and their mission was test flying new combat aircraft then ferrying them overseas to battlefields. When WWII was definitely leaning in the Allied Forces' favor, the WASPs were thanked for their contribution, and sent home. More than 35 years later, Senator Barry Goldwater from Arizona pushed a bill through Congress retroactively recognizing these women as a viable branch of military aviation, whereas before, they were hardly remembered. I attended the 1977 award ceremonies at the Antler's Hotel in Colorado Springs with a friend, and former WASP, Isabel Steiner Karkau, a Stanford graduate in Mechanical engineering.

Another group of women known as the Mercury Seven trained as astronauts in the 1950's and waited *decades* for their flights into space as male astronauts were launched. Their chance never came, and their existence as a group of exceptionally qualified pilots/astronauts is but a footnote in aviation history.

United States military academies began admitting women as cadets in the mid 1970's. Many asked when the services would allow women to fly in combat. Under pressure imposed by the mandates of the proposed Equal Rights Amendment, it took a long decade and a half before the all male institutions of Annapolis, West Point and the Air Force Academy, supported by taxpayer monies, admitted qualified women. News publications in the year 2000, reported female cadets attending the state institution of the Citadel in South Carolina were not safe.

In my late twenties, I was past the entrance age for the academies or military aviation. I would love to have attended West Point. Choosing ROTC (Reserve Officer Training Corps) financial assistance or a military academy for college, prospective military pilots have options. Given the opportunity, I certainly would have flown super military machines. I've often wondered how many professional pilots would have learned to fly if they had to pay for their flight training. Gaining experience at taxpayers' expense, military pilots are released from active duty to pursue civilian careers at the end of their obligation, which could entail as many as nine years, and involve combat. They are shoe-ins as pilots for the commercial airlines. Their security: nearly womb to tomb if they choose to stay; they circulate from one locker room onto the next.

Life wouldn't have been such a struggle if I had had Uncle Sam paying for my flight experience. I remember years of instructing when I was able to afford only an efficiency apartment and one meal a day: a bowl of soup, a glass of milk, and crackers at the airport restaurant counter. Existing on a flight instructor's pay of first five, then six dollars per flight hour was not really living even in the 1960's, so, I lived only to fly.

Ultimately, I didn't need the military. I got where I wanted to be on my own and through General Aviation. Taking my initial lessons at age 16 in a Beechcraft T-34 and a Cessna 172 at the Moffett Field Naval Air Station, I qualified for membership in the Aero Club because Dad was retired military. He worked just across the field at Lockheed Missiles and Space in Sunnyvale. As Satellite Systems Test Director, he eventually developed and flew the first synchronous orbital satellite from Vandenburg Air Force Base. Before this event, orbiting satellites rocketed around the Earth, virtually useless except to gather information, and after this event, their stationary position allowed development of communications and navigation satellites. While he worked there, my mother started her own company building electromagnetic filter interference devices, shielded test enclosures, and capacitors in Mountain View, the area that eventually became known as Silicon Valley.

Our moves as a military family had been often and varied: the South Pacific, Alaska, New York, Virginia, and California. When Dad was offered a vice presidency by Lockheed in Houston just after his historic launch, it came on the heels of our recent arrival in the Bay Area. The family was so against another move after so many prior ones, that he declined the position. In the end, it was an unfortunate decision for him. We'd settled pretty much permanently in the San Francisco Bay Area and I'd found flying again. It was so enjoyable that my instructor had me trying aerobatics in the T-34 before solo.

Sitting in my MG with the top down one day, waiting for my instructor, I watched in the rear view mirror as activities behind the nearly transparent screens at Ames Research Center intensified. Scientists and technicians in long white coats held clipboards and took notes as an airplane taxied out, jet engines running. Eventually, it lifted vertically off the ground and hovered like a helicopter. Most days when I was there, the plane just hung 20 feet in the air making an incredible racket, but one day it rose above the screens and hovered in slow forward flight toward the runway. The noise level increased and my heart beat faster as additional thrust was added. The fighter came alive with surreal, quivering energy poised in the air. Suddenly it shot forward with a tremendous roar, and disappeared at a high rate of speed into a speck on the horizon.

This scenario so fascinated me, that when my guidance counselor at Foothill College advised me of an opening at Ames Research Center for a "guinea pig" with flying experience, I hurried to apply. I got the job and found my physical and mental abilities were setting standards for space flight. There were several tests. In one, I tried to remain oriented in a chair placed in a darkened room. Designed to disorient, the chair was similar to but more sophisticated than one called a Vertigon. With my good eyesight, I was able to read not only the mandatory letters and numbers on the eye charts from way down the hall, but in jest, also read the tiny copyright information at the bottom of the poster for the dazzled Data Recording person. In flying, good eyesight means everything, and I was lucky enough to have it.

I found a very fine flight school called Flight Safety at the San Carlos Airport that was looking for a Girl Friday, and sandwiched this job in around college classes. To earn money for flying, I gave swimming lessons to neighborhood children whose families had pools in their backyards. Most of these pools were not fenced. My specialty was teaching babies. At only a few months old, I found they weren't afraid of water. We'd start by blowing bubbles on the surface, and then together we'd duck under the surface. Maintaining eye contact, their long baby eyelashes awash with water in their eyes, we'd continue blowing bubbles. This taught breath control. We would sit on the bottom and play paddy cake. When the infant could swim like a pollywog underwater, surface to take a breath, and cross the pool to crawl up the stairs, I was confident that if the child fell in, she or he could survive. This made me feel wonderful.

Flight Safety was on contract to several airlines to train Professional Flight Engineers for their flying licenses, making them viable members of an FAR (Federal Aviation Regulations) Part 121 crew. Initially, I did flight scheduling for these "Ninety Day Wonders." A puzzle of schedule coordination had to be solved every evening because at Flight Safety we had seven instructors, five airplanes, and two-dozen students going through the program at any one time. Primarily, we trained the flight engineers for Pan American, but also for Flying Tigers, Seaboard World, and American Airlines.

Flying was seeing big things little and feeling bigger inside; it represented freedom and independence for me, a young woman, but I was discovering this wasn't a particularly popular idea. Some people regarded this as dangerous new thinking; nonetheless, I was privileged to receive flying lessons from some *great* instructors at Flight Safety.

One distinguished instructor was Paul Adams, a retired Pan Am captain whose most interesting assignment, he felt, was in Rio de Janeiro on Flying Boats. Oh, the stories and the adventures of this era of flying! A pilot's trip in a Flying Boat was very nearly as adventuresome as an explorer's. Airports with hard surfaced runways were non-existent in many parts of the world so harbors - and sometimes the open ocean - became gateways for cities and commerce. Pan American was a flagship venturing into the unknown. Captain Paul Adams started his aviation career flying the airmail with Charles Lindbergh from Lambert Field in St. Louis. Paul thought Lindbergh took chances: "Once Lindy ran out of gas trying to land at a fogged-in airfield in Chicago. He had to parachute from his plane with the airmail bag in his hand."

At the start of each lesson, Paul would look over at me with a smile and say: "Why don't you be a nurse?" or, "Why don't you be a teacher?" Every lesson he had a different suggestion, and none had anything to do with flying. I would smile at him and say nothing. He was concerned for my future, my optimism, and my well being. I knew he knew what trials were ahead.

✈

Dwight Hansen, Ernest Gann's captain on the Matson Line, whom he wrote about in *Fate is the Hunter,* also instructed for Flight Safety. I was fortunate to take lessons from Dwight. And there were others: Glenn Ottsman (Standard Airways), Dallas Masterson (several), Dan Pearson (Pan Am), Carl Snyder (several), Ed Hill (PSA), Ried Saindon (General Aviation), all experienced instructors with thousands of hours flight time, often including extensive military and airlines flight experience. These were amazing prerequisites because the job only paid $5-6 dollars per flight hour. This experience level requirement held until the day I completed my instructor's rating with the FAA and my bosses offered me a job instructing. Seldom were applicants able to complete the flight instructor test successfully on the first try with the FAA; it usually took two or three attempts and this had been duly noted by management at Flight Safety. I recognized that persistence, determination, and preparation were required. Most applicants were unaware of what the FAA wanted to see in an instructor: teaching ability, insight, flying skill, and desire. I had the desire to teach.

✈

I flew every chance I got and that turned out to be mostly at night. Initially, I had the opportunity to ferry airplanes and parts for Flight Safety as the maintenance shop was built, and later, for fixed based operators who ordered new airplanes from the factories. My first ferry flight had to be made on the sly: at eighteen, Dad told me I couldn't fly out of the state of California. He intended to somehow assure my safety within a *geographical yard,* an amusing constraint given the topography of California. The state is large and the landscape as varied as anywhere in the world with its sea level to 14,000-foot elevations. This significance somehow eluded him as at 48, he was not yet a pilot, and had given terrain and elevation variance little thought. It would be ten years before he flew solo and I took him on his first cross-country.

I weighed the outcome, of getting caught leaving the state, with the importance of ferrying airplanes. I decided I couldn't pass on this chance. It might be a while before I would be lucky enough to find another.

✈

I took off in a Cessna 172 on a Friday morning with two men who were also planning to ferry Cessnas to California. One was a businessman who sold stock in airplane ownership for a flying club, and the other, his business associate. We turned east for Wichita.

I took the controls that cold, clear, winter day with unlimited visibilities. The irregular terrain of the Sierras Nevada gave way to the smooth horizons of eastern Colorado, which gives Kansas its "B Flat" fame. The 145 horsepower Continental engine droned on in sympathetic vibration while the countryside slipped beneath our wings. As if riding a magic carpet with a bird's eye view, we arrived over Wichita, nearing our destination. Looking down, the predominant color in the winter of 1965 seemed to be brown. There was no snow. The grass was long and beige and it lay over as if it *had* snowed, or was it the wind that tilted the tender blade tops? The trees were leafless, wooden sentinels. Everything was brown except the sky and it relieved this landscape with the bluest blue. I wondered if it would be pleasant to live in a climate that spent so much time in the *in-betweens*: *in-between* winter and spring, *in-between* fall and winter. I found suddenly I missed northern California and its two spring times: one, when the flowers bloom after a cool, wet winter, and two, when the extended heat of summer dissipates to the cooler temperatures of fall, and a gentle awakening rain begins. Within only a few days, the hills and valleys green up in the autumn just as in spring, because California around the Bay Area doesn't have a classic winter with snow cover.

Rooming at a large hotel on the airport in Wichita, the three of us met for dinner in the hotel restaurant. Patrons brought bottles of alcohol in brown paper bags; something I'd never seen before, though it really didn't matter, as I wasn't old enough to drink anyway. When our server arrived at the table topless, I wondered about the extent of the Floor Show. Obviously, these men had been here before.

I felt hot and flustered; I'm sure my face showed an embarrassed red. Their lack of chivalry and politeness was stunning; then I reminded myself of my circumstances: *How could they have thought differently of a girl who would fly half way across the country with near strangers?* Also, I realized I was witnessing an aspect of male behavior that equated to being out of town on a *kitchen pass*. I stayed for the meat and potatoes, but left before the floor show, and found myself being followed to my room by one of the men whom I had to shove out my door, while he pushed his way in.

The next morning at eight, I joined a tour of the Cessna factory sans my companions of the previous night, who advised they'd already taken the tour and preferred sleeping in. I strolled through the factory watching the manufacturing process. It was riveting, but I was most captivated by the people working on the assembly line. Male or female, they were nearly indistinguishable, wearing gray coveralls and safety glasses. They had graying brown hair, and pale, chalky-white complexions. They were methodical in their work and proceeded without expression. Unresponsive to my smiles and greetings, they were automatons. I promised myself I would *never* lose my love for life and wondered how they could settle for so little when there was *so much*.

Later that morning, I departed Wichita solo, heading southwest, having filed a flight plan with the FAA's Flight Service Station. As I climbed into the shiny, new, black and white Cessna 150 bearing the call sign November 8704 Golf, I noticed there were two hours on the Hobbs meter, a recording device for time spent with positive oil pressure, or when the engine is running. Two hours was just enough time to take a test flight. This was recorded in the aircraft logbook along with a notation that the aircraft was deemed *airworthy*.

Eventually, three hours elapsed since take-off. At 8,500 feet over the Panhandle of Texas, I noticed the magnetic compass vacillated from one heading to another. It was the only directional indicator on board because the aircraft came equipped with only a partial panel of flight instruments, the bare minimum for certification. Looking at the sectional chart in my hand, a boxed note in the corner stated that in this particular area, "A magnetic disturbance of up to 45 degrees exists." No wonder the compass was unreadable, and swinging from side to side.

I tuned Nancy Narco's ten channel Whistle Stop Radio to the Amarillo VOR navigational station by selecting the frequency from ten available ones noted at the side of the set. Pulling out the tuning knob and slowly cranking the coffee grinder handle, I waited for an audible whistle. When the whistle was loudest, the frequency was tuned to precisely the correct station. Pushing the tuning knob *in* locked the frequency and allowed reception of the VOR signal. Matching the aircraft heading with the selected bearing normally took me towards the station. But not now! The Course Deviation Indicator bounced back and forth as much as the compass. Either the station was too far away or I was too low to receive an accurate signal. VOR navigational stations radiate 360 degrees of possible courses and operate on line of sight. I tried climbing. At 10,500 feet the reception was not much better probably because I was out of range - over 100 miles away. I had been airborne more than three and a-half hours on a four hour fuel tank and would need to land, soon, for gas. I didn't have the adjoining chart to the west of the

Panhandle of Texas, and it occurred to me that I might have flown off the one in my hand. Nothing looked familiar. The faceless plain revealed little to compare with the chart.

Soon the gas gauges read empty and the indicator bounced with each little turbulent bump. I recalculated my fuel... I had less than thirty minutes fuel remaining; however, this was based on an optimistic fuel flow. I had climbed two thousand feet higher than planned, so thirty minutes fuel remaining was doubtful. No airports appeared below and none were in sight ahead. With a hand above my eyebrows shading the bright sunlight, I swept the horizon from left to right straining to see farther in the distance. I looked for many seconds and dropped my search to the area below the plane. How empty the countryside looked! I wondered how I would feel landing out in the middle of nowhere. I turned in the seat and assured myself I had my sleeping bag and emergency items of matches, flashlight, warm jacket and canteen in addition to my small suitcase. Sighing, I resolved it was time to ask Flight Service to give me a directional steer to an airport, preferably one that sold gas. I leaned the fuel-air mixture knob as lean as possible before picking up the microphone and tuning the Whistle Stop Radio to the Amarillo Flight Service Station frequency of 121.1 megahertz and receiving on the VOR frequency.

"Amarillo Radio. This is Cessna 8704 Golf," I spoke into the microphone.

"Cessna 8704 Golf. This is Amarillo Radio."

"Cessna 8704 Golf requesting a DF steer to the Amarillo Airport."

"8704 Golf. Was that a practice DF steer?"

Ulllluuup. " No, sir, Cessna 8704 Golf, the other kind..."

"Cessna 8704 Golf. Turn right 90 degrees for radar identification, and say new heading."

My heart was nearly in my mouth as I answered. Embarrassed by asking for a Direction Finding Steer, I had admitted I could not find my destination.

"8704 Golf, turn right 90 degrees." I banked the aircraft to a medium bank of 30 degrees and changed heading 90 degrees as accurately as possible, coping with the wobbly compass. Mostly I looked outside, spotting a distant hill on my right wingtip and turning until it was on my nose: I thought this would represent ninety degrees of heading change.

"8704 Golf. Turn left ninety degrees, and say your heading."

"8704 Golf turning to heading two zero zero degrees," I announced as my wings leveled and the magnetic compass steadied for a moment on 200 degrees.

"8704 Golf. Radar contact. Say souls on board and fuel remaining."

I sighed before I admitted that I was alone and estimated I had 25 minutes of fuel remaining.

"How about we take you into Borger, Texas? It's closer than Amarillo. The airport is at 11 o'clock and 32 miles. They have fuel available."

"That sounds fine to me." Soon Borger appeared on the horizon amidst oil pumps and feed lots. I was able to make a quick downwind and thankfully land with the engine *still* running.

Standing at the gas pump, watching the gallons added click over in the pump dispensing window, I watched with mounting concern as the counter showed figures approaching the useable capacity of the 22.5 gallon fuel tank: 20.8 gallons, 21.0 gallons, 21.4 gallons, 21.8 gallons. Mercifully, the gallons counter stopped. 21.8 gallons added to a 22.5-gallon tank! Seared by the realization of how close I had come to running out of gas, with a fuel consumption of 4 gallons per hour, having less than fifteen minutes fuel left a hollow feeling in the pit of my stomach. This trip was becoming memorable for its many firsts.

I tried to eat a hamburger at the airport restaurant but had no appetite. *Gee! If I can't even make it to my first point of landing, how am I going to make it all the way to San Francisco 17 hours away? Was Dad right to restrict me?* Doubts rose to confront me while sitting at the lunch counter, which had a view of the runway. People all around me were eating and scoring the airplane touchdowns. Alone with my thoughts, I wasn't paying much attention. Soon I smiled though, reminding myself of how much I loved flying, and decided to let this be just another adventure!

Soon, two shiny Cessna 150s touched down on the runway and taxied to the gas pumps. Minutes later, their pilots entered the restaurant asking for the pilot of the black and white Cessna 150. *Me. That's me.* I jumped up and introduced myself. They desired my company flying to California because mine was the only plane of the three with an operating radio, a fact they discovered back at the factory. They invited me to complete the trio.

Touching down in California, I waved goodbye to my flying companions in Long Beach and proceeded north to San Jose. "I'll be flying up the coast, landing about four this afternoon," I told my mother over the phone. The fog started to roll in over the hills north of Santa Cruz as shadows grew long. When I cleared the active runway, I was stunned to see my dad waiting for me at the gas pumps. I wavered momentarily. He didn't look particularly mad, and if anything, was pleased I arrived safely. Deciding to take the initiative, I gave him a whopping big hug.

My enthusiasm about the flight was contagious. At home, he got down beside me to look at the charts I had taped together and spread across the kitchen floor. I recounted the adventure. By the time my story came to an end, I felt he understood why I'd chosen to go.

"Do me a favor next time," he said with a smile, "just kick me in the shins and tell me you're going anyway. Then you won't have to make up stories for diversion."

"How did you know to meet me in San Jose?"

"One of your friends called asking you to wait for him because he had no radios or instruments on board his airplane. I tried to tell him you were skiing with friends but he insisted you were ferrying an airplane back from the factory in Wichita. Eventually he convinced me of what you were doing. I said if I heard from you I would relay the message. Now I've done it. Then I decided to see you fly in to San Jose for myself," he said, hugging me. "I'm glad you're home safe..."

When I first started flying "Gambler Specials," it was in the venerable Twin Beech. Usually configured to carry nine passengers, the Twin Beech was powered by two Pratt and Whitney R-985 radial engines rated at 450 horsepower each. With a tail wheel that trailed rather than a nose wheel that steered, landings could be an adventure and earned the airplane the reputation of a *mean machine*. It also caused many good pilots to eat humble pie. Everything would be fine until the tail wheel touched the ground. Then the pilot had to use good timing, coordination, and judicious application of brakes. When flying the Twin Beech, it was best to have an "educated toe." Because the tail fins were small in proportion to the rest of the plane and located at either end of the horizontal stabilizer of the tail assembly, there wasn't a lot of rudder surface for steering once the tail touched the ground. As speed diminished, airflow across the tail slowed, making the rudders less effective. Differential use of power from the engines and braking kept the plane straight on the runway. Finesse was definitely involved. More than one pilot had swapped ends in an embarrassing *ground loop*.

Another anomaly of the Twin Beech was that some higher capacity airplanes were built with *walking gear*. When making sharp angled turns during taxi, a lot of stress was put on the landing gear. To avert any collapse due to high forces imposed on the wheels and struts, Beechcraft engineers designed the landing gear so that it walked back and forth in the wheel well as a corner was turned. Many a tower controller remarked in dismay at seeing what they thought was a mechanical aberration. I can't recall another aircraft with gear of this type. The Twin Beech was neither the largest nor the smallest tail wheel aircraft and was similar in size and appearance to the one Amelia Earhart flew, though different. Hers was a Lockheed Vega.

Continued service of the Twin Beech precluded the public from considering a newer line of expensive, modern craft until suddenly one day, a wing fell off one in flight. The plane spun to the ground killing all the occupants. To avert further disasters, the fix would be a *spar mod*, an expensive modification usually consisting of a large strap extending from wingspar to wingspar, to hold the wings *on*. That was fine if the owner could afford it. Prices ranged from as low as $8,000 to over $20,000. Extinction was just ahead for this fine bird. Some pilots were relieved to see the Twin Beech parked in the Old Airplane Graveyard, used by aviation fire departments for practice. I wasn't. There was so much flying history lingering in the sounds of those radial engines, in the smells of oil and hydraulic fluids. In wistful moments, I hear the reverberation of those Pratt and Whitneys at taxi rpm sounding the truth in *a bucket of gas, a bucket of gas, a bucket of oil!*

The owner of Cardinal Airlines was also the Chief Pilot. It was a Mom and Pop operation. Mom booked the passengers and Pop, Rudy, flew the flights. He accompanied me a couple times over the Sierras to snowy gambling destinations. I had the requisite qualifications of a Commercial license, Instrument and Multi-Engine ratings and at nineteen, I was one year older than the minimum age to fly for hire.

Cardinal Airlines' departures were on Friday and Saturday nights, returning mid- morning the next day. One night we found our Twin Beech overbooked by two. Rudy politely gave up his pilot seat to one passenger and disappeared. I was sitting above our surprised guests as the tailwheel on the craft created a sloping cabin when on the ground. Rudy returned with a wooden chair from the office, which he placed just inside the rear cabin door. A murmur passed among the passengers. I was hoping for a smooth ride because this added seat wasn't attached to the floor and of course there wasn't a seat belt. His initial disappointment vanquished, the remaining passenger seemed happy to be aboard, but when an adjacent passenger questioned Rudy on the addition of the wooden chair: "Will he be safe if his chair isn't attached to the floor?"

Rudy took a moment to adjust his Homburg, which I suppose he wore to give the illusion of height he didn't have. Through clenched teeth that held an ever-present, unlit Lucky Strike - I think he was trying to quit smoking - he said with a wink at the passenger in the wooden chair and a nod to me: "Well, this *is* the **Gambler's Special!**" Things were sure different in the 60s!

My Lear 23 corporate job ended in disaster. The plane crashed in the Banning Pass with several investors and principals of the airline aboard. It was the premier demo model for corporate sales, operated by Flying Tiger Air Services out of Burbank and San Francisco in 1965. I was fortunate to be demonstration pilot, recommended by Flight Safety in the Bay Area where Flying Tiger pilots completed their simulator training. The chief pilot happened to be one of our students. Excused from flight that day because of college exams, I was hopeful this opportunity would turn into a good flying job. After the crash, I had nightmares about how I might have prevented the accident. I knew the old captain couldn't go rapidly from looking outside the aircraft to focusing inside on the instruments.

A new design for corporate aviation, the Lear 23 was turbine-powered and could fly from sea level to 10,000 feet in a flash. Another selling point explained in brochures was that "You can bring your dog along as copilot." I guess that summed it up!

The old captain departed the Palm Springs Airport with a private pilot in the right seat and tried to negotiate the Banning Pass visually on a foggy day. I guess he could have used my help. He ran at high speed into a low hill. After the crash there was no more airplane, and I was out of a job.

✈

Weekdays I worked at Flight Safety in the Bay Area from early until late. Arriving shortly before opening time, the chief pilot met me at the door with a copy of the *Wall Street Journal* in his hand. "I have something to show you," he said as he unlocked the door, turned on the lights and stepped inside. Always having been an advocate of mine and a fine gentleman as well, Dallas Masterson hired me at twenty-one as a flight instructor. Promptly afterward, President Al Ueltschi fired me from New York: "We don't hire women pilots!" he boomed over the phone.

Dallas threatened to shut the western division down if they didn't reinstall me in my new position. A year later the head office refused to let me be the chief flight instructor in the flight instructor program and we went through the same episode again. Funny thing, and that is not funny ha ha, but funny strange, before I became an instructor, Al Ueltschi, who was at one time personal pilot to Juan

Tripp, Chairman of Pan American, used to call me by name, and had me fly his VP, Bruce Whitman, around California. After I began instructing, I was always just "That girl!"

Dal laid the paper on the showcase for pilot supplies, and with reverent fingertips opened to the second page. In the middle was a four inch, two column ad which read: "Corporate President looking for a young, unencumbered female pilot capable of being type-rated in a large four engine airplane, free to travel internationally six months per year, excellent secretarial skills," and other particulars which filled the space. Apparently, the corporate president was a thermo-dynamics scientist who invented and manufactured respiratory devices for humans. He marketed his inventions by lecturing at universities around the world.

"Sounds like it was written just for you," Dal smiled, looking up to get my reaction. He was pleased to have brought it to my attention. At twenty-two, I didn't read the *Wall Street Journal* often, and the fact that there even *was* such an ad, that it was Dallas who found it and thought of me after he had stood up for me for so long, surely was fortune smiling.

I got excited; envisioned flying into the far pavilions of China and India that I'd read of as a child, exploring the bazaars of the East, flying low across Africa. For me, it was a dream come true, but the secretarial part gave me pause, and seemed like a return to *old thinking. Why would he want a woman if all he needs is a pilot?* This must have been the reason for the secretarial part. Try as I might to take the high road, I was niggled by the fact this man advertised for a *girl*.

The situation seemed perfect except that I had projected in my dreams. Normally, I wasn't given to discussing them, and I chose my audience carefully. I wanted to hear optimism - some inspiration - not cries of fear. My friends from work threw a going-away surprise party at a Coyote Point restaurant. They knew how much I wanted to fly and how I yearned to see the world. I was elated, riding on a cloud so much so that I didn't stop to think how this would impact my current flame. He didn't even come to the party. As I explained the ad to him later, my upcoming interview, and possible move to Palm Springs, he was irascible: "Sounds like he wants a mistress!" This appellation silenced me. I felt my eyes go wide; he'd addressed my fears. I decided to talk the whole thing over with my dad.

I called and asked to see him. I drove from my apartment in Redwood City to our family home in Los Altos Hills. When I arrived and followed Dad into the library, I noticed he seemed ebullient. He was always cheerful but this amount was unusual. Setting aside my concerns for the moment, I asked why he seemed so happy. It turned out he was basking in his own success: Lockheed had just offered him an advanced position.

After visiting about his news for a bit, we turned to mine. I showed him the ad. We discussed responsibilities of the job and particulars of the move. Finally, I felt almost distressed to ask: "Dad, you don't think this man just wants a girlfriend, do you?"

That question never entered his mind judging from the response he gave. Dad got agitated, sort of puffed up, as if he was offended I should even suggest such a thing. He became a little scary: "A President of a U.S. Corporation? Certainly not! Corporate officers are persons of the highest integrity. He must be married. Have a family." Dad's counsel revealed a fundamental optimism and courtesy he generally accorded people, especially in high positions. Clearly, he felt that a corporate officer, a capitalist, would be of the highest caliber not only in business but in his personal life. "Otherwise, how could he have possibly risen to such heights in the United States?"

Sitting across from him, I felt my chin drop to contact my chest. Looking at him out of the tops of my eyes, I couldn't decide if I was more chagrined by his response or by the fact that he sounded so chimerical and naive. Suddenly, I felt years older than he, and much more worldly. The encounter was almost embarrassing.

Some days after our discussion of integrity, my optimism revived. I felt lacking that I'd even entertained the notion that a corporate president might be advertising for a girlfriend in the *Wall Street Journal*. I decided to brush aside my qualms, those of my current flame, and press onward to this next adventure. The next thing I knew, I was in Palm Springs climbing around on a PBY converted from two to four engines, perusing a Super Ventura, a Howard 500, and a Lear Jet leased to Rexall Drugs, all parked and waiting either in or beside a very large hangar. Flying a Lockheed Lodestar, a PT-22 and a J-3 Cub around in the desert as part of my interview, though I'd never flown them, there followed a dictation and typing test. Spelling seemed important to this black-suited corporate president with a diamond stickpin in his tie. I could spell. I decided to throw caution to the winds and ignore the harpies who moaned in my ears as I concentrated and typed with the wind on his manual typewriter. At the end of these tests, he offered me the job.

The first couple of weeks I worked in his free respiratory clinic; the patients who came for treatment were generally in such bad shape from smoking and consequential diseases that many had permanently moved to Palm Springs. I learned some things about respiratory therapy and diseases related to breathing in films starring the corporate president, and from working in the clinic. A gardenia-colored limousine called for me each day.

I graduated from the clinic and relocated to corporate offices set in large hangars at the airport. The corporate president's office was unique in that it was a log cabin inside the hangar but with logs only on the *inside*. With a fireplace and illuminated paintings of Alaska on the walls, our desks were twenty feet apart but diagonally across from each other. I was sure the intent was to keep cool in the Palm

Springs heat, but I felt anything but cool when his orders turned to *ardor*.

He began trying to kiss me after I typed a letter with all his fifty-cent medical words spelled correctly. *Is it just that he's so happy to have someone who can spell, as well as type?* I hoped that was it, but in a heartbeat, his expression turned from happiness to passion. I hurriedly slid out of my chair and circled, keeping furniture between us, and at first excuse, escaped the room.

Distressed, over the next few weeks I began speaking to him about replacing me with a more willing and mature companion. He wasn't interested, and showed me a large drawer full of responses to his ad. "There are 320 of them."

"Surely there's someone more qualified than..."

"After months of looking, I chose you. You could take one of the visiting doctor's apartments here at the airport - in my hangar. We could be closer..." The walls began closing in, the harpies began singing, and the room seemed to darken. My throat got dry and I started coughing.

"Tomorrow you and I will be leaving on a six month flying tour lecturing at medical schools." He smiled, turning on the charm. "You might like some things for the trip. I'll have them sent over." I gulped, wondering what he meant.

"We'll go to eastern Canada, first, then fly to the Near East, up to and cross Europe to the Far East, then home. I have several new inventions to introduce to the international medical community. I don't advertise, you know, just lecture. My newest invention is a Cryogenic Nebulizer." I envisioned the correct spelling.

I understood why he wanted a secretary who could spell and who understood semantics because he named his inventions after their function. He seemed popular with the medical community, having advanced the field of respiratory therapy with his technology. Using his inventions in Vietnam, they were tested in the most extreme conditions. Attached to stretchers, the respirators breathed for critically wounded soldiers when they could not. The respirators were practical, and saved many lives in Vietnam; hospitals in the U.S. began using them, also.

As a pilot, the corporate president applied the principle of the venturi as canon to make his respirators work. Medicines were injected through a restricted orifice and accelerated into the lungs. I admired his inventive intellect, his entrepreneurial spirit, and his capitalism. He was a fine American to have given his inventions to the armed services.

It could be such an interesting job, I told myself. I tried to cope, to head off his advances with conversation, to stuff myself into this role. On the eve of our departure abroad, my presence was solicited at a dinner party of corporate acquaintances. The corporate president was not there. His absence puzzled me. The guests teased me about my upcoming trip but I really didn't need to be reminded of where all this was going. "When you pack, be sure to throw in your douche bag," one rough woman advised. Stunned by her crass allusion, I felt my face redden.

I looked down at my lap. I wasn't familiar with a douche bag and had only vaguely heard of one. *Are my worst fears coming to fruition? Obviously, they know their boss better than I. Maybe the point of this dinner is to warn me. Have I been naive in believing this job was above reproach? How could I possibly convey my innocence to this gathering, much less to the corporation?*

There was no alternative. Quickly I excused myself from the table before the second course. With amazed looks all around - *had they suddenly realized I might not be the person they thought I was* - I briefly thanked the hostess and rushed home.

I felt I was choking as I inserted the key in the door of my apartment. My roommate, a lovely widow with a crown of silver hair, rented me half her pretty garden apartment. There she was, in her customary place on the sofa, but in the midst of huge bouquets of long stemmed flowers nodding from tall vases. White garment boxes were stacked all over the room. Candy, jars of delicacies like lambs tongues, pickled pigs feet, and fig leaves crowded together on the counter tops. I looked at my roommate.

"Are these for you?"

"No, dear," I caught my breath: "They're for you."

I let it out. Water clouded my eyes. My shoulders involuntarily hunched over. My head hung in shame. I covered my face with my hands, and hurried toward the bedroom.

"Are you really going to fly around the world with *that man,* dear?"

"No... No... I don't know. I-I didn't think something like this would happen. I just want to fly, not all this other stuff..." Dad's words rang hollow in my ears.

"It's almost too late. You're leaving tomorrow, aren't you?"

I responded with fresh tears and rushed away.

Through the night I walked the hardwood floors, back and forth in my room. My slippers shuffled across the warm boards, which softly creaked with each step. I gazed out the window at the cascade of stars along the Milky Way and longed for things to be different.

"Why?" I asked the Man in the Moon, smiling huge and white in the heavens. He peered down, wordless, but with the wisdom of the ages. In my heart of hearts I knew I was choosing to do the right thing. I wouldn't be able to live with myself if I compromised my integrity and I wouldn't want a position where this would be required.

I had no inclination to pack for the trip because I knew I wasn't going. I was uncomfortable about leaving with nothing more than a letter but, *what more could I do?* I didn't want a confrontation, or to be talked out of leaving. Of the future, I guessed I'd just keep on instructing. At least I'd be independent and...and... honorable.

Oh, why can't I just get an airline job and be my own person! This last thought brought a fresh batch of tears.

When the waking hour was appropriate, I called home: "This isn't working out for me, Dad."

"What's the matter?"

"He wants a girlfriend."

A few moments passed. A gentleman, Dad told me he was deemed one by an act of Congress when he was commissioned as an officer in the regular army, he never asked how I knew, but he did console me with these words: "You have to decide the caliber of person you want to be and what kind of life you want to lead..."

"This isn't the kind of person I want to be, and this wouldn't be the life I hope for..."

"Then you don't owe him a thing."

"Not even an explanation?"

"No, not even an explanation, by your leaving, he will know. Come home. Just come home."

✈

I returned to instructing with nary a sideways glance toward corporations, which were springing up all around with flight departments. Eventually, I became Flight Safety's west coast Chief Pilot and remained in that interesting capacity until 1973. We did a lot of things for aviation at Flight Safety. We hosted the FAA-Lear Siegler experimental program that proved the value of simulation in general aviation. Eventually, this study resulted in changing the federal air regulations to include simulator time for advanced ratings and currency. We incorporated flying into college programs, issued fleets of military pilots their civilian licenses, trained scores of businessmen in their own planes, did proficiency and recurrent training for federal agencies abroad, and when the GI Bill was no longer approved for flight training, Flight Safety sold all our airplanes and redefined their facilities and programs for simulator training only.

I intently considered an offer at their new facility, training in simulators in Toulouse, France, on the Concorde and the A-300 Air Bus – the allure of Europe was almost too much and I had taken all those years of French when it was the international language, but the draw of actual flight was too much. As the instructors I'd known for so long parted for other jobs, I looked for something in Southern California that would allow me to continue attending Long Beach State University. I wanted to advance rather than go sideways in a new job if possible, but there were limited, if any, opportunities for women.

I was told by John Williams of an opening in Hawthorne with Hughes Tool Company. Colonel Williams was our chief simulator instructor and formerly Director of SAM Squadron, flying our presidents. In passing conversation with one of our recurrent customers, Hughes' Corporate Chief Pilot, my name came up as a candidate, because the company was looking to hire a minority.

The job entailed flying engineers around to military bases and out to desert test sights in an Italian built airplane I'd never flown called the Piaggio. When I appeared for the interview, I found the chief pilot was a severe, retired Air Force type: big and broad shouldered with icy blue-gray hair and steel-rimmed glasses. I wanted to call him *Colonel*. I noticed he was much older than his boss, the Hughes' Corporate Chief Pilot who had given me such a good recommendation.

From the moment I advanced the power levers for take-off, there was a view-limiting device placed in the windshield to block the view outside; it remained in place until touchdown. I flew a normal day's schedule with engineers aboard, and when the day was over, I departed with the colonel's promise to call. He had been uncommunicative throughout the series of flights, I adapted as professionally as I could, and made no mistakes.

Two weeks went by without a word, so I called him. I reminded him of who I was and asked if he had decided on a new pilot. He told me in severe tones: "This job, of course, goes to a man! A black man." I was surprised by his manner and the content of his message, but thanked him for "giving me the opportunity."

He said: "Humpfff," and hung up.

In retrospect, I think the chief pilot of Hughes' Piaggio Division of Flight, the "Colonel," was upset that the corporate chief pilot was recommending someone for *his* department. He and Colonel Williams had both given me good recommendations for the job. A few weeks later, during single engine training with his new pilot, the colonel spun into the ground.

✈

Chapter III

ACQUAINTANCES

At the end of my new hire class at Western Airlines, we were invited to a suite at the Airport Marriott Hotel. A welcome party was underway replete with Rangoon Rubies I was afraid to have touch my lips, much less drink. The concoction was the invention of Captain Wayne Touche` and looked like a red volcano bubbling up from a block of dry ice. Entertainment was a wet tee shirt contest and I wondered where they got the girls: bosomy, beautiful calendar-girl types. Guys hurried to get them wet by challenging them to drinking contests.

I watched in good humor and decided the whole airline thing could be fun. After all, it was 1976 in Cutting Edge, California. Free love and sport fucking were vogue. AIDS was yet to be part of the media craze though it lurked in dark bathhouses, and Women's Lib was in full bloom after more than a decade of the pill. Women's Lib was also Men's Lib but not everyone knew it. Partners fell in and out of marriage as easily as they fell in and out of bed, and monogamy was lying on the old relic heap somewhere near Candlestick Park.

The Vietnam War was in closure and young women and men were rife with *attitude*. At parties, exotic drugs were nearly served alongside liquor. An enterprise that challenged the Puritan work ethic arose with this era: drug running. To some pilots, it became the last bastion of capitalism. But government found it a threat to tax collection and revenues; a citizenry that chose an ethereal world didn't choose a working one. George Orwell's *1984* was a harbinger approaching in the distance. As time drew closer, it assumed a different face. It wasn't government who masked drugs in fluoridating water, we drugged ourselves, and eradication of drug traffic was forthcoming as an exercise for an idle military against its errant citizens.

I was not strong enough to capitulate to this revolution and opted for a safer path, though it was not without heartbreak and hazard. I chose, at a formative age, to become an airline pilot with hopes of someday flying internationally. Selecting this goal satisfied conditions I placed on my life. Challenged not only by the requisite education leading to credentials, but also by development of skills verging on more than just aptitude, I was fuelled by desire, and having a knack for flying, it became my calling. Pursuit of this mark gave me direction. Time was not on my hands; I was busy flying. When issues of the heart sought to derail me, I was reminded of my journey and got back on track. Flying was a balm. It comforted me knowing I was learning a skill I thought no one could take from me. That no women were employed by U.S. airlines before the Women's Liberation movement was a fact. It was a long stretch from introduction of the Equal Rights Amendment - assuring equal pay for equal work - in the early sixties, until the mid-seventies when women were finally hired by U.S. commercial airlines. I was fortunate to be one of the first hired.

✈

The dance band in the corner did a drum roll during every chug-a-lug and I expected to see a bikini-clad girl covered with icing jump from a cake. After an hour, the Rangoon Rubies loosened the crowd and the party went wild! I resolved to laugh at indiscretion and somehow become part of the joke rather than the brunt of it. I heard that pilot Lorelei Burch from Scenic Airlines was having a time of it at Western. Was she offended by the lack of professionalism, by the treatment she received from her peers? Perhaps her diplomacy wasn't working, or was it just that her fun meter was pegged? At first she was the butt of jokes, later, when she hadn't quit and gone away, she was the joke.

Lorelei and I knew each other for nearly a year before going to work for Western having first met while flying air tours in the Grand Canyon for Scenic Airlines. Surrounded by the Canyon's vermilion beauty each day was uplifting. As we flew eastbound after take off from Las Vegas and approached the gorge, the first buff cliffs rose to the horizon and sunlight slipped in silent revelation yawning black walls to red. As the Earth rotated into midmorning position, the angle of projection allowed brilliant illumination of geological character. Carved by wind and erosion, walls appeared redder than at other times, and monoliths along our aerial path extruded little shadow.

Flying as many as three tours a day this past year, the 10:30 a.m. tour took place during my favorite time of day. The air was smooth and there was genuine clarity. Unclouded by dust and illuminated by bright sunshine, geographical objects were lent prominence against the blue sky. Mechanical turbulence caused by winds swirling around vertical inclines had yet to kick up. Maneuvering an "S" pattern in Havasupai Canyon, waterfalls cascaded from holes in the canyon walls and bounced in travertine pools shined bluer by the angle of morning sun. Flowing 104 miles via natural underground flume from the San Francisco Peaks by Flagstaff, water exited the tunnels with dramatic frothing hydrology and fell stories below into Havasupai Canyon.

As days heated up and winds increased, afternoon flights became bumpy and "Qyatt Erp" bags depicting an amusing caricature of a cowboy got a lot of use. Solar radiation heated rocks, changing the temperature of the surrounding air, which rose in uneven columns, cooling with ascension, and if moisture was present, exploded into cumulus clouds. Every thunderstorm begins as a cumulus cloud, but not every cumulus cloud becomes a thunderstorm, Nature's most dramatic example of air rising at the moist adiabatic lapse rate. Summer rain was infrequent in the Grand Canyon, except what fell from thunderstorms. Water pooled in topo-dimples, mirroring rainbows of color as we flew past.

Our tour craft, the nine-passenger Turbo Star, was among several types we flew. It was an early predecessor to the Cessna Conquest but powered by two Allison turboprop engines. Scenic owners Elizabeth and John Seibold bought the STC for the engines and I was particularly fond of flying the airplane. The beauty of this airplane was twofold: it was flown with a single pilot and it slipped through the air unfettered by normal engine vibration. At the end of the day I lacked the vibrative fatigue residual inherent to flying straight props. Turbo props were smooooooth.

When the pilot selected a cue, passengers using earplugs could listen to the tour in their desired language. Having marketed these tours as part of Las Vegas packages – every passenger got his or her own window - Scenic Airlines assured itself international business in addition to domestic: it seemed people from everywhere wanted to see the natural wonders of that yawning chasm, the Grand Canyon.

In summer, a phenomenal thing occurred between flights: cumulonimbus clouds rose in the sky to more than twenty thousand feet. There were no flowers anywhere. On the next flight, if the cloud matured into a thunderstorm, there was rain *and* flowers. Suddenly dry red dirt went abloom: purple, pink, and yellow flowers appeared atop pinnacles. Pockets of color were tucked into nooks and crannies of magnificent schists. How long had seeds lain dormant? Were they transported to these isolated perches by birds, or did air currents lift them aloft?

With dispensation from the Park Service to fly tours through the Canyon, Scenic routinely operated planes a few hundred feet above the Inner Gorge but in the Outer Canyon. There were twenty-eight inspiring geological anomalies selected by the company from an endless array, and we framed each in passing with an elliptically-shaped wingtip fuel tank during pylon turns. The stunning country was eye-candy. Like butterflies in a blooming garden, our gaggle of planes flew from schist to schist. Tours began at Las Vegas' McCarran Field and ended at the Grand Canyon Airport. Passengers were flown directly back for connections after lunch and a bus tour. There was no aerial tour on the return and most passengers were grateful for straight flying and a distant view of the Canyon after the initial curvaceous flight path close to canyon walls and floor.

Lorelei and I became tentative friends. Our only similarity was we were both pilots. We weren't alike in many ways, but I often felt drawn to the extraordinary and in her case, I was once again. She invited me to lunch one day at the *Glide'r Inn* near the airport, rumored to have a good restaurant.

"Gene and I have been married for years," she began as we sat in the wing shadow of an elevated C-124 Flying Boxcar converted to business offices and a restaurant. "We've known each other since I was nine and he was eleven. Until now, we've been nearly inseparable." She paused, sipping her coffee. The rotating beacon cast a red glow now, now, now on her face as it turned round and round.

While she searched for courage to continue, for words to explain, I gave her an opportunity to divert the subject in case she didn't have the heart to go on. Her eyes were clouding with tears. I decided to ask a question about the attractive black pantsuit she wore.

"Your outfit's beautiful, Lorelei. Did you sew it yourself? "

"Yes, I love fashion." The jacket was an unusual cut with reveres stitched in perfectly sized, hand-sewn, white cross-stitches. Only a bold seamstress would embroider such contrasting stitches. It hadn't been too many years since pantsuits were accepted as public feminine attire. For women before the 1970's, a dress code of skirts extended from school to sidewalk. Pants were acceptable only in sports and at home. I visualized the jumpsuits I'd sewn hanging in my closet in royal blue, kelly green, fushia, and orchid.

"The stitches along your collar could pass for fabric airplane rib stitching, Lorelei. They're so neat and regular."

"Yes, I'm familiar with fabric airplanes. I've been rebuilding a Rearwin Cloudster in my living room for years."

"I thought only men took up their living rooms building airplanes..."

She tossed her head, laughing. "Gene and I have been building this one together." Once she mentioned Gene's name again, her eyes got sad. I waited to hear the rest of the story but had a feeling she was struggling to tell it.

"Do you have a Mechanic's License, Lorelei?"

"Yes, I have an A&P. You?"

"Yes, I went to A&P school, and..." but she was intent on continuing her story.

"Gene is flying out of Elko, Nevada," she resumed. "We're spending time apart. A year ago we lost our only child. It's shaken our marriage to its foundation. I haven't been able to get over losing my little boy."

I waited for her next passage. As time and space grew, I could hear the sadness coming in the sounds of silence.

"I wanted to have him at a large hospital in Reno with lifesaving equipment, but Gene thought I should have him where we lived and worked, in Elko. My son, Kenyon, strangled on his umbilical cord."

I listened to her heart-rending story and offered my hand in comfort. She held it lightly in hers as if a connection was considered, but not made. Impressed by how lonely that felt, I was compassionate about her loss and how she might feel about her husband. Poor man, loss of a child might be the worst thing that could ever happen to a woman.

✈

1976 was a paradoxical year. One morning at five the telephone awakened me. It was my husband calling me in Las Vegas from Silver City where he flew air tankers, protecting the Gila National Forest from fire. Ed told incredulous me, "I don't want to be married anymore," in a frightening tone I hadn't heard in years. "I'm moving in with our next-door neighbor from Berkeley." He paused dramatically, "Kitty...you know, the teacher..."

"Are you speaking of Katherine?" I asked, but to myself: *A teacher named Kitty? She calls herself Kitty!* Saying not another thing, I listened, stunned. Breathless, I had been expecting a call from Ed for some time. An awkward but compelling silence had grown between us. I waited to see what he would do. Every night, I sat by the phone waiting for the call that never came, until tonight, when I realized the admission was as hard for him to make, as it was for me to take. We weren't going down any more roads together.

He'd just confirmed my worst fear. His angry tone was more for himself than me. He wasn't going to commit to my venue - a profession - nor would he assume husbandly duties. "I don't want to be in harness..." Had I mistaken his intelligence for something else? Were his liberal roots now at the cutting edge? He chose to do the male thing, and escape with another woman. I was devastated by this news.

As he spoke, I visualized the two of them as a pair. *Isn't she about ten years older than he?* Vaguely, I heard him going on. "School's out for summer... she's coming to Silver to spend the fire season with me." I stopped listening. I just stopped. After the call, I realized I scarcely spoke a word, feeling the shock of abandonment. Or had I left him? I lay on my back, awake in the darkness and with a swelling heart, looked up at the ceiling through tears. They streamed towards my long hair, across my cheekbones, slid into my ears and dropped from my lobes, wetting the satin pillowcase. I tossed and turned, tangling my legs in the film of my negligee, trying to sleep, but the pain of our split was so intense that I could only roll from side to side, deeply sighing.

We'd often been apart flying on different jobs. *What changed?* I said aloud to the four walls. Could it have been my interviews with Western Airlines he worried about? Wait...wait. I hadn't even told him about Western.

Sometimes we'd taken flying jobs at the same company, like the time we flew Smoke Jumpers for Intermountain Aviation, headquartered in Marana, Arizona. This year we had jobs in different places: he was at Intermountain in Silver and I was at Scenic in LAS.

During winters, with savings earned from flying for contractors with the Forest Service, we attended classes at the University of California at Berkeley. Ed was a mechanic for World Airways and free-lanced as a mechanic in General Aviation. For living expenses, I taught at Gaffney Aviation at Buchanan Field in Concord. The Oakland FAA office asked me if I'd consider instructing there. Gaffney was operating an innovative airplane, the American Yankee, which had a laminar flow wing. Approaches had to be made at higher speeds, touching down nearly with power on. If Walter Mitty had been around, the Yankee would have been his choice of airplane because it flew like a tiny fighter and involved a new concept in landing approaches for some aspiring pilots.

It took straight A's for us to gain acceptance to Cal-Berkeley as transfer students from Long Beach State University in Southern California. Attending college was what we did in our time away from the forests during the school year. I was proud and independent, wouldn't ask my parents to pay for college. They had three other children and I was perfectly capable and self-sufficient, and never considered taking a student loan. Ed taught me that. "Staying out of debt is the key to freedom," he'd say. Eventually, I thought his was a different scenario of the Great American Dream from mine, and try though I might, I couldn't buy into his. I knew I wouldn't be happy living an austere life outside the "System." I thought I had to have "things," trappings important to the Establishment, the heritage of my gene pool. He apparently didn't.

I was ambitious to aspire to a commercial airline pilot's job when no other woman in the United States had one. The enormity of the challenge was of little importance to me. It's just that I loved to fly. I lived to fly. Would Ed view an airline job as conservative or establishment? Of course he would. It was definitely that.

"Ed, what do you want to be when you grow up?" I would ask that question. For years I encouraged him to seek a steadier vocation. He liked engineering but would not commit to it. He would be good at it. When I tried to discuss our future, he wouldn't address my concerns, looked over my head, and pretended not to hear. A wall of silence grew between us. This year, I took a flying job away from him, at Scenic Airlines, to give him what he called *breathing room*. I thought flying would take me where I wanted to go so when I reached for the sun and the stars by pursuing a commercial airline job, I was also grasping for the moon and losing a husband along the way.

In lonely moments when I tried understanding what changed between us - we took many of the same classes - I realized he was going left politically while I was going right. Eventually we couldn't discuss anything without getting into heated arguments. Our only connection was a troubled silence that ultimately influenced everything, even what went on under the covers.

It was breaking our hearts to realize that our legacies, our family heritage, something so fundamental, so genetic, was the reason we could no longer speak. He became a bleeding-heart liberal and I, a right-wing conservative. Earnestly, he tried one more time: "We'll be laughing about this in twenty years." He reached for my assurance that we'd still be together then. I looked down and couldn't speak. It was a deciding moment, a defining moment. In the silence that followed, we knew we'd reached that fork in the road.

Once I began feeling somewhat normal again and the initial pain of his bad news passed, I lay back and reviewed our marriage in vignettes: our flying, our adventures, our discussions about the world. His sweetness toward me, his endearing smiles, his dark hair and muscular body... though I had a profound feeling it could only have ended this way, it didn't make me feel any better. Some things are so bloody logical but still hurt like hell! Like the notch in Teddy's ear.

We were the Three Musketeers that summer, flying Smoke Jumpers out of the Redding Air Tanker Base near the end of the '74 fire season. Ted won the three of us a membership in the Enterprise Flying Club by winning a pool tournament. The Club was just across the freeway overpass from our apartment in the woods. Ed and I rode our bicycles over each evening for dinner and socializing. Our black and white dog, Poco, ran joyfully alongside, happy to be included. Ted drove in from his place in town.

Members' houses were spaced along the runway with taxiways into their yards. At the End of Season Party when everyone got roasted, Ed received a one-gallon can marked "Otter fuel," a dip stick, and an award for having made the shortest flight in Forest Service history: nine minutes, the time it took to take off from Redding, discover his plane hadn't been refueled during lunch, and go straight in to land at Red Bluff. One thing about Ed, he sure could cut his losses.

Teddy got the equivalent of a goalie's outfit including a helmet to protect him from harm. At the last Smoke Jumper party, when it was dark and time to go home, he got his 340- pound bulk headed downhill at an unbalanced run and came to an abrupt halt when he hit his head on the door jam of his truck. I was inside and it sounded like an ax hitting a watermelon. He bounced in reverse with the same speed he'd approached. He was so dazed and hurt that Ed had to help him up.

We three piled in the truck while Ted bled. I couldn't see where he was hurt on the right side of his head because I was driving, but there was an awful smell coming from his direction. Ed couldn't take his eyes off the wound and kept saying: "Ted, man, your ear is just hanging. We got to get you to the hospital..."

"I can't, man. I got to go home."

"Why? You're bleedin' pretty bad."

"I got to go home first," Ted insisted.

"But why?" I asked. There was a long silence from Ted.

"Because I shit my pants!"

I could hardly contain my laughter and drove Teddy straight home to change. We eventually found a demure Catholic hospital after driving all around town. The halls had figurines of saints on the walls and the nurses were nuns in white habits. Their head gear was of the flying nun type and when two passed in the hall they had to turn sideways to keep from knocking their hats off. They didn't look too pleased when the Three Musketeers stormed through the emergency room doors disturbing their peace at 2:30 in the morning, but never once did anyone say: "Shhh," bless them.

Once in the lighted hall of the emergency room where we could see, Dr. Ed proceeded with his diagnosis of Patient Ted. We must've been quite a sight: a trio surrounded by the flying nuns. We'd been on a fire all day in scorching temperatures and went straight to the Smoke Jumper party that night. I wore short shorts and combat boots, my long hair braided in pig tails; Ed had oil smudges on his cheeks, making him look more than ever like Popeye's buddy Bluto, his shock of dark, straight hair hanging in his eyes. His collared shirt was buttoned above a huge, obscene red flower and neatly tucked into his Frisco jeans. Teddy was wearing his too-short California Dreamin' tank top with his overhang showing: a foot of skin gaped below the bottom of his shirt and the top of his *clean* boxers.

Eventually, a groomed, nice looking slight fellow in a balloon-sleeved shirt and long Afro hairdo arrived to stand with us. For the tiniest moment Ed and Ted stopped talking to regard the newcomer. Then they disregarded him, turned back to each other and resumed talking. The young fellow disappeared for a few minutes and came back with a name badge. It said: *Dr. Newcomb*, which made me smile. Looking at the badge, the duo paused in their conversation, and directed an inquiry at him. "Are you sure you're a doctor? " Ted, 32, asked.

"Yeah, you look pretty young, man," Ed, 31, chimed in.

Teddy looked the Doc up and down and appeared beleaguered by the prospect of having someone younger than himself responsible for saving his precious ear. He was still bleeding. A normal sized person might have felt faint, but not Teddy. The pair looked down at Dr. Newcomb, who was dwarfed by their size, turned to each other again, and must have decided things were okay.

Teddy began climbing up onto the table. With his backside silhouetted against stark walls, his shorts crept down his considerable rear exposing most of the crack in his butt. To everyone's absolute glee, he mooned the entire lobby of the emergency room. It was a surprise that Ed and I were only asked to step a foot back from the action but we were never asked to leave the room. Teddy laid back for the examination while the nuns were a blur of angels. As the group cleaned and shined Teddy for the procedure, he suddenly sat upright: nuns fell off him and little pieces of blackened and bloody gauze floated to the floor. "Hey, Ed, should I be worried? The Doc just ordered a book with pictures of ears and there's eight pairs of 'em in the room!"

Ed looked at his friend, and growled in his deep voice, "I hope they don't have to amputate, man." With that unhappy possibility, Teddy lay back and quit squirming. When everything was done, his head was wrapped in a bandage that swung down to cover the offended vestigial appendage. He could have passed for one of the men in the World War I recreation, *Marching Soldier*.

A few days later we were at the Enterprise Air Park where houses lined the runway and airplanes were taxied into and parked in breezeways off the garage. Some Saturdays there were fly-ins. Pilots demonstrated their flying skills to judges seated on the front lawn of the Clubhouse. The events usually included Slow Flight, Flour Bombing, and Spot Landing contests. It was amazing how slow Ed could fly that Piper Cub. It seemed like it took him ten minutes to go by the judges. Invariably someone in that contest flew too slow, stalled, and dropped onto the runway. As the aerial arena was below fifty feet, usually no one got hurt. Planes didn't get damaged, just bounced really hard.

I was accurate in the Flour Bombing contest and hit the targets right on. In the Spot Landing Contest, Teddy kept missing his spot by only an inch. He'd land all around it, but not on it. And after too many $1 tries, his ego got involved. Teddy finally gave it up, beaten by a fellow who wasn't a particularly experienced or skillful pilot. Teddy was, after all, a Tanker pilot, somewhat of a hero who saved homes from forest fires by accurately dispensing retardant on the spot. It only goes to show that no amount of skill can take the place of pure, dumb luck.

Afterwards, Teddy felt discouraged and Ed wanted to leave but it was my turn to cook at the Club. I was making spicy black beans and rice with Mexican prawns on top for $2 a plate. Impatiently, Ed fired up his Twin Beech and gave the assembly rides over the kitchen while I grimaced skyward and cooked to the roar. He'd barrel-rolled the airplane at twenty feet after take-off with some of his passengers sitting on his toolbox which got a little light during the roll. Now, some people will roll a plane on take off, but Ed was the only person I ever knew who'd roll an old Twin Beech at twenty feet on take-off! He didn't do anything special like go faster; he would just lift off, pull the nose up and do a nice barrel roll, pretty as you please. Nearby Redding Tower could see the air show but Enterprise Air Park didn't have a tower and Redding couldn't do anything about it. I hear they're still looking for *that* pilot.

A few days later we were at the Redding Airport restaurant that specialized in huge hamburgers. They were tasty and patrons drove out from town to eat the half-pounders. Ed ordered the same thing every time: "Half-pounder, rare, *hold* the mayonnaise." While I hoped the cook would comply, Teddy decided to take off his bandage. He unwound and unwound the layers of gauze, letting it drop on the floor. His project gained the attention of the entire restaurant. His head appeared to be completely healed and his ear matched the other one except for a large notch in the lobe. When he felt the disfiguring wedge and exclaimed, Ed offered hope for future in his raspiest voice: "Tell 'em you're a guru, man."

Ed's hamburger came *with* mayonnaise. I couldn't believe it! What happened next was something a normal person would only *dream* of doing, but would probably never do. It was, however, an accurate representation of life with Ed. He stood up and launched his burger at high speed across the restaurant, through the pass window, and into the kitchen. It sailed like a Frisbee, turning round and round in the air. Due to centrifugal force the buns started to slide apart but because it had so much mayonnaise gluing it together, the garnish didn't leave, though I could see the tomatoes and pickles edging out in a colorful blur. It streaked over the heads of diners who looked up in awe as it flew by. With a loud *smack* it struck the burley cook in the back of the neck and stuck there, held by the mayonnaise. Everyone quieted as the cook slowly turned with a glint in his eye. It was Casey Rybeck, or might as well have been; he seemed to know right where to look. Then Ed boomed: "I said: half-pounder, rare, *no mayonnaise!*" It was the last time we ate at that restaurant.

For keeping Ed and Ted somewhat accountable during the last part of a bad fire season - we were paid by the fire - the Forest Service awarded me a Saint Christopher medal. I had found that the same thing that'll make you laugh will also make you cry.

✈

Three hours later the telephone rang. With some hesitation I answered hoping it wouldn't be Ed's cold voice heatedly addressing me again. It wasn't. It was Western Airlines calling to offer me a pilot's job. Hallelujah! How fortuitous, but oh, the irony! I must have completed the battery of interviews, medical exams, and simulator check successfully. Listening to the person on the line explain scheduling and class dates, I thought, *Oh, why can't we have everything at once?* My heart didn't know whether to sob or soar. I felt like I'd won the battle but lost the war.

✈

Conflict and heartbreak were unwanted companions as I drove my '63 TR-3 to Las Vegas' McCarran Field. Before beginning the day's flights I resolved to set my feelings aside while I flew, even though my emotions lampooned this decision. Arriving at Flight Operations, located in the second story of Scenic's huge, wood-paneled Quonset hut with a view of the ramp, I was reminded of the absurdity of aviation by the expanse and extravagance of the hangar. It was lost in a scam where an old Vampire jet was sawed in half, stretched to look like a corporate jet, and shares of its proposed success sold to investors. When I first started with Scenic, the Vampire was mounted as if in flight, hung in the entry lobby for investors to see. I passed it many mornings coming to work until one day it simply disappeared without a trace, just as the promoter had to South America with all the investor's money.

En route to my airplane with flight paperwork in hand, and nearly floating on the early morning breeze, the Director of Operations stopped me. "We'd like to offer you a new position - Director of Training," he said, smiling.

For a long moment I looked into his eyes. "This day is full of surprises," I grinned. How very comfortable and casual, asking me here rather than directing me to his office for this conversation. I considered doing both jobs simultaneously when I finished school and flew the line for Western. Though I'd flown as a line pilot for Scenic since my arrival nearly a year ago, much of my past flying had been as an instructor: my resume reflected that. I'd gotten along well at Scenic. As they expanded, they were interested in broadening their training department. I'd enjoy the position of Director of Training if I hadn't aspired to a commercial airline job and pursued Western Airlines. When I left Scenic, the other pilots chipped in and bought me a helicopter tour with Grand Canyon Helicopters as a parting present. I was touched by their thoughtfulness and promised to visit and stay in touch.

✈

Since I started instructing in 1967, I had heart-warming experiences teaching people to fly. Teaching was an opportunity to observe human behavior, to interact, and perhaps, make a difference in how well someone was trained to fly. At this writing in 2002, I can't improve on these thoughts as I review my intent to teach at Embry Riddle Aeronautical University.

One of my teaching jobs was in the Aeronautics Department at Cerritos College. An evening Professor, I worked during the day as Chief Pilot for Flight Safety and taught aeronautics at night. Teaching Golden West Airlines' new Captains, my logbook showed 52 candidates recommended in 1969 for their ATR's - Airline Transport Ratings. With that mark, the Long Beach GADO of the FAA nominated me for Flight Instructor of the Year. The award again went to a man, Bill Geonati, from the Bay Area.

I was lucky to be part of a team effort at Flight Safety on an experimental program conducted for two-and-a-half years in conjunction with the FAA and Lear Siegler out of our Long Beach facility. The results eventually changed the Federal Aviation Regulations to include the use of Simulators and Synthetic Trainers in General Aviation as viable alternatives to actual flight. Now time spent in simulation counted towards total flight time and could be recorded in a pilot's logbook.

✈

Before the era of the jet age in General Aviation, Flight Safety used the venerable Douglas DC-3 as trainer for the ATR. We taught corporate pilots in their company airplanes for proficiency and advanced ratings. One company we instructed for was NASA in their Queen Air. A NASA helicopter called for me in Long Beach and landed atop JPL's high-rise in Pasadena for ground school, then flew us across the city to the Burbank Airport, where the planes were kept. At the end of the session, I was helicoptered back to Long Beach; it was fun getting the VIP treatment *and* a bird's eye view of the city. Flight Safety had customers from one side of the world to the other, ultimately adding an additional word to the corporate name: *Flight Safety International.*

Among our many corporate customers were some celebrities. One was Ray Charles who had a four engine Vikker's Viscount and leased a Cessna 310 to us for use in our training program. Ray didn't himself fly because he was blind but while he waited for his plane to be brought up he played chess. He felt the shape of each piece. He remembered each move and usually won which was impressive.

When Flight Safety redefined their Long Beach facility for Simulator training only, and sold all their airplanes, I made preparations to leave. They came forward with a job at their new facility in Toulouse training on the Airbus and Concorde, but again, it would be in Simulators. I wanted to fly and politely declined, though the allure of France was almost too enticing - I could use all that French I'd studied - and I nearly relented. I remained at Flight Safety in Long Beach until the last Instructor departed.

Staying on, I wanted to do the test flying for FSI's new McDonnell Douglas DC-10 simulator and go on test flights. The new sim employed hydraulic motion through the use of telescoping arms that gave the pilot a sensation of flying, that the controls felt alive. Previously the only way to tell you were flying was to look at the instruments. From the new sim, I could see the world outside in daylight or darkness as the instructor preferred and with the new visual system a pilot could fly around the traffic pattern looking outside at the computer-generated countryside while shooting touch n' goes.

But there was another reason I stayed. I wanted to step-up to another position, not go sideways, and though I interviewed and flew flight tests several times with prominent corporations - I was coming very well recommended by the instructors who taught them - the job always went to a man. I resolved that until something changed in the industry - in the country - I would have to be content with another training position.

In 1973 I took a position as an instructor at IASCO - International Air Service Company - in Napa, California. Among other things, IASCO specialized in ab initio training for young Japan Air Lines pilots. Since the end of WWII when the Allies forbid Japan to have a military or airlines, IASCO pilots had flown the airplanes for Japan Air Lines. This last quarter century, a concentrated effort to nationalize the airline led to contracts for IASCO to train young Japanese men as pilots.

My employment interview consisted, first, of a panel of Japanese Boeing 747 Captains who spoke English well, and an American Chief Flight Instructor. My assignment was to teach them what happened to be one of my favorite subjects: comparing the difference between eights around pylons and eights on pylons by clarifying the term *pivotal altitude*. The second part consisted of a flight check in the Piper Aztec, performed under the hood and from the right seat. It was easy to know when Captain Kuahara was going to fail an engine: he put on his gloves!

This was a valuable instructing job as it set forth the habit of using procedures and required precise flying. My status was increased to Check Pilot after 100 percent of my students in Class A-17 passed the program successfully, and on their first try. This was a record for the previous thirteen years of IASCO's contracts with Japan, and I attributed my success to the judicious care I gave instructing each student, regardless of our apparent language differences. This event was not taken lightly by the American instructors working there who should have applauded the outcome as their Japanese bosses did, instead, I was accosted in the halls, outside the building, and off the premises. Usually, I just smiled and kept walking, choosing not to dignify their poor behavior by acknowledging them. What good would any of this do? They realized their performance limitations in that event and as I moved away they raised their voices to be heard. I wondered if they knew how foolish they looked and sounded...

✈

By 1976, I arrived at Scenic Airlines and flew the line for eight months before being presented with the offer of Director of Training. With nearly six thousand hours instruction given and even though instructing had been my forte, it didn't take but a few moments for me to realize I was ready for new horizons. I politely declined the offer to pursue a new idea in the San Francisco Bay Area: an Air Ambulance.

I chose my words carefully as I turned down Scenic's offer: "I was going to give you this later today, but now seems a good time," unzipping my 1938 Army Air Corps leather flight case given to me by a WASP, Isabel Steiner Karkau, who mentored my early days of flying. I handed the Chief Pilot my written resignation. I felt a little strange responding to his offer by giving him my resignation, but I wouldn't want him to harbor false hopes that I might change my mind. My letter politely thanked Scenic and gave my two weeks notice. "Thank you for giving me a new opportunity, but it looks like my star has risen." I smiled in supplication. To a pilot, an aspiring airline pilot, receiving an invitation for a class date with a major airline was tantamount to *being chosen.*

I reached to him offering my hand. He took mine in both of his: "If you change your mind, we'll be here, and we'd *love* to have you back."

"Thank you, thank you very much."

"Congratulations." He was genuinely happy for me. "We'll miss you."

Choking back a lump, I could feel tears coming to my eyes. "Inviting me back means a lot."

I gathered my flight equipment and proceeded to the airplane to begin the morning's preflight and engine run-up before meeting my passengers. Once boarded and briefed, we taxied to the active runway and flew eastbound on a Canyon Departure. A prescribed flight path for tour operators en route to the Grand Canyon, the distance from Las Vegas to where the tour began was about 70 miles. At our current speed of three miles per minute over the ground, we should arrive at the tour gate in 23 minutes.

Winter flying in Grand Canyon was enchanting. Snowfall on craggy pines attached to ledges looked filagree and the contrast against the red rocks was a visual treat. My breast swelled, enraptured by this sight and I voiced a passionate sigh at the fresh snow that only increased the beauty of the Canyon. During flights like this I imagined I heard symphonies.

Flying the tour, I thought back to memories of varied experiences collected over years spent in aviation: one year here, one year there, and recalled that only one or two adventuresome women have been present doing the same job. It was unusual, but there was a third woman at Scenic.

Billy Blue flew for the sister company, Grand Canyon Airlines, and lived at the Canyon. Her distinct radio-voice came over the airwaves as gruff and was immediately recognizable. On the rare occasion I had to stay at the Canyon overnight, she arrived to play pool with the guys carrying her own stick. She was an anomaly, and dressed like a man. Toward me, she was uncomfortably kind and inquisitive. I wondered if she had grown up in a family of men and somehow got confused. Though I acknowledged her presence and conversed at times – I thought she was very lonely - I chose to keep my distance. The other female pilot at Scenic was Lorelei Burch, whom I mentioned before and with whom I'd been paired in training. The three of us were flying as Captains, came from a General Aviation background, and paid for our early flight training.

The three of us were such a contrast: Billy was Billy, I was dark-haired and not thin, and Lorelei was shapely, blond, and thin, too thin, then. She was so pretty with her waist length blond tresses and large, limpid brown eyes that she could have been, and frequently was, mistaken for a Las Vegas showgirl. She, too, was so committed to her flying career that she elected to live in one place and fly, while her husband lived in another. They visited on days off whenever they could. Like me, she'd been working towards an airline career since she was a girl. Every waking moment she concentrated on her much-loved passion and worked toward her goal, hoping some day to have an opportunity to fly for a major commercial airline. This was one of several things Lorelei and I had in common. We started flying young and worked hard to get where we were. It was interesting to meet another woman with similar ambitions. It made the world feel a bit warmer, a little bit friendlier, knowing this dream was not mine alone.

The flying jobs available to women were few, but finally Lorelei, too, had been hired as a pilot by Western Airlines, and her class commenced before mine. She'd have greater seniority, and in the airline business in 1976, seniority was everything. It determined when you'd upgrade, when you'd be able to bid more advanced positions or larger equipment, and which bases you could hold. However, the one thing seniority didn't decide was retirement age. FAA mandated retirement age for commercial airline pilots was still an archaic 60 years old. This age was finally to change but not until 2007 when the mandatory retirement age was pushed ahead to 65, a reflective of improved health and longevity.

I lost track, no, I never kept track of Billy Berry until one day I heard her voice on the radio years later, but my acquaintance with Lorelei began at Scenic Airlines and continued through the years. Just short of a year after our meeting at the *Glide'r Inn*, we were both going through training for Western and when I spoke with her, she told me she and her husband were divorcing. Eventually, Lorelei took her late son's name as her surname and became Lorelei Kenyon.

A Western pilot was Lorelei's divorce attorney and graciously took her case gratis as he had never handled a female pilot's divorce before. Though his intentions were good, she ended up paying alimony. I took serious note that Women's Lib worked for both sexes. Captain Sunshine didn't forget this awkward outcome and years later when he was a check pilot on her airplane and she really needed fair assessment, he bravely evaluated her correctly and at his own peril.

✈

CHAPTER IV

THE CHECKRIDE

For four solid years after being hired by Western Airlines, I concentrated on doing a good job. It seemed best to be diplomatic and interpret every nuance with humor. So many practical jokes were played on me that after awhile I found myself laughing and smiling, and looking for the next. The first trip away from base on the 727, my luggage and flight case disappeared before we boarded the plane. I had to scuttle around collecting the necessary tools, flashlights and publications required to continue as a member of the flight crew. Three weeks after I'd filed a claims report, my luggage mysteriously appeared right outside Operations at the nosewheel of my departure airplane.

When I boarded one plane, sunscreens of nude women were considerately placed inside the cockpit windows by the pilots. They ate on picture placemats of their favorites in the buff, drank from personalized *titty* mugs kept in their flight cases, and wrote with pens shaped like women. When I checked the escape ropes stored in a compartment above our heads as part of the preflight, sexy pictures floated down. When I looked for the gear pins, they were strategically placed atop a centerfold of Burt Reynolds from *Playgirl's* first magazine.

On my first layover in MSP, I danced with pilots lined up in the hotel lounge before dinner. It wasn't something I expected, I had only gone to dinner. One introduced himself as Ben Dover; another with puppy dog eyes told me he felt like a bedspread, he'd been turned down so many times. Several twirled me around and into their arms, ending the dance with a surprising, passionate embrace. I knew they were teasing, having fun. Sometimes, I couldn't do anything but giggle.

In the crew lounge at hotels, soft drink machines dispensed beer instead of sodas. Once, tremendous thunderstorms kept me awake into the wee small hours. When at last they began dissipating, I moved outside onto the balcony to watch the distant lightning and listen to the gentle rain. I heard strange scuffing noises coming up the wall. I looked over the side of my fourth story room. In the hotel lights I could see a good looking, clean cut man in a tee shirt, shimmying up the downspout. I knew it wasn't one of *my* pilots as they'd strategically placed me between them in the middle room. When the climber saw me, he said, "Good evening," as if he might come this way often, and then began shimmying down.

Once I rode space available as a passenger in first class on a DC-10 going to Hawaii. After I helped a seat partner win the Captain's Halfway Sweepstake Game – the prize was a bottle of Western's "The Only Way to Fly" famous champagne – I noticed a very large woman go into the lavatory. She was a size requiring *two* seat belt extensions. A while later, I noticed she hadn't come out. I checked because I hoped I was next. Eventually, a service bell in the restroom must have summoned the flight attendant. I craned my neck to see as the door was opened, they spoke for a moment, and the helper began pulling, then tugging. The woman was apparently stuck because her ample bottom covered the entire toilet seat, creating a pressure seal. She couldn't be dislodged.

Soon, the second officer was summoned from the cockpit to help. He stepped in next to the lady and grasped her under her arms. By now, some of us were standing in the aisles watching with amusement. The S/O was a big guy and he must have been new or he would have realized that by raising the cabin to a higher altitude - decreasing the pressure - he could have broken her seal.

He pulled and yanked as hard as he could – she looked like a rag doll being tossed around – then he stepped back to take a breath and the expression on his face was one of dismay. He moved in closer, repositioned his arms under hers for another try, and, in the process, buried his face in her ample bosom. He began making mighty grunts and heaves. When this didn't work, he moved in even closer, inadvertently stepping into her underpants which were down around her ankles. The constant roar of the engines muffled some of our laughter because, by now, we were beside ourselves, holding our sides, and nearly rolling in the aisles.

Suddenly, the S/O decided he needed more help. He turned from the lavatory, tripped in the underpants, and fell flat on his face in front of the entire first class cabin. He writhed around on the floor, tangled up in the substantial-sized undergarments. Passengers vacated their seats to stand and watch. My eyes closed blinking back tears of hilarity. Everyone held their sides and laughed hysterically. Finally, he got free and literally dove for the cockpit as the door opened. A few minutes later - he must've gotten instructions - the cabin rose, and the fat lady walked without assistance. The S/O didn't leave the cockpit for the rest of the flight and the door remained closed during deplaning at our destination.

If you could imagine all the fun things that might have happened at an airline job, they probably did. When I was involved, there was a sweet aspect to these antics as if the guys weren't all that disappointed I was there. They were as confident and self-assured as the flying public would want their pilots to be, but at the same time, I felt as if they included me as one of them. It was a very special and fun time.

✈

First, I checked out on the Boeing 737 as GIB - an acronym for *guy in back*, which was Western's entry level, featherbedding position. There was only room for two pilots on this airplane and yet there were three, the pilot's union - ALPA's - answer to a plane built without a flight engineer and a production delivery occurring within contractual time limits. I had been flying captain for the minor leagues, and now, major airline or not, this GIB thing was demoralizing. Right away I bid for and got second officer, or flight engineer, followed shortly by first officer, or co-pilot, on the Boeing 727. Later, I checked out as second officer on the McDonnell Douglas DC-10.

Work took most of my energy with all the orals and checkrides, so I reduced my personal life to nothing more than mere dating. The new SFO chief pilot, whom I taught for his instructor ratings years before, invited me to be a check pilot, but a change of heart caused him to retire from his position before the issue of my increased status went any farther. An ambitious cohort, who stylishly sported an Afro hairdo though he was not African American, replaced him. His associates, most of whom wore short military haircuts no matter what the style, affectionately dubbed him *Curley*.

One week, our regular captain was displaced before pushback by a check captain who wanted to fly the leg from Los Angeles to San Francisco. As crew, we were mid month in a sequence of flights. Exercising his prerogative to maintain currency on the Boeing 727, the check captain elected to fly the leg and the scheduled captain stepped back to first class and rode in an available passenger seat. If a seat had not been available, he would have remained on the flight deck and occupied the jumpseat.

Upon rotation from the runway at LAX, oil pressure on the number one engine began decreasing during the take-off roll; normal for the 727 was approximately 30 psi. I quickly advised the check captain of this event and he turned in his seat to observe the decreasing pressure then and in subsequent minutes before we shut the engine down. As he turned out of the traffic pattern and continued to fly the departure path out of town, I read the numerous items on the emergency checklist for an engine shutdown. We noted the oil pressure was at zero, an unusual indication that we discussed, until the engine was secured by shutting the fuel off, at which point it should begin rotating in the air stream. At that time the oil pressure should have resumed a positive but low indication of 6 to 8 psi for the duration of the flight, but didn't.

Then another problem arose. The first officer and I were very concerned when the captain did not return to LAX for landing and continued to fly the departure towards San Francisco. Once we leveled off at FL 240, a lower than planned cruise altitude requested by the check captain and granted by Air Traffic Control, we would have higher fuel consumption. We pulled out our Operations Manuals nearly simultaneously and read through the engine failure procedures, which were specific. To continue onto a distant destination (SFO) when a perfectly good airport was still in the windows (LAX) wasn't reasonable. To fly along a coastal route where no adequate airports were available for landing was not safe: if we were to lose another engine, we would be running at one third power and might have to put down at a general aviation airport with too short runways, or in a farmer's field, or land in the ocean. None of this fazed him.

"It's a beeeautiful Sunday afternoon, Ladies and Gentlemen. We all want to get home to our families and loved ones even though we've had to shut down an engine. We'll be continuing on to SFO," the check captain advised passengers and crew in a deep and resonant voice. He chose to disregard regulations and his crew's recommendations to turn back to LAX. We continued advising him diplomatically that this was not a good choice and insisted he turn back. He ignored our concerns. Flying at the lower altitude afforded a closer view of California's rugged coast line but burned more fuel than planned. We were properly dispatched with enough to get to San Francisco plus 45 minutes, as the weather forecast for our destination was good. Should the forecast have included inclement weather we would have been dispatched carrying substantially more. I asked myself, *Does he think because he's a check captain he has special talents? Or is he just audacious, exposing his passengers and crew to additional danger?* I am astounded by his presumption, and angered at the inkling that as the junior officer the company might try to hang this one on me.

Soon the displaced captain knocked on the cockpit door, rang the bell, and requested entry over the telephone. It was likely he realized we'd lost an engine when we leveled off at a low cruising altitude. When admitted to the flight deck, he took the jumpseat behind the check captain. They began discussing the engine shutdown casually and with such élan it was as if they were flying a simulator. I was sure the gravity of our situation eluded them. Both the first officer and I sat quietly throughout the flight, wishing the check captain would turn back to our point of departure. When Los Angeles disappeared from view, we knew he wasn't going to return. I hoped we'd experience no further power losses as we proceeded up the coast at Flight Level 240.

When our flight arrived in the San Francisco Bay area, the check captain was cavalier with ATC, insisting we were not in an emergency situation and offered to follow traffic ahead. *Is he now trying to demonstrate what a super pilot he is?* Further, he refused ATC's offer to dispatch emergency vehicles to our runway. I held my breath, hoping nothing more would happen. He remained high on the downwind, then swooped to the runway and touched down without further ado, thank God.

I sat behind the captain at my flight engineer station as he stood beside the open cockpit door. He was strategically in line for comments and immediately recognizable looming over the passengers. He had put on the balance of his uniform. I noticed some deplaning passengers displayed reserve in thanking him for the flight, or completely avoided eye contact. Others verbally admired him and complimented him on his expertise. When the plane was cleared, the senior flight attendant stepped forward to the entry area to express her dismay at hearing *over the public address system* that we were in an emergency situation. The captain smiled and brushed her aside as he deplaned.

Before handing the airplane over to the maintenance foreman, the check captain read and approved my logbook entry by signing his name to the statement he told me to write. One of the sentences in the paragraph stated: "The oil pressure dropped to zero." It was this statement that precipitated a meeting between the new chief pilot, the first officer, and me.

Before my bottom sank into the leather chair in the chief pilot's office, Curley announced: "I'm giving you two weeks off without pay because you wrote in the aircraft logbook that *the oil pressure went to zero*. Because of this, a complete overhaul of the engine was required."

I blinked. "There was no oil pressure, sir. Zero oil pressure."

"Usually there is windmilling oil pressure of 6-8 psi." Curley lowered his head and looked at me through the tops of his eyes.

"There was no oil pressure for the remainder of the flight, sir. The check captain and I discussed this event at length."

"It meant a complete bearing failure if the oil pressure remained at zero."

"The oil pressure remained at zero, sir."

"It cost the company three men to overhaul the engine and 72 hours overtime because of your logbook write up."

I didn't know what to say. Throughout this exchange, the first officer remained silent.

I repeated: "I don't know what to say except the oil pressure remained at zero. There was no windmilling oil pressure indicated for the remainder of the flight."

The new chief pilot said: "Maintenance said there wasn't a teaspoon of oil left in that engine."

"So I don't see the problem, sir. I don't see why I should get two weeks off," my exasperation was beginning to show. I was right. He was trying to hang this one on me. "If there wasn't a teaspoon of oil left in the engine, sir, then a complete overhaul *was* necessary, otherwise, on the next flight a bearing failure might have caused a fire." Then I said quietly, "The check captain approved my logbook write up;" a summation which hung in the air. I resisted asking if *he* was getting two weeks off, too. *Should I press my defense further, perhaps be impertinent, and mention the check captain's most serious mistake of not returning?* I have an internal battle but decide to hold in the event I should need further ammunition by using the check captain's non-compliance with regulations. The new chief pilot gazed steadily at me without speaking for long a long time, as if he debated whether to bring up the issue.

In a tiny voice I said, "You aren't *really* going to give me two weeks off for writing what the check captain told me to write in the logbook, are you, sir?" I tried a little smile, hoping to humor him. Inside, I was furious.

"No, but I *am* going flying with you tomorrow."

✈

The first officer and I were scheduled for a coastal rotation with stops in Portland and Vancouver, returning to San Francisco at the end of the business day. The chief pilot displaced our regular captain to fly this trip.

It was a short taxi from Gate 67 to Runway One Left at San Francisco, making a busy and hurried few minutes for me, the second officer. From pushback, I started all three engines on the 727 while the final weights of passenger count, cargo and fuel were read to me over my headset by the load master in Flight Ops, stationed below Western's satellite concourse. Using a *flow pattern* to scan the engineer's panel, I started the engines and copied the weights at the same time. An analogy for the way a jet engine starts is *suck, squeeze, bang* and *blow.* The engine sucks in air delivered by the APU or another source and begins rotating. Then the air is squeezed, compressed to great density, fuel is added, then ignited: bang! Air blows out the back of the engine. Much as a released balloon, when accelerated, it goes!

Curley took the microphone from the first officer and called for take-off clearance as soon as we were waved away from the gate by the ground crew. He taxied faster than any captain I'd flown with. I called upon my training, proceeding rapidly though systematically through systems while at the same time copying the weights. Within about two minutes after leaving the gate, we were ready for take off.

As the engines accelerated toward idle with rising oil pressure, the generators came up to speed, oscillating at 390 to 410 cycles per second. Each generator was trimmed to its most stable operating velocity with a frequency control knob while observing a set of lights flashing slower and slower. Operating properly, it was joined with the two others on a common electrical line called a synchronous bus. This bus was the source for selecting electricity for application.

Switching was handled electrically, while components that moved and required muscle were hydraulic. Quickly paralleling the generators, the rest of the systems were activated while computing the weights and balance of the airplane. Center of gravity position was calculated and related to balance and controllability, while the gross weight determined the fastest the airplane could go before the pilot might decide to discontinue the take-off roll, able to stop before reaching the end of the runway. Gross weight total also determined speed of rotation and a take-off safety speed where the airplane could circle the field, clear all obstructions, and return for landing in the event of an engine failure.

Flap retraction speeds were determined at this time. Incrementally, the flaps were retracted as each speed was reached and by 200 knots or more, the 727 could fly clean, accelerating to 250 knots below 10,000 feet. This speed limit was imposed for two reasons: because of aerial congestion of military, commercial, and civilian aircraft operating near the surface, and because of possible bird strikes, which may break through the windshield injuring, perhaps fatally, the pilots, and depressurizing pressurized aircraft. Above 10,000 feet, there was no speed limit. Go. Go. *Go!*

As soon as ground control cleared the aircraft for taxi to the active runway, checklists were performed by habit and from memory in their appropriate sequence. The second officer reading the challenge expected an appropriate response. With experience, the reading became a score in a checklist symphony. Each note had to be played in order for the set to be complete. If any one piece was left out, any item left undone, a take-off might be attempted without proper speed bugs set, or with flaps improperly positioned, and human error would be read about in the next day's tabloids.

Transport manufacturers leave something as critical to flight as *flaps extended to the proper take off position* as the sole responsibility of the pilot. This pilot function could easily be replaced if the manufacturer would retrofit old and market new airplanes with flap extension systems that would automatically extend flaps to the proper take-off range as soon as engines are started, pressurizing hydraulic systems. The technology is available. Aviation history is littered with crashes since the inauguration of commercial jet transports in 1961 because pilots forgot to follow checklist procedures instructing them to extend flaps to the take-off position *before* take-off. The last crash involving this oversight happened in 1987 by a Delta Air Lines 727 taking off from Dallas – Ft.Worth International. Later, it was conclusive: the checklist heard over the voice recorder was rote, but the flaps were not positioned correctly for take-off. Since then, checklist procedures have been modified to assure the flaps are properly set for take off. Planes are still built with reliance on pilots to operate crucial systems in a timely manner. Transports will not take off and climb configured for cruise; they come down.

After calculating the weight of the airplane, I informed the new chief pilot we were too heavy for Runway One Left, our initial runway assignment. It was too short. We were carrying additional fuel to continue on to Seattle or Vancouver in the event existing fog in Portland did not lift. The new chief pilot advised the first officer, who relayed to the tower, that we would need a longer runway.

We taxied into position on Runway One Right, long enough for our heavy take-off weight. If we were a heavier plane, we would have used SFO's east-west runways which were able to accommodate the heaviest of aircraft.

I glanced over at the parking area. Dotted with cars and just east of the approach ends of the runways, I recalled years ago sitting in my car, eating a brown bag lunch, watching airplanes take off for places I could only dream about. Flying Tigers would hold position in a Canadair -CL44 awaiting take off clearance, followed by a Western Airlines Lockheed Electra, a Pan American Boeing 707, and a West

Coast Airlines Fairchild -F27. An era of aviation history has passed since then, and whole generations of airplanes have retired. What a surge I felt as those flagships advanced power for take-off. I dreamed of the day when I'd taxi into position in a transport going to some far-off place like we were today: Vancouver.

Quickly I completed all items and fastened my shoulder harness for take-off. Picking up the PA, I gave the passengers a brief, "Good morning Ladies and Gentlemen, on behalf of the Flight Deck Crew we would like to add our welcome aboard Western 's Flight 495, flying service to Vancouver, British Columbia, with a stop in Portland, Oregon. We've been cleared for take-off, flight attendants please be seated."

Leveled at our cruising altitude, the new chief pilot turned in his seat to study my flight engineer's panel. He didn't say anything, occasionally shook his head. I looked around my panel, carefully checking to see that I had it correctly configured. Discovering nothing out of the ordinary, I decided he was just trying to undermine my confidence, which gave me a twinge of anger. Finally, he commented on the position of the aircraft environmental cooling doors, which were on the low end of the importance scale.

"I've never seen the cooling doors in that position at cruise."

"You haven't?" I smiled and politely offered, "I believe that they're in the prescribed position for this regime of flight as described in the Operations Manual," and pulled out the book. Quickly, I referenced the table of contents and opened to the appropriate page where the doors pictured were in the same position for cruise as the ones appearing on my panel. I showed him the passage. As if thwarted and apparently annoyed that what I'd displayed on my panel was apparently correct, he then went through every system on the flight engineer's panel. By the time we began descent into Portland with statuesque Mt. St. Helens breaking the distant skyline in a graceful point, I was in a full-blown checkride.

When we reached the parking gate and the engines were shut down, the first officer vaulted from his seat with no regard for protocol: captain first. I understood why he did it and wanted to say, "Chicken," but refrained from this wit. There was nothing humorous about what was to come. I was steaming.

I'd been blamed for the expense of an engine overhaul because of the check captain's logbook write-up and threatened with two weeks' disciplinary time off without pay. I'd tried being rational with the new chief pilot and this had seemed to work; maybe he wasn't so unreasonable after all. But then to go flying with him, and make it a checkride, and a hard one, when he said it wasn't going to be a checkride – this bouncing back and forth de-stabilized the situation, and proved an interesting twist. Was this a pilot management character trait I could look forward to? I mentally filed it away for future reference.

The new chief pilot got out of the left seat just as I stood up in front of the flight engineer's panel. This momentarily blocked his exit from the small cockpit. I was nearly as tall as he and my line-of-sight went straight to his Adam's-apple, bobbing up and down on his long, thin neck.

"You said this wasn't going to be a checkride, sir."

He didn't answer right away and spent some seconds regarding his feet. I advanced my position.

"It seems I can't do anything right, sir. You've challenged every move I've made and taken exception to every procedure I've followed. I believe I've been correct in every way, but I can't seem to please you. Would you prefer I get off the airplane so crew scheduling can send another second officer?"

Realizing this would entail delay of our outbound flight because a replacement pilot would have to be flown in, perhaps on another carrier, made Curley pause. He didn't answer right away and when he did it was in a quiet voice: "I gave the check captain you flew with last week a congratulatory letter..."

I gasped. *Does this mean the chief pilot doesn't know the rules either?*

"...on the fine job he did handling the engine failure. First thing this week, the FAA gets a copy and the roof falls in. I guess the check captain should have returned to Los Angeles. The check captain has lost his check position and I nearly lost my new chief pilot position between my letter to the Feds and the additional expense incurred to overhaul the engine."

I appreciated that he was so candid. He paused a moment, then surprised me with an unexpected admission, "You know," his voice broke, "You're the fourth woman to admonish me today. First, it was my daughter and my wife, then my secretary, now you."

I tried not to chuckle, gazed at him with wide eyes, and remained silent. Then I moved away from the door so he could pass. I stepped downstairs to do the en route walk around inspection. Back on the flight deck, I resumed my position at the flight engineer's panel in preparation for departure; *this* checkride was over.

CHAPTER V

THE VIAL

Glenna McTavish's dark basement was too low to stand in erect. A single old light bulb turned on with the pull of a string. Illuminating the area with a yellow glow that cast light into corners, it defined the perimeters of her house. I followed her down the rickety staircase to select vases from her bounty of sterling silver sequestered in a place not unlike the Scottish castle where she grew up as a child.

Glancing around the dusty room, my eyes strained to look past shadows for the diffused webs of black widow spiders. I was aware my shoulders were drawn up in tension. I stepped in and out of the light, turning this way and that as Glenna stood under the bulb holding the string. Her slender figure was silhouetted in the triangle of light and her auburn hair shone, hanging in smooth waves around her shoulders.

Cling. "Oh!" Surprised I'd bumped into a vessel I couldn't see, I heard it rolling away.

"Careful. It's not too tidy down here," Glenna remarked in her mildly discernible accent. "In a few moments, our eyes will adjust and we will be able to see." As if someone focused the picture, details sharpened in the gloom. "We can choose any of these silver vases -

we'll need about two dozen, I suppose." Stacked in piles around the room, most were elegant; all were silver. They embodied her passion and she thought of them as her assurance of retirement.

"Will this one do?" I asked, pulling a tall pitcher with an elaborate handle from the pile.

"Yes, but we want to make sure the ones we pick are romantic," she held up a mug with a wicked face. "Not like this one."

"You must have traveled far to get that one." We smiled at each other. Glenna blew at the dust coating the monstrosity.

"Yes, this is an old Gaelic drinking mug." She gazed at her reflection.

I wondered how it entered her world and who last drank its contents?

Finally, after considering scores of bowls, plates, vases and chalices, we assembled a group and got busy carrying them up stairs to a lighter room.

"There's a lot of cleaning to be done by this afternoon," I remarked, unscrewing the lid of the English tin containing polishing gauze, unlike the silver cream I used.

"Yes, but we can finish if we work fast," Glenna said, dropping to her knees on the rug. Spreading newspapers over the floor, she began cleaning the surfaces with long, practiced strokes.

"What are your favorite flowers, Glenna? So I can tell Petunia at Flower Art." We laughed. "Do you think her name really is Petunia? Or is it just a clever idea to promote business?"

"A clever idea I suppose... Flowers? I like anything cheerful, spring-like, after so much rain, and so many clouds, I 'm ready for spring."

"Does Archie care what colors?"

"No, Archie doesn't care. Red would care, but not Archie. He just wants things to be pretty." Archie was Glenna's intended, who bore an amazing resemblance to Red but was a much larger man. Glenna insisted Red was six feet tall but at 5'9", I'd seen her looking over his head. I knew Red was larger than life, but could Glenna have been a stewardess who composed her own reality? Did this mean she could be deluded into thinking six inches was really a foot?

The mystery of this romance was that the two men looked so much alike. Both were captains for Western and flew the same equipment. Glenna was Red's paramour of many years, and he is thought to have wooed women all over Western's world. A colorful character, Red brandished moustaches so large they could be seen from behind. He hailed from Alaska and included Pacific Northern Airlines in his flying career until Western bought the airline in 1968. The acquisition brought new routes to Western and the airline gained more character with the addition of Alaskans like Red.

His reputation for loving life was renowned. Something of a cult hero among pilots, rumor had it he flew a daring helicopter rescue to pluck a friend from the yard of a South American prison. When Red retired, he was so popular that nearly every base threw a party for him. I never heard of anyone else at the airline having so many retirement parties.

Every few months, volatile Glenna broke off their relationship. Red never seemed to get around to marrying her and rumors of his latest interlude infuriated her. He arrived at her home in San Francisco to find she'd thrown his clothes out in the front yard again. To go into the arms of another man so soon after a twenty-two year romance, I wondered if she had given herself enough time to get over Red.

"With you there as the bride, Glenna, everything will be pretty. You look so happy these days, your cheeks are glowing." Glenna smiled and I smiled back. Then she dropped her eyes to the silver vase in her hands. Her copper hair hung forward in soft curls around her face. She was a real Scottish beauty. Tall, slim, "From good brrreeding," she'd tell me rolling her r's. I was pleasantly amused.

She told me her father was a "Physician," rather than a "doctor." Her enviable figure - a perfect size six below the waist and above, a twelve, was, she felt, the result of "prrroperrr genes." She let everyone know when first introduced that her name was Glenna with an N, and I heard this so often that "Glenna with an N" was the name she was referred to by her co-workers.

After polishing with no conversation for awhile, she asked:" Where are you going at one o'clock?"

Reluctantly, I told her. "I have a date."

"With someone I might know?"

"With Bill Lake, do you know him?"

"Yes, I do, if he's the same person. Is he a captain with Western Airlines based in San Francisco?"

"Yes, yes, he is."

"Well, you don't want to be involved with him. He's so, so... cavalier."

This was a surprise. I thought he was handsome to the extreme, and worldly. I admitted being somewhat dazzled by his attentions. I listened carefully. I wondered why Glenna felt this way. How well liked someone was by others was not part of my criteria in deciding whether or not I should know them. Yet, *I'm* most comfortable when people like me, so whether I enjoyed hearing about it or not, it was a matter of importance that I understand why Glenna had some question. She had been around the airline a long time.

"He's always been pleasant to me," I offered in appeal.

"It's not to say he's unkind, it's just that he's so...so confident. It appears there's nothing he doesn't know."

I wasn't sure this was a good recommendation. "Please tell me why?"

"You haven't beeeen around him as we at the airline have beeeen for years. He's suspect because he's such a mystery. It may only be a cover for an inadequate depth of character." To Glenna, good breeding and substantial character were synonymous.

This assessment took me so by surprise, I felt an uncomfortable twinge. He was certainly kind enough to me, in fact, he was warm and charming. I knew from experience that associates' disfavor could be disheartening, especially for arcane reasons. I left Glenna's on this questionable note.

Swaying in my seat to a Donna Summers' song, *I Will Survive*, I felt somewhat anxious. But my decision to reserve judgment on Bill Lake came intuitively. After dropping off the vases at Petunia's, I headed up the hill to his new home in Hillsborough.

A Hillsborough vantage point offered a view of the Bay Area from a southerly direction. If the cities of San Francisco and San Jose were due west and east of each other - bets have been won on this fact - they have always *seemed* to lie north and south. If San Francisco was the head and San Jose was the toe, then Hillsborough could be described as the southern shoulder.

Dusk and the early evening lights of Berkeley across the Bay appeared as jewels in the east hills. Mt. Diablo poked the violet sky with the profile of a single breast. How could such a lovely shape be called Devil Mountain?

The closest amusement was the San Francisco International Airport, sprawling like a monopoly game at my feet. Planes flew in and out looking like silver tokens. With company insignia illuminated by logo lights on their empennage, they lined up on final approach with their landing lights on. They looked like diamonds laced on a necklace, hanging looped in the air, spaced by Air Traffic Control's three miles separation required around congested areas. The Blue Ball of Pan American, the Red W of Western , and the modern art of Caulder's painting on Braniff airplanes were visible from my position high in the hills. *They're landing west at SFO*, I noted, ringing the doorbell of the captain's mansion.

This was my first exposure to a house size reflecting the rank of a pilot; there was a captain sized house, a first officer sized house, and a second officer sized house. As the paycheck increased so did the house size. This one was definitely a captain's house and large for a single man. New and gracious, it was nearly the size of my family home in Pink Horse Ranch, further down the peninsula. Just when I began to wonder if I was here on the right day, the door swung open. Two men stood in the entrance.

"Hello!"

I smiled. "Hello." One was my friend, Bill Lake.

"Come in. Come in." He stood aside, smiling while the other man brushed by, leaving. It took courage, but I looked into his eyes as we passed, knowing they mirrored his feelings. I wasn't sure what I saw – he didn't look directly at me – but his eyeballs were enlarged and protruded. They seemed too big for their sockets. Then he glared straight ahead, ignoring me. Lake didn't introduce us and called goodbye to his back. The man walked toward a car in the driveway, turning his head backwards toward Lake. They maintained steady eye contact until the man reached his car and drove away. Strange, I could feel electricity in the air.

At first I wondered if this hard look transpired because of me. If it had, the intensity and tension was not an appropriate reflection of the present relationship between Lake and me. I paused to wonder what it could mean. Bill and I were relatively new friends; we'd seen each other for different occasions the past several months: dinners, holiday parties. While he'd completed his new house, he'd camped out somewhere nearby, but I didn't know where. His house completed and beautifully furnished, he'd moved in and invited me for sunset cocktails.

I stepped inside onto a dark carpet. Crystal chandeliers lined up to point the way down the hall. I thought I smelled new paint on the walls. We walked for some seconds by the living room as he showed me the way to the den. Paneled in cherry, it had views across the Bay. New books with gold titles stood vertically on shelves and I could see my reflection in the desktop.

Captain Lake offered to pour me a drink. "What would you like?"

"Gin and tonic, please."

I stood in a set of windows overlooking the airport. The dark hardwood floor was cool beneath my feet and as I gazed at the view I felt him step into the space parallel to my back. I had heels on and he stood at least a head taller than me. He circled my body with his arm and held out my drink. I was acutely aware of him right behind me. Gazing at the view, we didn't speak: *breathe in, breathe out*. Ice cubes tinkled. Lights twinkled on in houses as dusk misted the hills. Captives of the moment, we watched the sky turn from clear to gray to evening black. He moved in closer, fitting himself into the curve of my back. I could feel his chest rise and fall. A scent of soap - he smelled freshly showered - I mused about knowing Lake for six months, and that while he built his new house we'd met either at his office or in town. He stepped away to the bar and cool air filled the gap.

"Would you like another?"

"No, thank you, this one's fine," I held up the crystal glass, showing it was nearly full. Boodles or Bombay gin were more to my liking - even tonic can't mask the bitter juniper taste of some expensive gins. I didn't mention my preference.

"I'll freshen mine, then." He filled his glass from a crystal decanter; straight, with ice cubes. "Would you like to see the house?"

"Yes, I would very much." He waited for me to step in front of him and I was amused that he first opened the door leading to the garage. A platform with a railing spanned the width of the garage and allowed a view of the cars. The cars were in primary colors and impeccable. Suddenly, the word *car* seemed too brief a word to describe them. These were automobiles and they gleamed!

Descending the stairs, I tilted my head from side to side looking for fingerprints on their surface. Not one. How did he drive them in the rain and return them looking like this? He must wipe them down afterward, even the tires. Did he change his clothes first? The smallest inkling of alarm passed through me. Watching him move around without touching them, the hair stood on the back of my neck and I wasn't quite sure why.

I began an inner dialogue to calm my beating heart. These feelings were all too familiar: I prepared to flee, justifying breaking things off by finding something wrong. It was always the same. To begin with, he wasn't really my type: he was too handsome with his deep blue eyes and lush black hair.

He opened the door of a black Jaguar sedan. Hesitating, I chanced a look over my shoulder to check the bottom of my shoe for chewing gum. In a moment, I'd look at the other one. Sitting inside, I saw no tiny pebbles under the gas pedal, such clean leather upholstery, no tissues, not even a trash sack. There was nothing in the ashtray because he didn't smoke, though almost everyone did. He wouldn't want the ashes.

As I got out, I glanced at his attire. He wore a long sleeved white shirt, unbuttoned at the collar, dark slacks, and highly polished loafers with matching, monogrammed socks. Was this his idea of casual? Impeccable, impeccable Bill Lake, every black hair smoothed in place. No gray. He would never be gray. Age would have to show itself in other ways.

At his age most men have softened around the waist. My dad politely described this bulge as a sign of prosperity. Or was it the dreaded Old Man's Disease? Somewhere around middle age, round, male button-bottoms defy gravity, leaving their posterior positions to end up in the stomach area. This condition is known as Dickey

Do: the stomach sticks out further than the dickey do. At 36, Bill had none of these early signs. We returned to the den.

"Your home is a showplace, Bill," I told him while running my hand across the back of a dark rose and green satin sofa. The material was sensuously smooth.

"Thank you. I've enjoyed working on this project."

The walls were gleaming dark cherry and each room seemed full of mirrors, glass doors, and crystal chandeliers. Nothing was out of place. There were no knick-knacks about; the house had the look of a fine hotel.

Bill sat in a wingback chair across from me. I picked up an embroidered pillow, the only thing that didn't go with the room. He observed my selection: "It's from my first marriage." I knew he must have been reading my thoughts; I found it a little unsettling, but maybe this was just a chance to get to know him better.

"Oh. How many times have you been married, Bill?"

"Twice." A pause hung in the air because the terseness of his response signaled there was little to explore. He leaned closer and asked, "What have you been doing since I saw you a week ago?" He seemed interested.

"Flying for Western and for the Air Ambulance. We're getting FAA authority to give our own six month proficiency checks under Part 135."

"Have you been anywhere interesting?"

"Yes, well, I flew to Salinas to pick up a donor's heart and eyes." I cringed when I saw his expression - maybe I shouldn't give too much information - and I proceeded carefully. "It's strange to transport such important things in iced Tupperware. I got to scrub for the operation. The surgeon let me watch over his shoulder and ask questions because I let him ride copilot in the Cessna 414. He said he always wanted to learn to fly."

"Yuk. How can you stand watching an operation?"

"It was fascinating, but it made me queasy, too, especially when they first open someone up. After awhile I can look past the blood and concentrate on the operation." I decided to forego describing how the surgeon popped the eyeballs out of their sockets and laid them on the donor's cheek while he cut the veins and attaching tendrils. From his initial expression, I was sure he didn't want to hear details. Too much information on this subject might give him the impression I was indelicate; I wasn't, just inquisitive. I stuck to the basic story and softened reality somewhat with another: "The team spent hours one evening in Ukiah trying to revive a little boy who drowned in his Grandmother's swimming pool. She'd watched him that weekend and hadn't been able to reach his parents. Try as they might, the team couldn't bring him back from blue and gray. I flew him on to Stanford Hospital and will never forget the Grandmother's expression as we taxied away from the ramp with her dead grandchild aboard. She was frozen to the ground watching the plane leave; I knew she was heartbroken."

Bill listened, shaking his head. I tried changing the subject: "What have you been doing between trips for Western and moving into your new home?"

"I've been trying to chase down that bastard, Greg Gertz. He stole money from my buddies and me." I squirmed a bit in my chair. Lake went from compassion to passion rather quickly. His face darkened. The subject aroused him and I was sorry I'd asked.

"Now Gertz is ducking out on his investors, I wish I hadn't signed his contract. He's quitting the airline. It'll be harder to keep track of him. He's taken a lot of pilots' money to invest in a low-income housing project in Oakland. It hasn't been too successful. I'm having him investigated..."

I decided not to pursue the subject, though I wished to add something but refrained from the position of Monday morning quarterback. At this time I had no money to speak of, but preferred to think I'd invest my own money rather than entrust it to strangers. I dreamed of having a horse ranch, investing my money in land. In listening to jokes during flights, I found that pilots are known for buying high, selling low. Usually they're not the best businessmen because they spend their energy honing their flying skills. Airline pilots made a good deal of money beyond their basic needs pooling the surplus with other pilots into one venture or another. Gold mines, oil wells, and other speculative "get rich quick" schemes were popular. I've never heard of *any* panning out. I was surprised Captain Bill Lake would get involved in such deals. It brought new light to his character. Maybe I was wrong thinking he was different, special - perhaps influenced by his handsome visage - when really, he was just another one of the boys.

His expression changed. He rose straight up from his chair, took a few long steps across the room, and pulled me up by the hand: "You haven't seen the bedroom yet."

The master bedroom was like the rest of the house. The drapes were softened by pale, filmy sheers that billowed on the evening breeze. The predominant color was burgundy on the side chairs and the love seat. Gilded prints of old-fashioned picnics and other pastoral scenes from a single artist decorated the walls. The bedspread was voluminous and half-covered with oddly shaped satin pillows.

At the head of the large bed was an alcove of mirrors. A large bouquet of silk flowers focused my attention on a silver vial that stood exactly in the center. I gazed at the small silhouette.

"Butyl nitrate."

"What?"

"The bottle - it's butyl nitrate." He must have followed my gaze and read my mind again. He sat on the edge of the bed.

"What's it for?"

"A rush, when I inhale it, it gives me a rush, lasts only a couple of minutes, then you inhale some more." He laid back on the bed, pulling me to him. He kissed my mouth and began moving his lips down the inner part of my neck. I was not too comfortable with this but goose bumps rose where his mouth touched. He reached for the vial, unscrewed the lid. Holding it under his nose, he inhaled fast and deep, filling his lungs until his chest swelled. Immediately, his blue eyes darkened and filled with water. His pupils dilated.

Could this be love potion #9? He handed me the vial. I hesitated.

"It's great stuff. Try some."

"I don't know... I've never tried anything like this before. What will it do?"

"It will do whatever you want it to do." He looked at me with sparkling eyes and moved in closer. I felt myself shrinking under his influence. He kissed my mouth, and artfully drew my tongue up through his lips into his mouth. For a moment I was lost in his long, deep kiss.

He took the bottle, put it under my nose, and I watched him inhale as he wanted me to do. I breathed in gently. The room brightened and began to swirl. He took it back. We were in concert. Soon I lost track. He wrapped his arm around me with his head below my chin. I could see white scalp through his luxurious dark hair. He moved my sweater off my shoulder and pulled the soft angora down to bare a breast. He paused to sigh - I felt his labored breathing - as he took the areola into his mouth. I heard raindrops gently splashing against the windows. Streetlights undulated in reflective light on the panes. Every sense was heightened, every sensation acute. I was enchanted by his caress. My clothes fell away. Our skin touched. He was ardent. I was hot.

Suddenly, he jumped up. "Want to see my new trees?"

I looked at him in surprise and glanced out the window. It was dark outside but I decided not to state the obvious. Dressing, I felt myself floating and dispossessed. I gathered my things and quietly followed him outside.

The new trees were tall standing in buckets lined up in the driveway. Lights from the garage illuminated their branches. *Some kind of cypress,* I thought. Soon Bill dragged the hose over to water them. I was stunned by his quick transformation while I was still dizzy. He was so absorbed in his task that he didn't even notice when I wished him good night.

✈

My Air Ambulance pager went off the next afternoon. Relieved, I looked forward to an interesting flight. Every experience with Air Ambulance had been memorable. Checking with dispatch, I found I'd fly a kidney transplant team to Monterey where a donor awaited.

A cascade of rainwater covered the windshield of the twin-engine Cessna. Peering out through the darkness, red reflections from lights on a sign reading *Butler Aviation* were artfully distorted in the puddles. I parked and waited inside the airplane with the logo light on, illuminating the company name of *Air Ambulance* on the tail. Owned by a consortium of eight doctors and brainchild of long-time friend, Dr. Michael Cowan, *Air Ambulance* flew both the Stanford University and University of California at San Francisco Hospital teams. The bulk of business was in transporting tiny, prematurely born babies from outlying places to either of the hospitals. The balance of business was in transporting patients, donor parts, and donors. In California, by simply signing the back of your driver's license, you could become an organ donor if you were killed and not too badly maimed.

Soon two figures were striding across the ramp in the rain. A tall man led with his nose, bending into the wind, sports jacket flying. The short man had a rolling walk as if one leg was longer than the other. He had a hard time keeping up and as he got closer, I saw he wore an elevated shoe. Light from overhead revealed a distinguishing proboscis on the first, and a great wad of gum being chewed - mouth gaping - by the second - mouth open, mouth closed, mouth open, mouth closed - in rhythm with his uneven steps. He pushed a brown wooden box extended to a height of three-and-a-half feet by crisscross, spider-like legs that moved along on wheels. Could it be a portable kidney machine? Perhaps this surgeon was the inventor.

This seemed an odd entourage, different from the other medical teams. I was distracted from my reverie by their unique appearance. Also, they arrived by taxi instead of ambulance or helicopter. No nurses dressed in pastels with stethoscopes hanging around their necks accompanied them. It was just these two individuals, loping across the ramp toward my airplane. They looked like characters from a Frankenstein movie and with some alarm, I wondered if I really wanted to take them flying.

Standing outside the door of the aircraft, I asked with amusement, "Dr. Livingston," *I presume?* The *'I presume'* I said to myself, but he was on to my humor and grinned. He extended his hand, asked my name, and climbed aboard.

"Would you like to sit in the copilot's, the right forward seat?"

"Love to. Never been in one of these 414's before," he said pleasantly, then turned in his seat to face rearward. "Yo! Giles. Plug into the inverter outlet - let's see if everything's working okay. Sit next to the machine in case it tries falling during the flight." This was strange: he nearly accorded the box a human impulse. I shivered.

Giles complied, wordlessly chewed his gum, collapsed the spindly legs and lifted the kidney machine aboard. During my emergency briefing I knelt next to it, aware that it hummed and vibrated as if alive. I closed the rear door and we departed for Monterrey.

There were only a few stars winking back through broken clouds, and the rain occasionally fell in shards against the windshield. The controller spoke to me over my headset and the surgeon, for the most part, sat quietly on my right. Infrequently, he asked a question about flying but was attuned enough to realize I was busy. It was turbulent intermittently, and I had the de-icing systems working on the airplane. I made an instrument approach through low clouds and rain, and we landed in Monterrey.

While we waited for the taxi, Dr. Livingston turned to me: "You've allowed me to see what you do, would you like to scrub and stand over my shoulder for the kidneys' extraction?"

His offer took me quite by surprise. "Yes, I'd like to very much!" What an unreal opportunity. I wasn't sure I'd even heard of kidneys being transplanted before, nor did I have any idea what they even looked like.

Arriving at the hospital, I proceeded with an extension of my job, providing liaison between the donor's family, insurance company, hospital, and our air ambulance service. Donor's family waited to say last goodbyes to their relative as his parents signed the donor affirmation papers. These people looked Polynesian - I checked my paperwork: they were Tongan. They had wavy dark hair, brown skin, and were enormous. Their nineteen-year-old son was fatally injured in a motorcycle accident. Riding at night without a helmet, he lost control in the rain, slid into a freeway retaining wall, and was hit by a large truck. His body was still alive, but his brain - what was left of it - was dead. He was hooked to life support machinery that would soon be disconnected. Each family member kissed him and tearfully departed, handkerchiefs to their eyes. Shortly after the last one left, nurses and orderlies arrived to disconnect life support and transport him to the operating room.

Coached - I did a mild scrub - and robed at the nurse's station, I entered the operating room. There were observers sitting above in a gallery separated by glass. Dr. Livingston placed a broad stool for me to stand on right behind him. I was surprised he even touched it. And I noticed he was still in his sports jacket, not surgical scrubs.

For some reason sterility wasn't important as donor would soon be dead. I was sure the opposite would be true where recipient was concerned.

Dr. Livingston was tall, but standing on this platform I could easily see two feet over his head. His technician, Giles the gum chewer, had stopped chewing, his face assuming a serious demeanor. He hadn't changed out of his street clothes, either.

In the transfer from the gurney, donor rolled onto the operating table and remained lying on his back. His great weight of more than three hundred pounds held him there in spite of the orderlies' and nurses' grunting and gasping efforts to roll him over onto his stomach, the most desirable position for accessing the kidneys. Gracious and smiling, Dr. Livingston allowed them to leave donor in this position and waved them away. Donor was disrobed. Even though his enormous head was bandaged, an indentation in his skull showed a large portion was missing.

Everyone quietly focused on Dr. Livingston as he lifted an enormous syringe from the tray. Holding it vertically, he squirted a tiny jet of fluid into the air. Did I see his eye go north to the audience above? He paused, took an audible, deep breath, and then forcefully plunged the huge syringe into donor's chest. An audible gasp swept the operating room. My heart felt that stab. I knew I was standing too close to the action.

"This is Heparin - to stop the heart muscle from beating. Once donor stops breathing, the coroner will pronounce him dead, and we may proceed." Like extras in a drama, we waited: doctors, nurses, coroner, and observers. Glancing up through the glass, I hoped to see none of the Tongan family present in the theater and felt relieved to see they were not.

Seconds ticked by. I breathed in, and breathed out through my mask. Nothing happened for a few moments but then, slowly, as if in farewell, a mast rose from the lower part of the body: it was donor's penis. First it grew to the normal six inches, then seven, eight, nine actual, measurable inches of masculine hardness. There were murmurs in the operating room and witnesses' eyes were wide in wonder as penis thickened, turned purple, and stood erect. My face was a mere four feet away. I grinned beneath my mask, as tickled and astounded as anyone. Such a waste but, alas, with a rueful sigh, I realized that what Bill Lake couldn't do alive, this donor was doing dead.

I had heard Tongans were the largest of people. Now I believed it! Nurses gaped. Men compared. Perhaps an additional organ could be transplanted. With that thought I felt my face get scarlet. Donor's erection hailed us farewell for what seemed a long time, through many preparations and much bustling about in the operating room. Dr. Livingston suddenly ordered a drape for donor's lower extremity.

Eventually, donor's chest stopped moving as the Heparin took effect. The mast under the drape slowly receded. The coroner stepped to the table as Dr. Livingston put a stethoscope for some seconds to donor's chest, listening for a heartbeat. He nodded at the coroner - donor must be dead. Coroner and doctor signed the Death Certificate, and Dr. Livingston looked straight at Giles with wide open, commanding eyes...

Giles picked up a circular saw, turned it on, and with a smooth whirr aimed it at donor's chest. He lowered it until it touched the skin. As soon as contact with bone was made, the volume and intensity of the rotation created an appalling noise: *Yerrrrrrrow.* Pieces of flesh and bone went flying. I flinched as a piece hit my face. I didn't exclaim and tried not to recoil. Thank goodness this debacle didn't take too long, perhaps a matter of some seconds. I stood at attention on my stool, trying to avert my eyes from the grisly scene, but not wanting to close them either, as if inattentive. When I chanced a glance, Giles was maneuvering the saw in total concentration with his tongue clenched between his teeth.

When he finished, Dr. Livingston said crisply: "Retractor."

Again, Giles was the heavy as he took a large implement resembling a blunt meat hook and pulled the rib cage up and away from the organs, exposing the precious kidneys. He braced himself by putting his leg with the stacked shoe up on the table as an anchor, lending further unreality to the situation.

Deftly, Livingston severed the attachment points and tissues with a scalpel. He gently encircled the kidneys with his hands and removed them from the cavity. One by one, he flipped them gently but with a slight flourish onto a tray much as a buffet chef might serve up an omelet.

Giles dropped the retractor onto donor's chest as soon as removal was complete and walked around the table to the kidney machine. Orderlies and nurses stepped forward and began restoring order to a scene that was the focus of everyone's attention moments ago. Giles opened the glass top of the box, which had indicating dials along one side. He placed the tray holding the brown, spongy, pocket-like kidneys inside. Then he stood back to allow Dr. Livingston to attach lifelines to each kidney. Once secured, Livingston nodded. Giles turned a key on the side, and the box sprang to life.

"Boom ba boom ba boom, Wheeeee! Boom ba boom ba boom, Wheeeee!"

Everyone gathered around curiously to see Dr. Livingston's amazing machine. In 1978 it was unusual for kidney transplants to take place when donors were geographically distant from recipients. As soon as the box was stabilized and operating to specification, Dr. Livingston instructed Giles: "Gather your things. Wash them. Call for a cab. I'll be in the coffee shop. Let me know when our cab arrives. We need thirty minutes to make sure the batteries are charged enough to disconnect electricity."

Giles nodded in assent.

"Miss," he turned to me, "Would you care for a cup of coffee? The pie is great here." Dr. Livingston took my elbow and steered me down the hall towards the cafeteria. It was 2 a.m. and our mission was half complete. We still needed to return to the Bay Area and install the kidneys in a recipient.

As we walked down the hall, people from the operating room stood aside, smiling in wonder and admiration. There were murmurs of approbation for the good doctor as we passed. He nodded and smiled pleasantly. I realized I had witnessed, perhaps, the first part of a medical miracle.

Seated in the hospital cafeteria, by the time we'd selected our pecan and cherry pies, I discovered Dr. Livingston was congenial, sensitive, and witty. Add these qualities to innovator and inventor, and he seemed extraordinary.

"What did you think of all that back there?" He asked after a bite of pie and a sip of coffee.

"I feel privileged to witness this event. It's a landmark for me. I've never been present at a kidney extraction before. Thank you for giving me the opportunity to be an observer, and for your commentary, Dr. Livingston."

We chatted for a few minutes and as he spoke I suddenly realized this was a chance to ask about Butyl Nitrate. *But first... first... I'll carefully ask about Heparin.*

"Heparin is a muscle relaxant and the heart is a muscle," he was affable in explaining.

"Wwwhhhaat is Butyl Nitrate?" I breathlessly asked.

He regarded his long surgeon's fingers for a moment, hesitated, then explained. "Butyl Nitrate is a stimulant."

"A stimulant... for what?" I carefully asked, leaning closer to hear the explanation.

"It is the drug of choice in the homosexual community. It's commonly used as an erotic stimulant to acquire and sustain erection."

With these answers ringing in my ears, I returned the surgeon, his assistant, and their vibrating box to the San Francisco Airport, politely declining the good doctor's offer to accompany them to the hospital, explaining I was on call all that next day. They proceeded on to the University of California Hospital in San Francisco, again, via cab, to install donor's kidneys in a new body.

I began feeling tired as first light brightened the eastern horizon. Dodging early morning clouds, I flew the short distance from San Francisco to San Carlos in a few quick minutes and headed home for bed.

If I previously had any inclination to stay around SFO to see how my relationship with Captain Lake might turn out, I was now decisive. I submitted my bid for co-pilot on the Boeing 727 at Western's new base in Minneapolis-St. Paul the very next day and looked forward to fair skies and good flying.

✈

CHAPTER VI

FURLOUGH

The twin cities of Minneapolis and St. Paul are entwined at the confluence of the Mississippi and Minnesota Rivers. Headwaters of the Mississippi are located 100 miles north at Lake Itasca. Did I hear Garrison Keillor say during live performances of *A Prairie Home Companion* that the Minnesota River begins at Lake Wobegone? I enjoyed his entertainment at an ancient theater in St. Paul with friend and roommate, Dorothy Halleran. Sometimes the temperature was forty below zero when the show was over and patrons had difficulty starting their cars. Except for the sound of idling engines, a Minnesota winter night is usually clear, cold, and quiet. Exhaust fumed the lowest twenty feet of air with an automotive smell trapped by a temperature inversion.

The first time I rode a snowmobile or went ice fishing was with Dorothy, in 1979, on the Mississippi River riding south toward Red Wing, city-of-shoe fame. We were dressed in bright yellow snowsuits, a barrier to wind chill this cold February day. The snowsuits were lent by *our* date, Dan McGann. She called him *Dan the Murder Man* when he wasn't around. He was a homicide detective with the St. Paul Police Department whom she'd been dating for some time. I began to understand why their romance had lasted so long: he captivated her with old murder mysteries. He could have been a writer except he didn't seem introspective, instead, he was pure action. I wondered how he'd ever make Captain with this limitation, but bookish Dorothy probably loved him for it. She had other boyfriends, too, and equally humorous pseudonyms for them which conjured images of their persona: one was *High Dive*, another, *Willie Wonka*.

Where river ice ended and riverbank began, there was a scary stretch of water we traversed in a flying leap. Holding tight to Dan's waist, we got airborne between the bank and the river. Dorothy followed on a sled towed by our short lead. I turned to see if she'd clear the stretch of water and land on the ice as we had, but she was airborne, then, and landed with a thud on the ice. They were gracious to include me in their ice fishing trip as I'd only recently arrived in Minnesota.

Dorothy and I were introduced on a flight by our mutual acquaintance, Dee Router, who taught aircraft systems ground school for Western Airlines. Dorothy was a meteorologist who worked for the National Weather Service. She was observing a flight from the cockpit when we met. Pretty and witty, her presence on the flight deck enlivened the crew on the long flight from San Francisco. We became friends. Ultimately, she transferred to Washington D.C. to appear for a time as Meteorologist on the long-lived FAA weather program, *AM Weather*.

Miles of laughter and smiles later, we perched on our sleds on the ice in the middle of the Mississippi River. Dan jabbed holes in the foot thick ice with a steel pole, and hand over hand, let our lines down into the water. Each line had eight small, shiny brass hooks knotted down its length, but no bait. I guess the fish were small and attracted to the shine. I sipped icy beer, held my line, and chatted. Icy beer seemed incompatible with the temperature and I wished we'd brought something warmer. The beer made my cold lips numb, and they felt bulbously awkward as I tried to articulate, but beer was a boy thing, and though this outing was not one Dorothy would pick, she liked Dan's company, and Dan liked to go fishing on Saturday.

The sound of water rippling over rocks and ice added background music to our conversation as we visited, often laughing, catching blue gill and perch. Occasionally, our voices were drowned by the *whoosh* of an icy breeze through naked trees. I shivered in my heavy snowmobile clothes. Smiling, I stepped inside, introspective, for a moment, reflecting that single life was beginning to feel akin to my spirit, and the cold winds of divorce didn't haunt me so often with that vacant, lost, and lonely feeling of disconnection. I was meeting new people, making friends, renewing old friendships. There were lots of things to do, places to go, people to meet, and I did so, happily. It was obvious that with such mobility it would be difficult to settle down. I lived in Minnesota while working, and in San Francisco and Nevada when not. I felt somewhat guilty that at 34 I wasn't married or even involved, but it just wasn't going to happen right now. So, rather than feeling I was somehow wrong in this situation, and fighting the elation of being free, I decided not to worry and to be happy. I was in an extraordinary set of circumstances, but then, what is life if not an adventure?

✈

I had one male friend to ski with, another for gliding, one for sailing, one for endurance riding; friends for this and friends for that. A brother asked: "Who's the Man of the Moment?"

I answered: "What's the activity?"

My airline career was now several years old, and I found I spent most of my time alone. Though I slept in the finest hotels on layovers, had a commuter apartment, and lots of friends, I missed returning to the warm feeling of being home. Having horses and dogs, since I wasn't lucky enough to have a family, became important to me.

As a salve for some of these longings, I bought an exquisite home in Nevada in partnership with my aging parents. They cared for my animals, were a presence I appreciated, and just having them there when I arrived, gave me that warm fuzzy feeling of being home.

My new home was just over the mountain to the east of Lake Tahoe at the foot of Kingsbury Grade. There are many beautiful places in the world and this was certainly one of them. Heavenly Valley ski area on the Nevada side was above and behind our house. It was only a drive up the mountain to Lake Tahoe. Situated in Nevada's oldest town of Genoa, the area was picturesque with the Sierras as a regal backdrop.

When I was home, my folks and I enjoyed each other's company. In some ways it was a renewal, spending time with them. I hadn't been home for nearly twenty years. It was good to know them again, hear what they had to say about life, and travel to places we wanted to see.

Not five miles away, across the beautiful Carson Valley, situated in the afternoon shadow of the Sierras, I towed and flew gliders for fun out of the Douglas County - Minden – Airport, a country airport with long runways from the civilian pilot training days during WWII. Minden evolved to a multi-dimensional regional airport, still uncontrolled, home to a fine crop-dusting school after the war.

Some of the best gliding in the world occurs on the Sierra "wave." Only a few minutes flight from Minden, competitive soaring championships are frequently held and altitude records have been set as, on the east face of the mountains around Lake Tahoe, there is a notch in the ridgeline that causes a venturi affect. When the wind blows at more than 25 knots, vertical movement of air lifted up the mountainside accelerates with decreased atmospheric pressure causing a pulse in the atmosphere. Identifiable on moist days, by a characteristic lens-shaped cloud called a lenticular, the area can be dangerous on clear, "blue" days, when it was invisible. The waves often extend a hundred miles or more from the lee side of the mountain, rising and descending, much as waves on the ocean, above the valley floors.

Glider pilots fly up into the stratosphere attaining altitude records on the Sierra Wave. Some glider pilots like friend Linda Draper joined an elite cadre known as FL500 where they ascended to 50,000 feet or more garbed in special pressure suits which made them look like astronauts. They took advantage of a "window" in what was called Positive Control Airspace, created just for gliders that could be activated by Air Traffic Control with just a radio call. With inbound commercial flights to the Bay Area alerted, they were steered around the small window, which extended from FL180 on up toward heaven.

I'd always wanted to fly gliders and some very fine ones were parked at the airport. Generally, gliders are built in Europe - ever more since the end of WWII when the Axis weren't allowed powered craft by the Allies. Glider pilots from all over the world come to fly on the Sierra Wave in these exotic craft, some with great air-penetrating ability and glide ratios approaching 60 to 1.

I exchanged glider towing for glider flying in a couple of different airplanes. One was a French-built Ralley with moveable leading edges allowing the airplane to fly slowly without ever stalling, and the other, the tail-dragging Piper Pawnee, normally used as a crop-duster. It was a thrill towing gliders up through the turbulence of the rotor cloud. At times the tow plane and I rolled right on around in the vortex with our glider still in tow. Finding the smooth leading edge of the standing wave, we were lifted aloft by this powerful, silent elevator.

When I started instructing in gliders, my first student and I went up in his Blanek to practice for his commercial license. After spending awhile practicing commercial maneuvers of chandelles and lazy eights, the sun dipped below the horizon and took with it, the warm temperatures generating lift off the Carson Valley floor. As we turned homeward, flying in sinking air, the air tanker fire bell must have gone off. We were on a three-mile final when a Siskyou Aviation DC-6 pulled into position and began his engine run-up before take-off. For several minutes he remained there; he may have been talking to Air-Net about the fire, but it was much longer than we expected. We couldn't land over the top of him on the same runway - he didn't even know we were there and we had no radio contact with him - so we had to land out in the sagebrush on a peripheral farm road and walk the glider around the airport to the flight line. It seemed like miles!

Another time, a soaring school contracted with Hewlett Packard to give glider rides to its employees who were in the area during the Memorial Day holiday. I flew maybe a dozen rides over the Sierras in view of Lake Tahoe and bald eagles who shared our lift. A character I didn't particularly care for was our tow pilot; he was the only one available because it was a holiday.

I'd met him earlier, the previous winter at a Christmas party given by a neighbor who'd been in the Air Force with him. I found myself backed up against a wall by this midget motorman, who might have come as high as my shoulder. I had on five inch heels with my hair done up on top of my head, making me over six feet tall. The quintessence of what he said was that he didn't approve of women in aviation.

I smiled and tried to make light of his misgivings, eventually asking if he'd had a daughter interested in aviation, would he be supportive? This approach didn't seem to faze him – he told me he didn't have a daughter - and he railed on, looking up at me like an infuriated dwarf, until people at the party stopped their conversations and turned to stare. It was embarrassing being the brunt of this spectacle. I wondered if alcohol had anything to do with the force of it. I tried to keep from turning angry red and bonking him on the top of his little head. Somehow I maintained my cool, and smiled as broad a smile as I could muster, though the corners of my lips resisted turning upward. He didn't stop, just blustered on. He wouldn't let me talk, and finally, I just slipped away, leaving him there in a blue funk, yammering at my back.

Well, here he was as my tow pilot for the day and his tow speeds were getting faster and faster. I indulged him as long as I could, then spoke to him before my next flight with my very pregnant ride standing beside me. Politely, I asked that he tow at more reasonable speeds. He said nothing and we adjourned to our respective craft.

I quizzed my new rider if she and her baby would be all right given the possibility of turbulence and pressure changes. She assured me she would be. "I've never had problems with my pregnancy during recent flying lessons, and I'm very much looking forward to experiencing powerless flight." We chatted as we walked to the glider at the side of the runway, tipped to one side with the wing resting on its tiny wheel.

My passenger approached our 20-30 minute flight with the enthusiasm of an engineer because she'd studied aerodynamics at some point and thought experiencing powerless flight would be fascinating. I smiled, assuring her it would be, and glanced again at her big tummy, shrugged some, and hoped the seat belt restraints would extend far enough for her to be comfortable. It was her call. We did the briefing and preflight, strapped her and little junior in, and went gliding.

I was astounded when the tow pilot took off and flew us in a direction opposite where we would find lift! Then he descended at high speed down the side of a hill into a small valley in direct violation of my request. I wondered what he'd do when he reached the bottom. His flying was hard to believe! I wondered if he was okay or having some kind of problem. I flew as long as I could on tow, but as soon as I realized he was setting us up for disaster, I pulled the release. My front seat passenger turned and looked at me saying, "Wow!" She knew enough to recognize our danger. We struggled to soar back up the sides of the hills in ridge-lift, gaining just enough altitude to skim over the tops, returning safely to the airport.

I apologized to my passenger for this aberrant behavior. She was relieved that we made it back safely and wondered, feigning ignorance, "What's his problem? I've had jealous men treat me similarly."

"I'm not quite sure, but I'm going to find out!" I answered her first question then bid her goodbye as we parked the glider, then I went looking for the midget with blood in my eye.

"He's gone for the day," the flight school owner spoke from in front of the crowd of HP people. "He said you're the worst glider pilot he's ever towed, and he should know. He used to fly 747s for United."

I felt like telling the flight school owner he was an idiot, but chose not to stoop to his level, and insult him in front of customers. "Well, do you still want me to give the rest of these people their rides?"

"Of course."

Oh, brother!

I knew for sure he was an idiot, then, and headed across the field to find a *good* tow pilot. When I showed up with Monty alongside me, the flight school owner made another announcement to the group that the mini-motorman had lost his medical certification *and* his airline job because of alcohol, which was later verified by asking the FAA. I listened to this second blast, and wondered about the mental balance of the flight school owner in revealing this diminishing information to customers, some whom this character had just towed. Monty and I finished without incident, giving the rest of the HP people their money's worth.

Since I'd been made aware the flight school owner was giving commercial rides, even though he wasn't a licensed pilot, and at one point asked if I would sign student logbooks as if I'd given the lessons, this latest fiasco involving him was probably the excuse I'd waited for. I couldn't believe the irresponsibility of those two yahoos, and left their association immediately.

✈

When I wasn't flying, I skied in the winter, water-skied on Lake Tahoe in a wet suit in the summer, and went fly-fishing. There were no state income taxes in Nevada, certainly an advantage for a single person making a salary of about $75,000 per year. I commuted out of Reno on the airline to my pilot base in the twin cities of Minneapolis - St. Paul.

A group of professional women I enjoyed doing things with, lived in Minnesota all of their lives. I thought I must have been a good influence as one of them, a nurse, began studying to be a doctor. That spring I had a team of polo ponies to keep in condition by riding them around the lakes and cross country on my days off from flying; they were owned by a Twin Cities businessman who thought they needed diversion between matches. Because I needed five years with the company before I could get travel privileges of taxes-only passes, I could afford to go home no more than once a month. The rest of the time I spent in MSP.

I was enjoying flying co-pilot on the Boeing 727. The great way things were going at Western, with the upscale economy of the country, I should make captain soon. Crop dusting was on the horizon in a Super Cub and a Pawnee out of Welch, Minnesota, with friends Captain Bub Kelly and First Officer Slim Breaker. Welch was one of the few places the big glacier missed in Minnesota, so there were plenty of sharp little hills to maneuver around.

✈

The line jiggled in my hand. I pulled it in, hand over hand, admiring the row of iridescent blue bodies wiggling on the hooks. Maybe there were seven. All the lines got hit at once. Dan removed the fish to a creel and we dropped the lines down our respective holes again. We repeated this activity until they stopped biting which was about three-thirty in the afternoon, when the sun got low and the temperature noticeably colder. We packed our things and headed upriver to Dan's house.

There would be plenty of fish for dinner. Dan poured us a hot drink, mulled wine. The roaring fire was inviting. Dan's music was too hard rock for me and I tried to ignore it by tuning it out, but it was tough, so I joined Dan in the washroom. He was cleaning the fish and things were a lot quieter. Initially, I liked Dan, except now he was scraping the scales off the poor fish before he killed them.

"How can you do that?"

"Do what?"

"Scrape the scales off the fish before they're dead."

"They don't feel it."

I didn't want to argue, but I knew they *could* feel the sharp knife slicing away at their little bodies because they struggled and flipped as Dan scraped. I risked sparking his ire but: "If they don't feel it, why are they struggling so?"

"Fish don't have feelings," he insisted, continuing to focus on the one in his hand, not lifting his eyes to look at me. I wasn't getting through to him.

I was about to continue when Dorothy appeared in the doorway. She must have heard our voices, wondered what we were doing. Her eyes fell to the fish in Dan's hand. He moved the knife blade up and down the fish, removing the scales. I took a large gulp from my wine, then another; maybe I could numb my aching heart.

"Shouldn't you kill them before you scrape the scales off?" Dorothy asked, the pupils of her eyes distended into little points. "It seems like the humane thing to do."

"They can't feel it," Dan said slowly, exasperation in his voice. He went on scraping. We stood quietly. Suddenly, as if a light came on, he stopped and lifted his head to look as us. We both had said the same thing. With knife in mid-stroke he met Dorothy's eyes. Had the message gotten through? We were objecting. Could his years of dealing with death have desensitized him to life? We didn't have much appetite for the little creatures, and soon left. Dorothy chose not to see *Dan the Murder Man* again.

Rumors spread around the airline as fast as it took us to rocket from one city to the next. Crews visited in operations while collecting flight paperwork. "When the length of the paperwork equals the length of the airplane, you've got enough to go," my Captain, Lon Felson, told me as he folded the many sheets of the computer readout into a manageable package. The dispatcher smiled at us though the glass of his office, then handed us more.

"See. What'd I tell you?" a pleasant smile, a sweet smile with a cupid's bow for lips. "Let's see, weather, flight release, flight plan, load plan and passenger manifest. Yep, got them all! Computers are so great. They do all the busy work. The dispatcher just plugs in the new numbers." After a review of paperwork concerning our flight, Cap says, "coach is full, first class has one passenger. Flight attendants, hmmm, an all male crew."

Captain and dispatcher share joint responsibility for planning the flight. The captain signed his acceptance and approval at the bottom, then the dispatcher did the same.

"Good flying," the dispatcher wished us well as he turned from the window.

"Thank you, we both said in unison."

Sequentially, in three days, I had three turn-arounds from Minneapolis-St. Paul to Phoenix with the same schedule all month. Today was a clear, winter day. We should have a smooth flight. My captain, Lon Felson, was a good-looking guy with blond hair and blue eyes. He was about six feet tall and had a golden tan. The cupid-bow on his upper lip gave his face angelic appeal – I bet he'd stop traffic in the girl's locker room and cause quite a stir. Did he say he'd only been married twice?

Quickly, we established he was one month younger than me. I'd heard of him referred to as one of the *Kid Captains* who was hired at 21, which was an anomaly, because it was difficult for someone to gain the necessary flight experience to be hired by an airline at that young age. As with many aviators, he came from a family background of flying; his dad had a fixed base operation for years. I often asked pilots who or what interested them in flying. Usually, it was a father, an uncle or a grandfather; no one mentioned a *she*.

Just as we rotated the 727 off the ground taking off from Minneapolis-St. Paul and began climbing, a large *boom ta boom* vibration came up from below our feet. We froze a moment to listen. No one ventured a guess as to what it might be... *Boom ta boom* continued without stopping.

"Could someone be locked in the baggage compartment?" The noise sounded as if someone was jumping up to hit the cockpit floor in constant rhythm.

"Call the ramp and ask them to account for the ground crews," Felson ordered, a trace of excitement in his voice.

Oh, boy, another adventure. We continued to fly the departure from MSP during the exchange. A few long minutes went by and the vibration continued.

"Nope, captain," the second officer turned to speak. "Ramp says all are accounted for: baggage handlers, mechanics. No one's missing."

"Western 546, Western Operations."

"Western 546." The captain took the microphone. "Go ahead Ramp."

"Do you have an all male flight attendant crew?"

The second officer checked the crew list. "Aye, captain. We have an all male cabin crew."

"Yes, ramp. Our list shows all males... Paul, open the door and ask the *A* Flight Attendant to step in here." Paul reached around to his right and opened the door that joined the cockpit with the first class cabin. We were turned in our seats watching. As our door opened, the first class lavatory door was closing about three feet away. A tall male flight attendant stood in the doorway with a smaller flight attendant in front of him.

The look on the captain's face mirrored what he was thinking. He looked down, collecting his words: "We opened the cockpit door to ask if you knew anything about this vibration we've had since lift off. It seems to have just stopped. We've been getting clearance to return to base because we haven't been able to determine the source."

The two flight attendants looked at each other and simultaneously said: "Calisthenics. We were doing calisthenics, captain."

Together, we flight crew said, "Calisthenics, huh?"

"Calisthenics, captain." They smiled, nodding agreement, and quickly closed the cockpit door.

We notified the ramp that our vibration had stopped and we were proceeding to Phoenix. We were relieved we didn't have to return to base because it signaled a serious and expensive problem for the airline, involving paperwork and explanations. After awhile ramp asked: "Western 546, what was the source of your vibration?"

The captain paused a beat, and then said, "Calisthenics."

"What?" ramp asked.

"Calisthenics."

"Calisthenics, huh, captain?"

"Affirmative. Western 546 proceeding to Phoenix."

When we arrived in Phoenix operations, the dispatcher inquired about our problem. The captain related our story. The dispatcher pursed his lips in thought and walked away shaking his head. "Things ain't what they used to be around here." I felt my shoulders involuntarily hunch forward a little. For better or worse, I knew I was part of the change.

Next morning when Captain Felson and I checked in at MSP operations, the same dispatcher was on duty. "Weren't you the crew on Flight 546 to Phoenix, yesterday?"

"Yes, we were..." Felson replied, as if knowing the rest.

Suddenly, the glass enclosure housing operations filled with people. They looked in drawers and lifted papers from the desktops. They read notices stapled to cork boards. There were many bodies in the small space, intent on listening to the captain's story firsthand.

After telling it, suddenly they all snapped their heads towards us at the window and chanted, in unison: "Calisthenics, huh?!"

We completed our set of three turn-arounds, and on each stop, our calisthenics story was retold by an outbound crew or by an inbound crew. Sometimes we insisted it was our story and they didn't have it quite right, and other times, we listened to the flourishes and just let it go...

✈

Captain Felson invited me, a fishing enthusiast, to join the rest of the base in The Great Northern Fishing Contest. It was to be held in early fall on Gull Lake, way north of MSP near the Canadian border. First prize was $1500 for catching the biggest fish - called a *Northern*

- a pike. A predatory fish, indigenous to the lakes of Minnesota, it was a sporting fish, and one featured on local restaurant menus as fine fare.

We launched our Lund boat for several days as early as four-thirty in the morning, came in briefly for lunch and dinner, and fished until dark trying to catch that $1500 fish for the glory of Western Airlines. Gull Lake was a large lake in a region filled with lakes and surrounded by tall broadleaf trees. Western's fish camp was a set of cabins, each with a sitting room and fireplace.

Fireplaces roaring and fish stories aching to be told, we gathered in the great room. I'd never fished so intensely. My right arm was sore from casting out and reeling in. I relaxed in an overstuffed chair after dinner in town, and listened to Minnesota jokes about Sven and Ole, like this one: "And now, Captain Ole Ohlinger, from Brainerd, Minnesota, you're winner of our national beer naming contest. Tell us, Captain Ohlinger, how did you come to name our beer Schlager Lager Beer?"

And in the best imitation of a Scandinavian accent: "Vell, you see, ve like to take our girlfriends out in the boat at sunset. Ve have somesing to eat, somesing to drink. Pretty soon ve're holding hands, then ve're a huggin' and a kissin', and pretty soon ve're in the bottom of the boat. Then, vell, Schlager Lager."

"Now, Captain Ohlinger, what do you mean by Schlager Lager?"

"Vell, it means fucking near water, and its juusst like yer beer is!"

Sunday morning, just as Captain Felson stepped up on the boat seat to cast his line, fishing partner and fellow captain, Paddy, cast his, too. Something caught his line immediately, and Paddy set the hook with a mighty yank. "I've got a big one!" Paddy yelled. He sure did.

Felson paled, stepped down from the seat holding his neck. When he took his hand away, visible was only one prong of a four-pronged Northern hook. The other hooks were imbedded in the soft tissue at the base of his head. The area was bleeding. We were stunned by the accident. We tried removing it by gently twisting it this way and that, but the barbs kept the three-inch prongs securely in place. This made the bleeding worse. Though Felson said nothing, not a moan or a groan, I knew by his pallor, he was really hurting.

I was glad he couldn't see the back of his own head. Paddy was very upset he'd hurt his friend. I could barely look at the wound. It was gaping and bloody, and we were only making things worse trying to wiggle the hook out. It got imbedded deeper in the soft tissue. Just where the neck ended and the brain stem began was not something I cared to guess.

Paddy pull-started the motor and we raced for shore. We were twenty minutes out as sun lightened the morning sky. When we got to shore, he leaped out of the boat and ran for the tool chest to get some pliers. With that big hook hanging out of his neck, I was afraid Felson would get caught on something. "How about I get some wire cutters and cut it off?" Paddy ran to the car to find more tools. He cut one hook off leaving three others inside. All that remained were shiny gold spots flush with the skin.

It was hard to believe the whole affair was lodged inside the back of his neck. My toes curled and my stomach churned just looking at the wound. We decided it would take more expertise and artistry than we had to remove the hooks.

We climbed into the car after I poured Felson a straight whiskey, which he refused, so I drank it myself. The guys sat in front, and I sat in back holding a hand towel to his head. Slowly, his blood soaked the towel and dripped to the floorboard where it made a slick puddle under my feet. His color blanched as we roared toward town on a gravel road, trailing a rooster tail of rocks and dust.

We had trouble finding a doctor. No clinics were open on Sunday. Felson protested, he wanted to get back to fishing. Everything seemed to be closed. Finally, someone told us the nearest hospital was in Brainerd, Ole's home, forty miles away on a dirt road. We groaned.

An hour later, we slid into a hospital parking lot in Brainerd and hurried to the Emergency Entrance. Swinging open the glass doors, we were stopped mid-stride by the sight of a life-sized paper doll painted as a fisherman. Every appendage, every imaginable spot on the doll's body had a fishing hook stuck in it, duplicating the places hooks had been removed. There were hooks in unmentionable places and I could hardly keep from laughing; my companions were less impressed. I knew we'd come to the right place.

We waited for what seemed to be forever after checking in at the front desk. A doctor on call had been summoned. Felson got grumpier and grumpier. He couldn't sit. He stood. I continued holding the soaking red towel to the back of his head and kept quiet. There was no humoring him.

When the doctor arrived, he acted put out. Responding to fishing hook duty, today, was apparently not what he had in mind. Our predicament must have been a common occurrence and evidently, not terribly important compared with his Sunday golf game. He still had on his ridiculous plaid pants and striped shirt, and the cleats on his shoes clicked against the floor as he walked. In the lobby, without a word, Doc twirled Felson around by the shoulders and administered a great big shot of Novocain to the base of his neck. He took hardly a glance at the wound. We were shocked by his bedside manner. Then Doc disappeared.

In twenty minutes, Doc returned with a pair of regular old pliers. Without cleaning the wound or prepping Felson's head, without escorting our friend to a cubicle or offering him a bed, he closed the pliers on the fishing hook. Bending his considerable forearm around

Felson's forehead and putting muscle into the brace, Doc ripped the hooks from Felson's head. An egg-sized chunk of flesh came out with the hooks. Paddy and I gasped and looked at each other: *We could have done that.* Without a stitch or a swab of iodine, the doc walked off with the pliers holding the hooks, never to return. *Poor Felson. His brains might have come out on that hook!*

It would be heartening to know Western Airlines management could respond to the Deregulation Act of 1976 in a timely manner, and rise to the challenge that unrestrained competition would bring. Without the Civil Aeronautics Board setting fares, or government subsidies on unprofitable routes, futures of U.S. commercial airlines would be in the competitive world of business, not the closed, assured world of a public utility. By the late 1970's, because nothing apparent had happened at Western Airlines in response to deregulation, nothing changed. We still operated as if there was no tomorrow, while all around us other airlines rearranged or changed their game plans. It seemed deregulation was only a mysterious and so far, hollow word. But by 1981, Western was beyond action and reactively dissolving jobs. The entire revenue System Flight Schedule was the size of a single piece of legal paper, folded.

A prospective new president from Alaska, Neal Bergt, was contracted for one year. He owned and operated a versatile airline called *Mark Air.* Previous presidents with company longevity perhaps didn't have the heart to terminate faithful employees of America's oldest airline. I was present at corporate headquarters in Los Angeles when he arrived, flying his Westwind jet from Fairbanks, to pitch for the job.

The bulging midriff of Western's middle management was slimmed right away to skinny by Mr. Bergt. Seventy-one vice presidents who walked the property in $2500 suits, smiling and shaking hands, were given summary retirements. Whole departments disappeared. One day I called Western's Aircraft Sales and Leasing Department and began speaking with Vice President Ray Hammond to arrange a lease, and the next day when I called back, there was a recording of departmental dissolution. I was breathless.

The pilot seniority list shrank with furloughs. Some of these fine people would never reappear on Western property. They moved on to other airlines or took jobs outside aviation. An interesting phenomena known as The Pool was developed by the Air Line Pilot's Association and Western management to maintain a percentage of pilots held in abeyance, current and ready, should the airline spool up to greater operating potential and need pilots beyond the present skeleton of crews. Though perhaps better than furlough, finding myself in The Pool, as the thirteenth person from the plug, was not without jeopardy. This awkward circumstance found me at 85% pay and on standby, having to call in every two weeks to see if I was to be furloughed (no job) or still in The Pool. I found the whole thing nerve-wracking because I had a mortgage to pay and had to live up to my responsibilities involving my parents' investment. Living with uncertainty and fending off financial disaster should I be furloughed, I decided to do something constructive: find another job.

To choose something other than aviation was not even a consideration; I was a pilot, and I flew airplanes for a living. But finding employment in an interim, when a new employer knew you would return to your original job when reactivated, was difficult. It would have to be a special type of job. I found that job at Evergreen International in their air tanker division. Flying the Lockheed P2V-5 Neptune guarding the forests and homes around Lake Tahoe from fire, this was the first time I had ever had a flying job right down the road from my house. Mandated to protect personal property and forests from fire, like firemen, we were on standby at the tanker base at Douglas County Airport where I flew gliders. It was an exciting job when the fire bell rang and it often did that dry year.

After completing forest service requirements of accurately dropping water on targets, I lacked only real experience dropping retardant on fires. Fos-Check and Fire-Stol were brand names used for the red powder mixed with water to the consistency of taffy and air-dropped to smother a fire. Once the water evaporated, it became a fertilizer, encouraging new growth. The airplane I was to fly was of 1950's vintage and started service as an anti-submarine reconnaissance aircraft used in various configurations – land and pure seaplane - by the U.S. Navy. Contractors to the Forest Service found it to be a very fine air tanker. Powered by two Wright Radial 3350 carbureted engines, this power was augmented by two jet engines configured to run on aviation gas rather than jet fuel. The aircraft had plenty of power to haul thousands of pounds of retardant to a fire, and would continue safely should one engine fail. This was something not all air tankers could do.

At the tanker base one day, we dozed on army cots in the shade of a cottonwood tree in the 100-degree heat when the fire bell sounded. As firemen, we jumped to the bell and into our Nomex suits and helmets. I ran up the nose wheel well ladder, then out onto the wing to close all the upper hatches. Secured, I strapped-in, knowing I would get the checkride I'd been waiting for. The Chief Pilot and I each started two engines as the ground crew finished loading 17,000 pounds of retardant into the hopper, and within a couple minutes we were rolling down the southeast runway on take-off. Helmets on, there was only a dull roar as background noise in our headsets. But if we had to remove our wired headgear for any reason, the noise was so loud it sounded as if the world was coming to an end.

Over the intercom, Ken told me: "We're not making a lot of history here today, maybe only a little bit of history, checking you out as an air tanker pilot *with* initial attack rating." He endeared me with his comments, though I was unaccustomed to recognition. Evergreen Tanker 141 rolled the entire length of Minden's seven thousand foot runway toward town before rotating off the ground and lumbering into the air. It would be a left turn to the fire in the Sierras near Truckee. When we had a positive rate of climb away from the ground, I moved the gear handle to the up position - but the gear didn't come up.

"Oh, shit!" Ken exploded. We looked to the airspace between our seats. It was a two-story drop to the ground. Long grass bent over with our passing. The nose wheel ladder we used for aircraft entry was still hanging down in the air stream, preventing the nose gear from retracting. "I'll get it!" Ken boomed as he took off his helmet and climbed out of the seat. Apparently, he'd forgotten to stow the nose wheel ladder.

I added forward pressure on the elevator to level off and accelerate. The plane seemed to be flying okay with the gear down. It wouldn't be necessary to jettison slurry to stay airborne; the P2 was such a good airplane! Returning for another load would not make the Forest Service happy. Reaching climb speed of 140 knots, I stayed low, banked into a thirty degree - medium banked turn - towards the fire, north of Lake Tahoe. Once airborne, it was easy to see the smoke. Glancing down between the seats, I could see Ken in his yellow *No Mex* suit with his 6'9" frame stretched out on the floor. He had hold of the ladder and splash plate, trying to fold them up. His thick mantle of hair was slicked back in the 140 knot blast, and his *No Mex* suit rapped against his body in the wind.

I looked back up through the windshield at the tall green grass scooting by just below the plane, then back down just a few seconds later to the space between the seats - Ken was gone! Only a matter of seconds since I last saw him. But the ladder was stowed. I put the landing gear handle to the Up position and the gear retracted. I continued toward the fire.

Adrenaline surged. Ken must have fallen out! I was solo. Just as I keyed the microphone - to let the Forest Service know via the Air Net channel - that if they looked about a thousand feet off the end of Runway 12, they'd see a guy in what used to be a yellow No Mex suit - Ken climbed back into his seat. My skin prickled with sensation. It gave me the willies. No time to tell him I thought he fell out - now we were advancing on the fire.

At cruise we'd secured the jet engines and flown in ear-splitting silence. The airplane was so loud it was impossible to speak more than a few basic phrases over the intercom. As we approached the fire, I reached up and started the jets. There was a noticeable increase in thrust as additional power was added and our speed increased slightly. The fire looked like a river of flames in the bottom of a long, narrow canyon not too far from Truckee. Imperiled homes lined each ridge.

"Well now, who have we here?" The voice of the Forest Service Air Coordinator came over Air Net.

"Tanker 141 - Ken Louder."

"Bill Ice, here." Ice led us onto the fire, the Air Coordinator's job. He would direct the attack by either leading us through the smoke to the spot he wanted retardant dropped, or directing the attack from above, which was safer for him. Leading air tankers into smoke filled valleys was hazardous. I didn't say a word on Air Net because our lives were in Ice's hands. He could easily have maneuvered us too close to terrain and I wouldn't want to give him a reason to do that. Hearing his voice over the airwaves was a surprise. It had been several years since I worked with him in Redding. Then I flew for Intermountain Aviation, Evergreen's predecessor.

Ice did his best to keep me from flying that season, which only frustrated me. With a barrage of ramp inspections and equipment checks no one else had to endure, he tried making me late for every fire. I had to think and fly fast - faster than anyone else - to get there on time. Once he'd detained me so long I was late. Of course he wrote me up and sent word along to Intermountain. He would send for me, accuse me of obscure infractions he must have laid awake thinking of at night because nothing was ever written down. Other than a few Golden Rules for tanker pilots, like never fly uphill and don't taxi with your wings folded, there were no manuals.

During these interrogations, Ice repeatedly called me by names other than my own as if waiting for me to correct him. I didn't take the bait, ignored his rudeness, and assumed the high road, gazing steadily at him with sullen eyes. His lips curled back from his teeth and his spittle flew at me across his desk. His tiny blue eyes were distended in glaring points. Ice was prominent in the Forest Service and I never remembered being treated so badly. What an example he set, in direct violation of published government policy. It was more than an attempt at humiliation or rudeness on his part; it was misogynous hatred, and coming from a government worker with a high government service rating. I wondered how this could be with all their rules against harassment?

He may have told Intermountain I was late because I got lost en route to the fire or any of another dozen lies. But all that hadn't seemed to matter because Evergreen hired me anyway. Maybe they knew he was a misogynist; at any rate, he was just another government employee. Finally, he was able to take me off contract long before anyone else. When I asked why, he gave no reason. But I knew he did it because he had the power and I was a woman, a young woman.

I tried to understand his anger by listening between the lines of his monologues. I tried to understand the problem: he was given to making me the problem, but no, it wasn't me: *he* was the problem. I was doing the job he formerly did: flying the big airplanes. Now he putted around in a light twin, leading *me* into the fire. It must have been unbearable for him and certainly dangerous for me... Seeing him below us, flying the same old orange and white forest service Beech Baron, a gripping reminder of those days. What a contrast to the jovial acceptance I'd received earlier that same season in Silver City. On my maiden run, I was mooned by as many smoke jumpers as there were runway lights on either side of the runway! I hadn't heard of that happening before.

Wouldn't it be easy to accidentally hit a pickle switch, now, and knock Ice out of the air with a load of retardant? I would, of course, first say hello - from out of the blue -so he would hear my voice - he couldn't have forgotten *my voice!* The act would be final and probably fatal for Bill, but it might put him out of his misery. There he was below us, in my sights. He would never know...but Ken was doing all the talking.

Pine trees nearly brushed our wings. There was no bottom restriction on our altitude and we slid across the flames. They were hot and tall and we trail-dropped a line in three runs, pickling open two doors on each pass. The fire was red hot and the wind from it fanned it into a moving inferno, but the line of retardant prevented it from ascending the tree-covered canyon walls toward houses. Homeowners who stayed to fight were standing on their roofs with hoses in their hands, waving and grinning as we flew by at eye level. They were glad to see us.

Flying back and forth to Minden for reloading, the fire was eventually under control of the Hot Shot ground crews. As evening approached, afternoon winds subsided and the flames stopped jumping the ridges. Not until debriefing at the Oldest Bar in Nevada did I get a chance to tell Ken that because he was gone so long stowing the nose wheel ladder, I thought he'd fallen out of the airplane. He had no idea of my consternation. With a big smile he said: "You distracted me as I climbed, and I forgot to stow the ladder!"

✈

One cold morning earlier that spring, a neighbor appeared on my doorstep. I was an hour away from leaving for the Minden Airport. Fred Fisher lived on my road and was principal stockholder in AMFAC Corporation, owner of hotels, Carnation Tuna, Yellow Cab and other companies. I was mystified by his presence in my home. We settled in front of the fire in my living room. As I gazed across the Carson Valley he let me know why he had come to speak with me and began: "I'm interested in closing my airport on Kaanapaali Beach on the Hawaiian island of Maui, and building hotels on the site. The real estate is worth a great deal because it's right on the water. I want to move the airport to one of the sugar cane fields inland from the beach. I have some 60,000 acres available along the base of a mountain to build another runway."

"Isn't there a large airport at Lahaina?" I asked, recalling my island geography.

"Yes, but there's a two-lane road with a lot of slow pineapple and sugar cane trucks coming all the way from Lahaina to our side of the island. If a person has only a weekend to enjoy Maui, he doesn't want to spend several hours on a slow two-lane road driving to our hotel. It will be a long time before the roads are improved."

Fred paused for a moment and regarded the outstretched fingers of his left hand before continuing. "I want to be able to fly non-stop from Maui to the mainland without going to Honolulu for fuel; Maui direct to the mainland. One concern is the environmentalists. Apparently, the whales are everywhere on this side of the island, and low flying planes scare them. Would you consider helping me by going over there and doing a feasibility study? I have some nice hotels on Kaanapaali Beach."

I paused a moment, thinking. Accepting the project might mean, among other things, I could offer work to one of the several DC-10's I 'd seen in Los Angeles, permanently parked and idle on Western's ramp. It also meant soon I would vacation on Maui.

Traveling to the island on my days off from Evergreen, I caught a ride on a small airline from Honolulu to Fred's airport on Kaanapali Beach. I looked out the airplane window hoping to see whales, but the water was a placid blue and rose and fell in empty swells as if breathing for the islands. As we approached Maui, I noticed the shape of the island was a profile of a cartoon character with an enormous nose. Fred's airport was right where a nostril would be. The runway began just inland from Kaanapali Beach, the white beach about a hundred feet from the water, stretching slightly uphill into a sugar cane field. A general aviation airport without a control tower, it adequately accommodated the ten-passenger airplane I was riding in. From the air the runway looked to be about a quarter mile long but it wouldn't be of sufficient length, width, or compaction strength to support large transports. The last quarter mile of our final approach was flown low over water and our wheels touched down where sand ended and asphalt began.

An open-air tram took me to my hotel just several hundred yards away. I registered at the hotel desk situated in a lobby filled with planters of red Happy plants from nearby fields. Finding my room, I opened the door and threw my bags on the bed. When I opened the sliding glass doors, silken curtains billowed in the tropical breeze and I stepped out onto the patio to look at the view. The sun was a golden ball approaching the water line. Palm trees swayed along the beach in rhythmic waves of green. After my long flight it was energizing to know paradise waited just outside my door. I changed into shorts and hurried to catch the sunset.

Striding northwest on the beach away from hotels which lined the shore, the sun set with magnificent shards of light jutting from the horizon. Clouds reflected gold, then the pinks of evening. Hurrying, I wanted to walk off the length and width of Fred's runway before it got dark. A mango and banyan forest lined the beach on the inland side and tall sugar cane plants rose to eight feet or more around the perimeter of the runway. The warm surface felt good to my bare feet as I paced off the measurements, sandals in hand. No need for concern about snakes lolling on the asphalt - none were endemic to the Hawaiian Islands.

While I completed the measurements - the runway was 2500 feet long and 50 feet wide - the tropical sky dimmed from a panoramic splash of gold to nearly black within minutes. Sighing, I asked the disappearing sun why the most exquisite moments in life were so brief...Turning toward hotel lights and away from the darkness, I found the lonely beach edged by a line of towering Banyan trees. I walked in bare feet, savoring the elegant sensation between my toes, which sank into the cooling sands. Suddenly, a large figure came dashing from the trees with a bead on me. I paused in mid-step momentarily to determine if he was heading my way for certain. I looked around fast to see if there were any others. The beach was vacant. He was charging straight for me at a fast, ground covering run. There was no doubt what his intentions were as his head was bent down, and in the dwindling light, I could see his wide-open eyes fixed on me. I've heard crews talking about this Hawaiian pastime. It was reasonable to assume I was going to be in trouble shortly unless I could evade him some way. Rape wasn't on my agenda for the evening. There wasn't one moment to spare. The distance between us was getting down to yards. I dropped my sandals, turned and sprinted for the water. It was only forty feet away. I took a really deep breath and dove into the blackness. Staying underwater, I made a sharp turn away from the lights. I swam in the unexpected direction – away from civilization. Counting on this expectation from him, I stroked mightily from the beach, distancing myself from shore in a diverging angle. I discovered I could do my fastest underwater swimming four feet below the surface. Stroking a modified crawl, arms coming smoothly and rapidly up my sides to an outstretched position, I dug at the water for distance accompanied by my strongest frog kick for speed. Stroke after stroke - I was sure my aggressor could swim - he looked like a young Hawaiian about nineteen and was absolutely huge. I hoped he wasn't in the water right behind me. After what seemed a long time, I quietly broke the surface.

I allowed only my nose and mouth to touch the air. My lungs wanted to burst with carbon dioxide but I painfully settled for a quiet blow. Inhaling treasured air, I lay back in the water and scanned the beach. The air was really dark, but I could make out a figure pacing up and down where I dove in. I treaded water for some minutes, hoping he would turn away and disappear back into the Mango and Banyan forest. My rising and falling breast relaxed to a slower, rhythmic expression. I could feel perspiration and my skin tingled as my body cooled. At least he was still on the beach. I started to relax and began a steady sidestroke that allowed my head to remain above water. Present danger averted, my inner tension returned with another thought to worry about: an article in that day's local paper about missing swimmers on Kaanapali Beach. It reported that at this time of evening twenty to thirty-foot Tiger sharks swam just offshore in shallow waters. They were territorial, fed off reefs, and would eat anything in their area. Evening swimmers disappeared. When one shark was caught, contents of its stomach revealed swimwear.

I couldn't decide which danger was worse, the large human on the beach or the possibility of sharks with me in the water. I decided to stay in the water because of the certainty of what lurked on the beach. If there were any Tiger sharks around, I hoped they were *man-eaters*. I began a vigorous sidestroke to close the distance between the hotel lights and me. On my side, I watched the beach from a hundred feet offshore. Minutes went by. I was able to finally exit the water safely into the company of hotel patrons eating seaside on the patio. They glanced at me in wide-eyed surprise as I stepped out of the water in shorts and tee shirt. I smiled, dripping, and went directly to my room. *Think I'll skip dinner this evening.* My spirits were dampened for sunset walks along the beach. I confined my evening excursions to lighted, populated areas.

Circumspection and the specter of what could have happened the night before were jarring companions as I lay in the sunshine, bikini-clad, soaking up rays. I was happy and thankful to bask in brightness. The previous night was so black. Suddenly, into my line of sight, zoom: a face. "Hello." Placed between the sun and me, it was dark and I couldn't see his features. I hoped he wasn't a solicitor.

"How're you doin' today?"

I said nothing, waiting.

"Say, that's my ship out there," he stood up tall and directed my gaze with a pointing finger. In my reverie, I hadn't noticed the three-mast Schooner slipping into the bay. "Would you help me swim my payroll out? I can't seem to get anyone's attention on board, and I'm a little nervous with all this money." He held up two large sacks. I could see the outline of coins through the material. "Will you help me?" he asked sweetly.

I hope he hadn't just robbed a bank. I looked into his sparkling blue eyes to see what I could see. His features were too open, too golden and clear for a bank robber's. So, I smiled. "I'll be glad to."

We walked to the water and got in. I balanced the heavy sack on my head as he did, holding it with one hand and stroking with the other. It was a long swim – maybe two thousand feet - and I wondered how he'd thought I could make it without dropping the money to the bottom, hundreds of feet below.

Once aboard, he thanked me - and I him - "I've never been on board a schooner before -" and he showed me around. He walked in front of me and I admired his golden tan and muscular body in his speedo. He told me it was his ship and he gave whale-watching tours around the islands. Every open space below decks was decorated with the loveliest Weyland paintings of whales. They brightened dark wooden walls and lent a poignant, gallery-like atmosphere to the vessel.

"Would you like to sail with me around the islands? We're leaving tomorrow morning." He bent down and gave me an irresistible kiss.

"I'd love to but I have a prior commitment: it's called work." His face was sad, but he said he understood.

Later, his stevedore ran me ashore in a speedboat. Rather than looking ahead, I was turned watching my golden friend wave farewell and almost wishing I could call in sick...

✈

The results of my study were compatible with Fred's. When I reported to him at home in Nevada, documents in hand, the first thing he said was: "This is a much more expensive undertaking than I had initially thought." The cost to build a 10,000 foot runway, with button turnarounds and a button apron in the middle that would support a heavy transport, was going to be expensive, much more expensive than my initial estimate. In addition, leasing a DC-10-10 airplane from Western wasn't proving to be easy. No one in the Sales and Leasing Department would return my calls.

Returning from Hawaii, it was another week before I was able to fly to Los Angeles. After spending time on the phone with no success, I thought I should appear in person to try to lease a DC-10 from Western Airlines. I stayed with the lovely people I always stayed with whenever I came for training or had business, John and Jacquie Stowe. John stood on the sidelines while I tried to get through to Western to lease an airplane. It amazed him that no one would return my calls. He thought maybe the Chief Inspector in his office might have some ideas. I accompanied John on a visit to his office at the international airport to meet Western's principal operations inspector, Chief Inspector Anthony Reas. We visited in his office.

"How does a person get to be the Principal Operations Inspector, Mr. Reas?"

"Your presence is requested."

"By the airline?"

"By the airline."

"Would it be reasonable to think there was a certain amount of professional respect and willingness to accomplish common goals, like enhancing safety or addressing problems? Would that be correct?"

"Correct."

"If the airline decides they would prefer another Principal Operations Inspector, would this change be possible?"

"Possible, but not good for the outgoing inspector's career."

"Why?" I tried to ask the obvious as carefully as possible.

"Because part of the job is working together for the mutual attainment of the goals of safety and proficiency. If a fellow can't get along with the airline, he has no business working in this office. It's because of the airlines we're here and have these jobs."

This was astounding: An FAA man who thought and said the FAA was there for aviation.

Finally, my friend John intervened and said: "She's been trying to lease a DC-10 from Western, her own company, and no one will return her call."

"You mean you're trying to put one of their idle planes to work and no one will call you to say thank you?"

"Thank you? I haven't even spoken to anyone about setting it up."

"How long have you been trying?"

"Nearly two weeks." He shook his head and picked up the phone, dialed a number, got a secretary. "Chief Inspector Anthony Reas, making a cordial call to Western Vice President Seth Oberg," he covered the mouthpiece with his hand and looked at me: "This should get some action."

Then later that afternoon, "Western is delighted if you can lease one of our airplanes," Vice President Seth Oberg said in his call to me.

✈

Fred's findings were a duplicate of my own. Just the drilling to discover composition of the lava base substructure would be five million dollars. It would just cover the contractor's feasibility study. I had planned to build the runway for that amount and implement a landing fee schedule payback plan to recoup the investment. Special machinery to compact the material sufficiently to support a thick layer of cement - thick enough to support a DC-10 – would have to be barged in. Cost of the runway construction according to the bid I had gotten from a construction company with experience building airports in the islands would conservatively be twenty five million dollars. We were stunned by the price tag. Fred advanced his plan but more slowly than at the onset.

✈

A casualty of the furlough times was Western pilot Cindy Rucker. After being furloughed, she joined a traveling air show with her new Acroduster, a small, single place, acrobatic airplane. From reports I'd read, it was excellent but tricky to fly in acrobatic flight. Cindy died doing an airshow in Hesperia, California, from injuries sustained when she pancaked in at the bottom of her very first loop. She had shared a commuter apartment with me in Minneapolis from time to time.

Her death came when we were mourning the demise of our treasured Western Airlines. The Missing Plane Formation was a tribute to her as small biplanes passed over the congregation at her Santa Monica funeral. Looking skyward, squinting into the afternoon sun, the symbolism of this formation was not lost on me. I thought it might also extend to Western Airlines, missing from the airline array and it left an uncomfortable lump in my throat. It was the end of an era for Western Airlines and one of her women pilots, buried with honors.

A wake at a bar in Santa Monica was long and wet when suddenly, out of the crowd, bounced the cutest dark-haired girl. She introduced herself as Gurley Cameron. "Your abilities are so well thought of in the Training Department at Western that I've really wanted to meet you."

I discovered she was an aspiring airline pilot, and - I should have known, since she was a beautiful dark-haired colleen - one of Bill Lake's ex-wives. As evening shadows danced on the boardwalk at Venice Beach, Gurley explained her ambitions and the demise of her marriage. She was forthright and candid. I just listened.

"Bill was totally unreceptive to my learning to fly. He didn't support me in any way - philosophically, financially, or emotionally. He wanted me to just be his wife, and it wasn't enough for me." She paused, seemed to be choosing her words carefully: "*He* wasn't enough for me." There was a pregnant pause, then an admission: "He drinks too much."

"Yes, I've noticed. But he's not an alcoholic, is he?"

"I don't think so, but drinking causes other problems..." She looked at me with a wordless gaze, hoping I would catch her drift. I didn't let on that I might understand her meaning because I wanted to hear the words, so I said nothing and tried to keep my face expressionless.

"He can't do *it* most of the time. I left him because I need a man who can do *it* if not all the time, at least some of the time."

✈

Several weeks later I was at a health club in the Bay Area. Soaking in the hot tub after working out on the Nautilus machines, I was joined by a flight attendant, Penny Purfect. She was anxious to tell me about her intended, Bill Lake. I was not surprised as his taste in women seemed to run to raven haired beauties, and she certainly was one. But I fell silent and wondered as she told *me*, a recent acquaintance, "I don't love Bill, I just feel it's time for me, after several failed marriages, to get married and settle down. I want to have a nice life and... children."

I was speechless at her disclosure. I wanted to ask her how she could marry a man she didn't love. It seemed she might be missing an important point, and as I listened to her speak, I was aware I was floating away with the bubbles. Poor Bill, was he so blinded by her extravagant beauty he couldn't tell she didn't love him? Maybe he could think of nothing more than how fine he would appear with her on his arm. If he knew she didn't love him and he was going ahead with plans to marry her anyway... these were forces at work I couldn't understand, whole sets of values I thought had somehow gotten twisted.

Two months later Bill married Penny in a civil ceremony. That evening, I attended a reception at his house, taking time to slip away from my roommate's holiday party. Bill was immaculately groomed and standing stiffly in a line greeting guests. Penny was stunning in an exquisite white blouse with a royal standup collar. It framed her shoulder length dark hair and delicate features. She looked every bit the lovely temptress, Veronica, in the *Archie* comic series but her expression was a mystery. She looked wary, frightened, as if she shouldn't be there and was about to run. Her features were tense. Her brow was raised and her eyes were wide, a surprising expression for a happy bride.

I passed through the reception line offering congratulations, including assuring Penny's anxious parents that I thought Bill Lake was a nice man. They had the same expressions as Penny. Maybe she had confided in them, too. I tried to speak with them cordially, but they were speechless, unable to converse. Eventually, I gave up trying to visit with them and moved on about the house.

I passed from room to room weaving in and out of the guests with an empty champagne glass in my hand and questions in my heart. No one engaged me in conversation, though I got some nods and smiles. It was safe to assume the bulk of guests were pilots. A few were in uniform. There was one in particular who caught my eye. He was handsome with dark curly hair, and though I went by him several times, he didn't venture to speak. He turned and followed me with his eyes as I went by but continued speaking with other guests. I was wearing a long scarlet dress cut on the bias. The bulk of it fastened off the shoulders and around my neck. The back was low cut, and a sensational tickle from the blue fox made me want to take the coat off but somehow I just couldn't. I visited the powder room nearly gasping for breath, hoping for a few minutes free from *his* stares.

Having regained my composure, I ventured out into the hall and turned away from staring eyes, finding myself in the master bedroom. Many coats were on the bed and I considered leaving mine. I was alone and there was a new aura I hadn't noticed before. Sweeping the contents of the room with my eyes, I realized the silver vial was missing from the mirrored alcove at the head of the bed.

After my brief cruise among the guests and early departure to return to my *own* party, I received a call a few days later from *the* pilot. His name was Raul Chogge and he asked for: "The honor of your presence at a black tie affair at the Mark Hopkins Hotel in San Francisco." I was mildly surprised as I didn't know him but the formality of his invitation intrigued me. He turned out to be my handsome admirer at Lake's reception.

He must have asked Bill for my name and number. Chogge turned out to be a fine gentleman who bore a resemblance to the young actor Omar Sharif, though Chogge was a much larger man. We dated for several years. Raul was a charming, charming man. Educated, articulate beyond others, a real gentleman. While in the military as an officer and mechanical engineer, he designed a way for missiles to keep from falling over and getting stuck in their silos once the restraints were removed for firing. As a result, the military told him he could do whatever he wanted. He told them he wanted to fly.

They trained him as an Air Force pilot and he flew their heavy bombers and transports during the Vietnam War. Eventually, he found his way to Western Airlines. It was a charming story; he was a charming man. But I worried he was like a chess piece, shelved and idle, until the next time needed. With no apparent interests other than restoring an old boat and an antique car, he sat in his chair, reading, looking out over his valley, waiting for the day of his next assignment. Raul called for a date about twice a year and made an assumption we were an item. I welcomed him when I saw him, but I was much more intense. Twice a year wasn't enough for me. I went on with my life.

✈

Penny and Bill adopted a tiny son who had dark hair and looked like Penny. She wasn't able to become pregnant and like so many women, blamed herself. But she was hoping to be a mother and have children even if they were adopted. I visited in their home with other friends celebrating their new arrival.

While fixing dinner for a number of couples in the party, Penny supported her new baby son in the cradle of her arm. She held a bottle under her chin as she stirred the sauce. Bill sat in the living room telling us: "She's a sloppy, sloppy girl."

Guests gulped and faces turned red. No one even murmured. My heart went out to Penny. She was such a lovely, desirable woman. She didn't know that while she was making dinner for eight in the kitchen, he was talking about her in the next room. What on earth had she gotten herself into? I hoped Penny was happy. The treasure of children who are wanted may compensate for many things. Two years later, they adopted another child. This time, it was a sweet, little fair-haired girl.

CHAPTER VII

PUTTING OUT FIRES

I was in Western's uniform of midnight blue and wearing the new female pilot fedora with silver wings on the hat. As I stepped off the flight from New York and hurried to catch my commuter flight home, I chose to go *un-pressurized* - outside the terminal as only flight crews could do - as opposed to in. Crossing the snowy ramp before the days of security, the soft blue scarf of my uniform blouse blew across my face in the wind. I was reminded that the look was feminine. How thoughtful of management to let us still look like women.

I climbed the outer jetway stairs, suitcase in hand, joining the rear of a passenger line awaiting entrance to the airplane. I realized my fatigue, having just completed a four-day flight sequence, arriving back at the Salt Lake base after an early - o'dark thirty - departure from New York. Suddenly, the terminal door opened back up the jetway and I heard big footsteps striding down the darkened hall. I turned to see the source, which rattled the tube with each heavy footfall. A tall man came around the corner. He was attractive, fair, rugged, with broad shoulders. I saw the outline of muscles under a cashmere sweater. The planes of his face were angular, and he had a reddish moustache that framed a dazzling smile. I caught my breath.

"Goooood morning," he sang out, radiating exuberance and cheer. His voice echoed a clear, unobstructed tone. I felt myself awakening, smiling, beginning to soften. The male was definitely a hunk and worth a closer look. However, little Seraph sat invisibly on my shoulder, smoothed her wings, and whispered: "He's jus' the kind of man your mama tole you to watch out for!"

"Sorry, but he's just the kinda man that I like!" Allowing him to engage me in conversation, I discovered this was one of several times we'd met over the past twenty years, in general aviation terminals and at fixed base operators where I had worked. He introduced himself as John Knight and I remembered him vaguely... he remembered me not at all.

He was on his way to Reno and normally would fly his own plane, but today he was meeting the Nevada State Criminal Investigator arriving from Las Vegas in Reno at nearly the same time. John said he was scheduled to testify for the prosecution at an embezzlement trial for Bingo Truck Stops. He traveled with me via Western Airlines, flight 795, my commuter flight home to Reno. As a way of conversing while I checked him out, I addressed the manual he held in one big hand. "Are you attending one of Flight Safety's airplane schools?

"Yes, I recently checked out in our company's new Cessna Conquest."

"Oh. I was lucky to fly the Conquest's predecessor for Scenic Airlines in Las Vegas before joining Western," I smiled.

As we stood in line waiting to board, I enjoyed his voice, impressively deep and full. We visited about flying and other things. He had naturally beautiful teeth and a broad smile. Our turn came to sit and we went to our respective seats. I sat in first class and he was just behind the bulkhead on the aisle.

I waited until we were airborne then asked the senior flight attendant if I might have a man I just met sit with me. He said it was fine as there were few people in first class. In the lavatory, I changed out of my uniform shirt into an orange silk blouse, ran a comb through my hair, then stepped back to invite John to come sit with me.

As we visited, I noticed his strong profile. I was really into noses and his was a straight one, no bob there. He was muscular and chest hair floated out his collar. I guessed he was about 6'4" tall and I could see by the size of his shoes he had big feet. Big feet, big hands: always a good sign. His physical attributes were appealing but what impressed me most was the confidence in his voice. He was a commanding package. He told me he had been single for years.

He invited me to dinner that evening in *my* town, Genoa. He was meeting the Nevada State Criminal Investigator, Chuck Rikalo and his wife Pat, at the Pink House. Later, I explained that the Pink House was my hangout after gliding - one of the reasons I chose to live in this part of the world: to soar the Sierra Wave. The Pink House was formally a station where Kit Carson and Hank Monk staged wagon trains of Mormon immigrants going to California. Genoa is the oldest of Nevada's towns.

That evening, dining by a fireplace in the historic old house, flames danced across our cheeks. Our shadows moved on the walls and crossed the vintage furniture of reds and pinks. While we visited in monotones inside, I was sure I could hear the rustle of harnesses, horses and wagons outside...

✈

Months later, I stood in the Salt Lake Chief Pilot's office, shifting from one foot to the other at the secretary's desk. Charmagne tried persuading me to take a chance and put John down as my buddy for six months worth of airline passes. I could choose only one person. She was sweet and patiently waited at her desk with her face tilted up to mine. As sole provider for her husband and seven children, she ran the chief pilot's office. Years ago, her husband lost a leg at the hip working on the railroad. Crushed between hitches while making up a train, he couldn't work, so Charmagne did. The aura she exuded was bright, cheerful, and warm. I felt golden in her presence.

"Why don't you sign on the line?" The line she was referring to was the one designating my buddy.

"It's a commitment, Charmagne. Something I haven't done for years." Charmagne looked up at me with a patient gaze. My shoulders ached under the weight of my overcoat. The air around me felt heavy and close. I was suddenly hot inside my clothes.

"Go on, take a risk. It might turn out to be a good thing," she smiled.

I breathed in audibly for a moment, then held my breath. I pointed the pen at the paper, and wrote *John Knight* on the line.

✈

On dates, we saw the world via buddy passes on Western or bought tickets on other airlines. Other times we flew around in John's Aero Star. He included me when he began showing his truck stops to prospective buyers. It was interesting that he considered these selling-tours dating. We carried the principals aboard and visited each station. I noticed they were all accessible by air and in remote locations where truck drivers might need fuel, a meal, or a shower. They were a network of service, an innovative concept in the fuel industry, connecting four dozen or so Bingo truck stops across the country. It was apparent John worked all the time. I didn't mind because he was constructive, but I teased him about it, and the next thing I knew, truck stops east of the Mississippi River sold to Sohio, the ones in the Northwest sold to Burns Brothers out of Portland, and those in the Southwest went to Beacon Oil, owned by Ultramar of London. The negotiations concluding each deal went into the wee small hours and were fraught with intriguing calculation.

We skied between my trips that winter and in the spring, rode horses, either in the Sierras or in Utah's Wasatch Mountains. I took a bid on the DC-10 as Second Officer, and spent July and most of August of 1985 attending school in Los Angeles. It was a hot, smoky summer. Fires in the hills of Los Angeles were near enough the Stowe's home where I gratefully stayed as a guest during training. We could see and smell the smoke.

One easy weekend off during classes, I hopped a flight to Tucson where John met me with his plane. I was riding the 737 jumpseat when we heard him call Tucson Tower. My pilots said "Hi" and followed him in for landing. John had promised I could study aboard John Lyddon's boat, scheduled to meet us in La Paz. We were going fishing and diving. I never dove with tanks except for certification in college. I looked forward to the weekend away from school and with John.

As we flew southwest over the Sea of Cortez, azure water sparkled in the afternoon sun. A few islands scattered across the middle of the expanse were rocky, with no inhabitants other than seabirds. Mountains chained down the center of the Baja Peninsula and rose dramatically from the sea to ten thousand feet in places. At our two o'clock position, palm tree forests planted long ago by the Jesuits and townspeople lined the river in Mulege. Approaching the east coast, I glanced north toward the Bay of Concepcion knowing that in July it would be without romancing whales.

As close to a colonial town as could be found on the Baja Peninsula, the city of La Paz lay below us. With her sheltered port, university, and treed market place, she was the capital and center of commerce for the state of Baja del Sud. We landed and cleared customs, then rode in a taxi to the harbor. Our driver was skillful, steering around goat herders and the occasional wooden-wheeled produce cart going to market. When the driver honked, the farmers moved to the side, smiled, and waved their willow canes. With the windows open for air conditioning, I inhaled the ambiance of sea-air, appreciated the laboriously hand-cultivated fields, and admired the myriad colors of trailing bougenvilla blanketing adobe walls. It has been said that once the dust of Mexico settles on your shoulders, you can never shake it off.

New condos lined the harbor, priced with optimism for La Paz's future. The *Don Juan* swayed in her lines awaiting our arrival. John's friends stood around the wharf and turned to greet us. Once aboard and underway, I kept my promise to myself and *really* did study.

Perched in my swimsuit on the top deck of the boat, I caught the sounds of gulls and sea lions squawking on my tape recordings of verbal notes. I memorized checklists and referenced manuals for system operations and limitations. There was no breeze to flutter the pages spread out across white cushions in the afternoon sun. I talked to myself while I studied and watched the fishing and diving. Everything seemed so bright. We motored to a large lone rock where sea lions basked in the sunshine and barked as we came near. We found an arch with underwater gardens growing along its sides. The many colors of coral and plant life were visible from above but distorted by the tiny waves in the blue-blue water. I longed to see the colors firsthand. While I studied, John fished and snorkeled. Circling schools of herring, giant groupers swam up through the middle with such speed that they jumped out of the water, their arcing bodies in formation several feet above the surface. Little fish jumped high out of the water ahead of them trying to get away. Friends snorkeling speared the giants and struggled to hold their catch above the water for me to see.

Finally, I reached an impasse - I'd had enough studying - it was time for fun. I couldn't wait to explore the underwater gardens. From the swim step, I V-jumped with fins on my feet into the water, pressing my snorkel and mask into my face to keep them in place. John and I swam hand-in-hand around the base of the arch. The plant-life colors were spectacular. Small sea lions swam out to meet us, swam with us, between us, and all around us. Suddenly a bull swam to parallel me, his face in mine. He was as long as I was tall. Then he lagged a moment as I went by and bit a round chunk in the shape of his mouth from my fin. When this happened, I decided we were encroaching on his territory, and left the water. Sea lions have aptly earned their name. Soon, the other snorkelers joined me back on the boat; they were lithe and tanned.

Considerately, our hosts motored for over an hour at top speed to a special place where they said the bottom was flat and sandy and the currents weren't too strong. The boat Captain promised: "If you can take a breath from the end of a twenty foot hose, swim another twenty feet to the bottom, and bring up a handful of sand, I'll put a tank on you." I was able to do what he asked and we put on our tanks. John handed me a red scooter and we backed toward the side of the boat. I was careful not to step on my fins and to keep my head clear of the tank as we somersaulted backwards into the water. We floated downward weighted by our belts toward the flat, sandy bottom. He circled his thumb and forefinger asking if I was okay. I grinned and returned the gesture. When we got to the bottom, we turned on our scooters. They extended our range and we zoomed around at about 2 mph. I loved it. Presumably, our hosts had chosen this spot for safety on my first tank dive, but the only thing they didn't seem to know about were the orchard-like rows of sea snake holes spaced about a foot apart. A head poised in each and undulated with the current. I assumed they were harmless, as John didn't seem to notice them, otherwise why would we dive here? Years later on another outing up the Inland Passage of Alaska, I mentioned the sea snake colony to our hosts. Barbara was mortified. "Sea snakes are so poisonous! Of course we had no idea they were there!" John just grinned in his inimitable way and said nothing. It made me love him even more.

Back in school on Monday morning, the class discussed an item before the instructor arrived. I thought I had the information on my tape recorder. In playing it, I had quite forgotten that the sounds of seagulls and sea lions were in the background of my recording. "Where were you when you recorded this? The Sea of Cortez?" One pilot smiled and teased.

"Yes," I answered with a happy smile.

"And what were you doing there, young lady?" he parented.

"I was sitting on a boat, mostly studying, learning to dive."

"Oh, fine. We sat in our murky hotel rooms all weekend poring through books, while you were out getting a tan." Another pilot feigned a groan, but I could tell they would all rather have been diving. I savored their reactions and felt exceptionally lucky for the richness of my new life. In the future, I decided it was better to disclose little of my life with John.

On a break outside class one morning, Captain Lon Felson appeared in the doorway. Through the extensive grapevine, he must have found out I was in class. Leaning against the hall wall, he addressed me as always by looking at me out of the tops of his eyes. "Have lunch with me at the employee cafeteria today, okay?"

I had earlier kissed John goodbye; we had moved into the Sheraton Hotel for the duration of class, but he was presently en route to his offices in Provo. I offered a somewhat reluctant "Okay," and appeared around noon. Once we were seated on the sunny patio, I couldn't help but notice Captain Felson had a distant, detached look. He also looked kind of pale. I waited to hear what he had to say.

"My... my wife is divorcing me."

"Ohhhh," my voice seemed to purr. He was very upset. I had never seen him this way. I didn't ask why she was divorcing him. It was none of my business.

"I think it's her mother. She doesn't think I'm around enough, and she's moved into our house to help with the kids. My wife returned to flying after our second one was born."

"Your mother-in-law's now a part of your household?" It was unfathomable.

"She has kind of taken over. I guess I should have seen it coming. At first, I thought it would be good to have her around to help, a grandmother's presence, and all." He got upset. I wasn't quite sure what to do, never having seen him this way.

To change the subject to a happier one, I gave him news of my engagement and forthcoming marriage. "Lon, I've met a really fine man. I hope you can meet him someday," thinking he would be glad for me, as I would be for him. Suddenly, he was on his feet slapping the table with open palms. I was aware all conversation around us had stopped and everyone's eyes were on us.

"First her and now you!" I blinked, amazed. What was happening? What was he talking about?

Confused and embarrassed, I looked up at him standing over me and softly cajoled, "I thought you'd be happy to hear I've found a really nice man." This was a side of Lon I hadn't seen before. I smiled and tried making conversation by telling him what fun we were having and our plans for the future, but he went on fuming and sputtering through the meal. Relieved when the check came, I counted out my share and stood back from the table. "I have to get back to class." I felt my lips tilt in a little farewell smile. He pushed back from the table and turned to leave. I called "Goodbye" as he stomped away. I shook my head in disbelief - I thought we had always just been friends.

✈

I knew I had gone places and done things, but for the life of me, I couldn't remember with whom, before I met John. Now, I felt somewhat chagrined by this lack of commitment. How long had it been, ten years since I was in a relationship? Memories of my past were becoming a colorful collage. Intuitively, I'd known these men weren't right for me, so I gave them up - even the memory of them - and sat at home in Nevada. One day, I realized I missed John when he wasn't around - I could even hear his voice in my head. I looked out over the beautiful Carson Valley with its waving green pastures and mountainous backdrop, and wished I could be with him. I knew my inner strength came from taking the high road, imagining and attempting things not normally imagined by others, and I got the impression John lived that way, too. I approached life as if any of many things were possible. It was only necessary to choose. When detractors wailed *impossible,* I considered their words but pressed on with my plans.

John's father insisted: "There's no such word as *can't,*" and John lived life as if this were true. He always put his best foot forward and made his best effort, which was substantial. I admired these qualities but realized he was intolerant of anything less in others, and certainly he would expect me to be exemplary. He called me often, and asked about and took an active interest in my airline career. We seemed to be together on important points or I couldn't have pursued the relationship. I was impressed that nearly all his truck stop managers were women. With John's positive outlook and dimension, I knew anything was possible.

Then he did the most considerate thing. My sweet Great Dane, Piedade, (Pia-dady – one with a kind heart) died after losing all in puppy birth. They said it was cancer but I suspected it was really a broken heart. I was terribly upset about my friend and companion, and felt awful about leaving her lifeless body at the vet in Utah. Sweetly, John and his son, James, flew her home to be buried in my back yard in Nevada. I was genuinely touched. He had my mind, and with this gesture, he warmed my heart. When he surprised me and asked if I would marry him, I breathlessly obliged. He'd chosen a most romantic mountaintop setting with an endless view of the Utah Valley. He uncorked an exquisite bottle of Spanish champagne, which, after the curvaceous ride, sprayed all over in jubilation, leaving us only two sips.

Our wedding morning, with snowflakes the size of doilies floating down from the Sierras behind my mountain home, we were married by an Episcopal minister in front of the fire. Our reception was held at the Pink House where we had our first date. The wedding cake topknot was a frosting replica of John with a frog sitting on his head. My likeness was kissing him on the cheek and the caption said: "I had to kiss a lot of frogs before I found the handsome prince."

John expressed some concern: "One of the frogs might show for the wedding and shoot the place up!" He was referring to my mining friend who wasn't too happy when they were introduced. Fortunately, *we* were the only rockets in-air, and our guests spent days celebrating what Lake Tahoe and the Carson Valley offered in December: skiing, gliding and trail riding.

A happy year later, John bought me a horse ranch a dozen miles south of Provo. We moved there and found ranch life such pleasure: the croak of frogs, the smell of freshly mowed hay, animals grazing, and foals playing. In marital bliss with my raffish husband who was all my men rolled into one, I whispered to the night: "Thank you, Charmagne."

✈

A year later, when Delta was going through the process of buying Western and times were looking up, John had sold his truck stops; I wanted to take a leave of absence from the airline to travel with him. Encountering a stonewall from the pilot's union when I called to discuss an excerpt in the contract granting leaves, it took several calls and some time before I made contact with ALPA's attorney. This happened only when I finally demanded that I speak with him citing that I had paid my dues through good times and bad, when a percentage of our pay went to support other airlines' pilots who were on strike, and I felt I deserved a few minutes of his time. He was reluctant to approve my intentions though what I had in mind was clearly spelled out in the contract with the company. In a screeching voice, he warned me of: "the perilous course you are undertaking!" Listening through his dramatics, he assailed me with: "There will be a reduction in your seniority commensurate with the time spent on leave!"

"But the contract clearly said this would not be true, there will be no loss of seniority." I wondered if he was familiar with this part of the contract, it didn't seem he was as he was extolling the exact opposite. I knew loss of seniority could be a contentious point, though in all fairness, a reduction in seniority as he described could be the price to pay for a leave the contract allowed and could be as much as ten years.

I swept away his concerns as theatrics, and embraced my good feelings about stepping out. I'd hung in there during the tough times of furlough, *the pool,* and fifty percent pay cuts, and told him so. I asked why I'd be at risk if I was acting within the constraints of the contract. He emphatically repeated his perilous line.

"With Delta in Western's future," I offered in supplication, "the hard times for everyone are surely over." I remained positive throughout our conversation.

My leave was granted, and for a year John and I explored the world together. We considered buying a ranch in Australia which was advertised in the Wall Street Journal, and "just stepping out." "A dollar an acre with miles of shoreline," the ad said. When it came to actually signing on the dotted line, we hesitated, looking deep into each other's eyes, and realized we enjoyed our present lives too much: John looked forward to creating more businesses, and I'd not yet made captain.

While traveling in Thailand, we were intrigued that patrons were advised in the Oriental Hotel brochure not to drink the tap water. "A five star hotel, and you can't drink the water. They advise that we not even brush our teeth with it," John read from the brochure. The water we did use tasted boiled. He held a glass from the tap up to the light. Black things were suspended in it. We stepped closer to study the contents. What we saw was scary. "How can a Third World country ever hope to advance if its people are battling dysentery and hepatitis all their lives?" I asked.

"They can't," John said grimacing at the floaters.

"If you don't feel good, then you don't feel like doing good," I watched the little things moving in the liquid. It was a mess, and the only water natives had to drink. I didn't even consider drinking it.

Sitting under the canopy of our little boat at the floating market in Bangkok, we took in the busy scene of merchants bartering from ponga to ponga, women washing clothes on shore in the muddy water, others filling jugs to carry home.

We watched a snake show in a floating pavilion where a young Thai held a black mamba in each hand and maneuvered to pick up a third in his mouth. John was invited to hold a Python, allowing the twenty-foot snake to wrap around him as I watched from the back row, terrified of it contracting. I remembered seeing this happen in a college biology class. The teacher's shoulders were dislocated and his ribs broken.

With a name as complex as the traffic that moved on it, the broad river passed only a few feet from our hotel windows. Lifeblood of the city, everything seemed to happen either around it or on it. Long-tailed pongas pulled distant barges with heavy ropes. Floating houses built with artistic curves and decks piled high with grains or wood glided by with families living aboard. The boats floated down from the highlands on the current, steered by the father with a single long oar. This constant pageant continued but slowed after dark.

I spoke in low tones to my husband as we watched the Fingernail Dance, savoring Thai food from the pagoda across the river. This was the advent of a new era for us. With my hand on his shoulder I voiced encouragement. "You have great ability in business. You envision ideas and are also able to market them. Have you thought of doing something humanitarian like... cleaning up dirty water?"

We talked for hours about the water, exploring the possibilities, and left Thailand with a bottle of hotel tap water in our luggage. Once home, we had the contents analyzed. It had eight parts per million ecoli. Zero ecoli was acceptable in the U.S. Two years later, *Pura* was patented: an ultraviolet water purification process that sterilized the water combined with a custom filter to remove specific minerals. It was housed in a cylindrical unit that fit under the kitchen sink. Power supplies could be electrical, battery, or solar. John moved manufacturing to his hangar at the Provo Airport because of the larger space available and the units were assembled around our aviation activities. Marketing the units through hardware stores abroad, we attended water technology shows in the United States to advance the product. Eventually the company was sold to a larger conglomerate called *Hydro Tech*, which added the dimension of precise electronic controls.

✈

One day, Captain John DeMerritus, Delta's new Salt Lake Chief Pilot, called me at home on the ranch, inviting me to his office for a visit because Delta wanted me to return to line flying. "Delta wants its pilots actively working, not on leave." This was understandable and I'd already decided to continue my flying career.

After driving the sixty miles to Captain DeMerritus' office, he asked me what I'd done during my leave of absence to maintain my flying skills.

"I... have a King Air I fly." I hesitated, wondering if I should say more when I saw his surprised expression. I decided to continue and answer his question honestly and completely, and I was proud to tell him the rest "... and I have been designated by the FAA as Flight Examiner for certificates and ratings in General Aviation."

"Which are?"

"Private through Airline Transport, including Flight Instructor."

"What area?"

"The Intermountain Region."

"Delta does not allow its pilots to have other flying jobs! You'll have to give it up!"

I gasped in surprise. "Reserve military pilots have jobs flying outside of Delta."

"We make exceptions for military pilots."

"But they could quit."

He chose not to answer. I was immediately angry at his boorish manner. I'd never been spoken to in such harsh tones. For a hot moment I considered telling him that I didn't want the job, that I wasn't accustomed to this treatment, but somehow, responding to his theatrically irrational anger didn't make sense. My inner voice reminded me of the years I'd spent pursuing a flying career in single-minded purpose to the exclusion of much of normal life including having children. I wanted to finish what I'd started, but this treatment was a worry, certainly a bump in the road.

I stifled my temper, though in doing so I nearly gagged. I agreed to return from leave sooner than anticipated. Then he told me what I couldn't do on my days off. For a moment, I collected my thoughts. I needed to present my reasons for wanting to maintain the coveted position of Flight Examiner without adversity from Delta. I knew of other Delta pilots who did so. It was something I'd always wanted to do, and only now that I was settled had I become stationary enough to hang out my shingle.

"Does Delta perceive my being a Flight Examiner as having another flying job?" I asked politely.

"It damn well does!" He exploded. The use of expletives by management came as a shock. It changed the entire tone of the interview to one of impropriety.

I chose my words carefully and continued speaking in congenial, soothing tones. "A Flight Examiner is a judge of flying - like any other judge who's knowledgeable and asked to sit in decision. I'm not pilot-in-command. If there's a problem, I have insurance for these contingencies. I'm only a judge of flying, an observer and grader of ability. I am not flying the airplane."

"Delta will not allow you to have another damn flying job, young lady!" He pounded the table. His manner, delivery, and use of profanity were disrespectful and unacceptable. Could this be Delta Air Lines style, conducting business in a predatory atmosphere, pounding the table, screaming at employees, managing by intimidation? It was surprising that this could happen in the United States, one might expect it behind the Iron Curtain or in Third World dictatorships, but never here. It didn't seem to matter what I thought and I didn't seem to be making headway. The man was a hothead. He treated me as if we were in the military and I was insubordinate.

I decided to try another strategy though I was bothered it might be demeaning. Keeping the Flight Examiner position as well as my job at Delta meant a lot and almost anything was worth a try. I never heard the company give the other flight examiners ultimatums like the one I was getting. Because of them, I thought acquiring this position would be fine with the company; I knew Western would have been proud. I didn't think I'd ever been relegated to begging, and I was uncomfortable. I was proud and this was very unlike me, but it was worth a try. "Please don't make me give this designation up. It is an honor bestowed on me by the General Aviation Community, the community I come from."

"Delta hires military pilots." I knew this was partially true but they had plenty of pilots from General Aviation as well.

"It's my chance to give something back to the general aviation community. I can help assure awareness between the airlines and general aviation. Issues that concern big airplanes, like traffic separation and near misses, could be a focus. I would be donating my time. I've set up an aviation scholarship funded by applicant fees. I don't keep the money for myself."

"You send me a letter stating your case and I will take it under consideration."

I stood when he began shuffling papers on his desk. Apparently, the interrogation was over and I was dismissed, but I decided to verbally acknowledge his instructions: "I'll send you the letter you've requested, and will report to Atlanta next Monday for indoctrination, as directed. I'll pick up my deadhead authorizations for travel from operations before leaving today." He didn't acknowledge any of these statements. As I left his office, I wondered if I had lost something. Was this the 1990's corporate way? Ranching looked better and better.

In the end, I declined leaving my treasured airline job, realizing that people in power come and go, as DeMerritus eventually did a couple years later to become a principal at an upstart, short-lived airline called *Value Jet*. I hoped he'd taken his management style with him but, unfortunately, Delta was left with his legacy.

Review of seniority and standing on different equipment lead me to submit my bid for the Lockheed 1011, international, putting me one step closer to seeing the world. My dream softened as it was about to become reality. I'd written the letter DeMerritus demanded, and assumed it was in my file. I heard nothing further, no acknowledgement of receipt from the chief pilot's office about the flight examiner issue. This lack of communication made me wonder. I continued to give checkrides and issue licenses on my days off from Delta.

My flights as First Officer on the 1011 over the next year and a half were generally to Hawaii. It was the spring of 1990; DeMerritus left the SLC Chief Pilot's position and took the same job in Portland. He was generally known as a whip. His caustic, demeaning letters to pilots about various misgivings hung in pilot lounges for all to read. They struck anger and fear in our hearts, regardless, the Western troops were not falling in. The Delta modus operandi was completely different. There was no appreciation of individuality or assertiveness, two characteristics normally found desirable in pilots. Rather, the company was so large with some 9,000 pilots that they apparently thought only mindless adherence to rules was acceptable. At first, most Western pilots refused to drink the Delta *kool aid*, remaining loyal to their past, but time changed everything. Eventually we all drank.

This wasn't fun like the Western Airlines days. The demeanor was competitive and all seriousness. No smiles, no light-hearted banter or camaraderie. What happened to all the cockpit jokes? Some decided to give it up and elected not only to drink the kool aid but swallowed it in great gulps. Perhaps the Delta way was more comfortable, more predictable for them. Everything was written down. Every expectation, every response, every decision must come from a decision tree written by lawyers. Among these limited people was Dirk Bullman, a former Western pilot with an unpopular reputation. Dirk had the personality of a dry clam at low tide and become obsessed with the possibility that he might have a chance at chief pilot. No expense too great, he quickly sold out, even bought a shiny new uniform. Eventually as assistant to the newest chief pilot in SLC, Dirk got his indoctrination to Delta ways. His job was like that of a vice principal in high school: an enforcer, a screamer. He didn't win any popularity contests with the pilots. Perhaps he felt he didn't have to as he had the iron hand of the company and its policy manuals to back him up.

Replacing DeMerritus as new chief pilot in SLC was a short, thick man from the east, a Captain Chicago. His politics must have been incisive; you don't get to be a chief pilot at Delta Air Lines by being naive. A dark skinned Bella Lugosi type, he looked straight out of the mob. His mannerisms were flamboyant and he used a huge cigar as a prop. His ego was barely contained in the ample office space below Delta's concourses in Salt Lake City. Chicago had an arresting malevolence, everyone seemed his enemy. He told me once in a meeting: "I'm Armenian," but he had the round eye of a Sicilian and the charm of an asp.

✈

CHAPTER VIII

THE AMERICAN DREAM

Suzy Q was a tad shorter than the rest of us Amazons at the airline, but she had a big personality. I'd never been able to confirm stories about her being stretched on a chiropractor's rack to reach the requisite five foot six inch minimum for pilots, which she didn't quite attain. Her structure may have attracted Delta's attention but I think it was the magnitude of her bearing that made her a target.

Wearing her long, pale, naturally blonde hair back in an attractive chignon at the nape of her neck, Suzy Q was the epitome of her Scandinavian heritage. Intelligence emanated from large, round, blue eyes through a steady, no nonsense gaze. Before coming to work for Western as a pilot, Suzy flew captain for Zantop Airlines on DC-4 and 6's. When furloughed by Western, she and her husband took the opportunity to start a family and had two little girls. She showed me pictures of them while we were having breakfast at the training pilots' hotel in Atlanta. They were as blonde as she was.

"I want to bring you up to date on a situation..." She began her story.

"When Delta acquired Western, and furloughed pilots were recalled, I found myself in a simulator check with Captain Clyde

Bohr. Formerly with Western as Director of Simulator Training on the 737, Bohr fast peddled to keep his prestigious position in Salt Lake for Delta by making training much more difficult than it had to be. He's proud his program is tougher than any other at Delta."

"Yes, I've heard this."

With mountain flying and an elaborate Performance and Navigational System on the 737-300, Bohr's demands didn't show favoritism towards Western pilots, if anything, his standards of excellence were way above the norm. Ostensibly, because the airplane was operated in the mountains, and generally it was former Western people based in SLC who flew there, he felt they should be kept to a higher standard. If his program was better, it wouldn't be disbanded and taken to Atlanta as all other training programs at Delta have.

"To assure his power, he's become a fearsome taskmaster," she began. "His beefy size backs up his tough demeanor. His name is fitting. He growls instead of speaks and hostility oozes from each of his large pores."

Suzy was failed on her simulator check, the first failure of her flying career. The reason given for her failure was insufficient rudder in a single engine operation resulting in a heading change of two more than the allowed ten degrees. "That's taking the standard to the extreme. He takes his responsibilities too literally. Most pilots can't read the compass within two degrees."

Part of the advantage of being designated to give checkrides was to soften the literal interpretation without compromising the end result. Had he gotten the concept mixed up in the execution of his duties? While she told me this, I listened, amazed that with all the effort it took to get this far in aviation, especially for a woman, that Delta would put forth such effort to fail its finest. Did they make a practice of professionally embarrassing their pilots? Was this how they assured conformity? Or were some men set on dethroning the queens?

"I contended I was within parameters; Bohr denied it. A heated argument followed. As part of a crew, I've often seen male pilots well out of parameters who were passed, and told him so. For contesting his decision, I was escorted like a criminal to the chief pilot's office."

"How so?"

"By his Assistant, Dirk Bullman, as if I was a prisoner – like he was holding a 45. In the office, he didn't just reprimand me, he screamed at the top of his lungs." The pilot group had noted Bullman's reputation for behavior becoming his name, as ambitious and histrionic. I thought it was an interesting way to play his hand. "Bullman was furious that I dared challenge Bohr's decision. He screamed so loud I knew everyone in the pilot's lounge could hear him through the door! Several times I tried to tell my side of the story. They refused to listen. They took me off the line. For attempting to defend myself, I was perceived as insulting and insubordinate. As punishment, I was removed *indefinitely* from line flying."

I was speechless.

Suzy went on: "I wonder what happens to command ability when Delta won't allow a person to speak in his or her own defense? How can pilots always be deferential to management? Make proper decisions, use good judgment, and command an aircraft? To be successful in our careers at Delta, do we have to be pilot clones? If we're submissive, we have no command ability." She paused a moment and drank some juice. "With these attitudes, how safely are passengers conveyed? How do we survive flying the airplane?"

If assertive, are we perceived as a threat to administrative power and dealt with as Suzy Q? This was not the first time I'd heard stories like this. The men I've known who took exception to this treatment quit the company before their retirement, before they were ready to stop flying. Some went to greener pastures at other airlines to begin again with a low seniority number, and others never flew again.

In conflicts with administration, it was easy for pilots to become targets, singled out for humiliation. Checkrides were a convenient way to professionally embarrass a pilot. Fail them on a checkride and there was little more the pilot could say or do, as they could just be failed again, perhaps even more troubling, if one pilot could be surreptitiously failed on a checkride, could another be surreptitiously passed?

Suzy Q's checkride occurred in November and her second chance to redeem her job was in March of the following year. She was removed from line flying in November, which meant no pay and no practice, to await her fate. Failing twice at Delta, meant you're fired! I was in Atlanta for my own simulator proficiency checkride on the Lockheed 1011 in March, when I found her trying to choke down bacon and eggs before her marathon. In a lowered voice - she was pale and worried - she explained the events of the last several months. She couldn't understand what had preempted this company behavior or why she was being treated like a criminal. She blamed the newest SLC Chief Pilot, Captain Chicago. "Chicago is an RD" - Real Delta - and she wrote his animosity off as legacy following DeMerritus' style of reprimands and derogatory letters to pilots. I thought there was more. He would not appeal to women and because of this, he was a misogynist as well.

"Before this simulator episode, when I had a meeting with the chief pilot, it was as if he demanded I play a game I wouldn't play."

"What game was that, Suzy?"

"He wants me to kiss his ass. I don't operate that way. I'm direct and don't mince words." That she was, and didn't, was an understatement. Suzy Q was her own person. A complete independent, the way a pilot should be: clear vision, clear thinking, uncomplicated and forward.

"And because you won't, you have all this trouble?"

"Yes, he's the reason I'm being treated like a criminal. I'm sure he gave orders to give me a real hard time on my simulator check last fall."

"Who gave you the check?"

"Cldye Bohr. That's when all this began."

"I don't know him. Are you all right about yourself in your heart? Are you confident in your flying skills?"

"Yes. I've not compromised myself. My integrity is still intact. I'm a good pilot and I know it. But Delta doesn't want me flying if I will not defer to the likes of..."

Just then, an average-sized, gray-haired man clenching a pipe stem between his teeth and wearing a red bow tie popped up at our table. Suzy paused mid-sentence.

"Ready?" He interrupted, saying to Suzy. "Let's go!" He blurted out commands without social preliminary. I wondered at his rudeness and who he thought he was.

"Have you met?" Suzy gestured toward me and introduced us as if to soften his blow. "She's here for simulator on the 1011."

I smiled and began extending my hand, when he snapped. "I hope *you're* prepared!" As if Suzy Q might not be? Then he turned on his heel and walked briskly away with Suzy trailing behind as if this encounter was a misuse of his precious time.

I guessed he represented the pilots' union. As if I might not be prepared for the most important day of each year- my simulator checkride -as he assumed Suzy was not - how insulting! Obviously, his barb was not lost on me. I said nothing, inhaled deeply, trying to maintain a neutral expression. I wanted to say something offensive, to tell him not to interrupt and to wait outside, but this wouldn't have been in Suzy's best interests. I was quiet and gazed at the gracious captain that the airline pilot's union sent to be her objective witness, on this, possibly, the most important simulator checkride of her life.

I resumed sitting in my chair and tried to eat my tepid eggs. There was hostility oozing from every corner of this airline. It wasn't fun flying here like it used to be in the days of Western. There was no good-natured humor; rarely was a joke told. I would never dream of doing something the company might construe as counterproductive because it would mean losing my job. Western people referred to the acquisition as a merger, while Delta people referred to it, if at all, as a buy-out, assets as well as liabilities. Did Delta perceive intelligent, assertive pilots, as liabilities? Did the men running the show perceive us as only threats to their infrastructure and power base? It was so ridiculous. Our lives were complex enough without this extra burden. We just wanted to go flying and get on with our version of the American Dream.

Chapter IX

THE GLASS CEILING

I had bid for and was awarded a First Officer's position on Delta's most coveted airplane, the L1011, a couple of years after the acquisition of Western. Mostly I flew with RD's (original Delta pilots) out of Salt Lake City because not many former Western pilots had the necessary seniority after the acquisition to hold positions on this aircraft. Additionally, several former Western pilots made attempts to check out on the 1011 aircraft, couldn't get through the school, and were summarily fired, retired, or dismissed from the program. Delta allowed two failures: some airlines allowed none.

One day a check pilot I'd known for years, Ned Farmer, stopped me in the hall and asked me what I was doing. This phrase translated to: "What equipment and position are you flying?"

I answered, "First Officer on the 1011."

"Wow. You're doing that! A lot of people haven't been able to get through the school."

This comment mystified me. I had no idea the school was regarded as difficult. I thought it was interesting and a lot of fun, especially because our systems teacher, Paul Benetta, was someone I knew from the past. It was great sitting in his class in Atlanta. The last time I saw him was in the Bay Area 23 years earlier, enrolled in a college flight program at Flight Safety. His nickname then was Deadstick Benetta because he artfully landed a Cessna 150 *deadstick* on top of a mountain of garbage at the city dump. When the engine quit for mechanical reasons he was further than gliding distance back to the airport. Rather than land in the water, and water was all around him, he maneuvered to land on the only terra firma he could find - an island of garbage - and did a super job! Forever after he was dubbed Deadstick Benetta.

The other pilots in our 1011 class in Atlanta were whiz kids. One had led the raid on Moamar Khadafi's headquarters in Libya, and another vied for a seat on the Blackbird – the SR-71. Their stories were spectacularly riveting.

"Ned, I can't tell you how much I love flying the airplane. There were several airplanes I've always wanted to fly, and the Lockheed 1011 is one of them." I didn't bother him with details of *why* I wanted to fly the 1011 because it couldn't be told in a couple sentences. It was the Lockheed-built airplane I began hearing about from my dad when he worked for Lockheed as Satellite Systems Test Director while I took flying lessons across the field at the Moffet Field Aero Club. He was first to know if I was overdue or forgot to close a flight plan. Seeking common ground as a father with a teenage daughter, he told me about the very fine transport aircraft Lockheed was building called the Lockheed 1011. He explained how Lockheed's previous civil aviation transport, the L-188 Electra, had incidences of wings falling off in flight due to resonant vibration. To assure the 1011 wouldn't have such problems, the new transport was well engineered. There were backup systems for backup systems, making it fairly complex for new pilots to learn and continuing pilots to recall.

I stood by as a reserve pilot from our ranch south of Salt Lake City and wore my electronic pager everywhere, allowing a measure of freedom because the length of my leash was longer: I didn't have to always sit by the phone. Once, in the saddle, separating cows and moving them to another pasture, my horse, Basko, jumped a stream with a mighty leap and my pager flew out of my pocket, past my face, and disappeared in the tall meadow grass. John had to dial the pager number from the house while I stood in the field near the spot I thought I'd lost it, listening for the beeping tone. It worked. I found it.

Giving the benefit of doubt to people is considerate and often the case in polite situations, but change a situation to one of adversity and often no benefit is given at all. As a new First Officer on the 1011 flying the Pacific, I found myself on reserve, filling in for pilots who were sick or otherwise unavailable for duty. On reserve I was given varied and interesting flight assignments, training for example, done entirely in the wee hours when revenue flying was finished for the day, or ferrying airplanes with mechanical problems or in need of heavy maintenance to major bases across the country. These special assignments meant I flew exclusively with check pilots. My reserve status continued for nearly one-and-a-half years, and I seldom flew more than once every sixty to ninety days. It was a worrisome situation. How could I ever hope to become really proficient on a new airplane if I seldom got to practice?

The 1011 aircraft is a wide body jet with unique flying characteristics due to the greater volume of air displaced, when compared with narrow body jets. It has great air penetrating ability. The avionics and autoflight systems were complex and interrelated compared with the uncomplicated 727. Reading about these systems was good and wise, but it was more helpful to actually get to use them in flight. The legs, a take off to a landing, were long in international flying, and each of the two pilots normally flew one complete leg. The other pilot, the non-flying pilot - NFP - handled communications and acted upon the flying pilot's - PF - commands.

On the L1011 we had a second officer who performed the duties of a flight engineer. Riding sideways in front of his or her panel, the second officer was usually the most junior pilot of the group. Some retired captains elected to rotate back to this position once past the FAA mandated retirement age in order to keep flying, accrue additional years with the company, and partake of the handsome income. They were known double dippers. Some were triple dippers if they also retired from the military. They got retirement *and* a lucrative position with their pre-retirement seniority. Their continued presence often chagrined their younger flying partners who felt blocked from advancing in seniority. Sometimes that real old pilot's - *ROPE's* -seniority number was Number One. What the younger folk seemed to disregard was that someday they, too, might find themselves flying after retirement age for a number of reasons: financial necessity, loneliness, or the inability to adjust to any other kind of existence.

If the two L1011 flights departing SLC each day were gone by 11:30 AM, and I was not assigned a rotation from another base, I would be free for the rest of the day. If the following day began a sequence of days off, John and I would fly to Lake Powell. Landing at Page Airport, we'd van down the hill to Wahweep Marina. John would get the propane and I'd buy the groceries. He'd take the houseboat up the scenic lake while I flew ahead in a blue and gold Lake Amphibian we affectionately called Butch, scouting for a good place to beach the houseboat and moor the plane.

We'd monitor the Marine Band radio channel 14 or 16. Delta Dispatch could get a phone patch through in the event there was an emergency. Knowing this allowed me to enjoy my time away from home, free to water ski or swim; Lake Powell is an enchanting playground for water lovers. I envisioned heaven looking like this landscape with tall mountains rising vertically from the blue-blue water. Friends came to play. An especially fun-loving bunch was a group of teachers from Salt Lake we'd known for years. We horsed around all day riding a plastic log in groups of six or eight, boogie boarding and swirling around on giant donuts pulled at high speed behind John's Scarab. There were a lot of arrowheads around, just lying in the sand, and we climbed up hills to get a better view of cliff dwellings hanging off vertical walls in tight canyons. We water-skied and swam until dark, then built bonfires on the beach and cooked dinner in the coals. If we were lucky, we got to eat striped bass caught at dusk along canyon walls.

One teacher was the most graceful water skier of the group, a perfect silhouette arcing across the lake. The first woman principal in Utah, Nancy Moore was now Superintendent of Schools. She and I sat on rocks enjoying enchanting Lake Powell views and discussing our careers. She confided that she and her husband talked daily about having children, weighing the feasibility of mixing children with careers. So far they hadn't come to a decision. She felt her biological clock ticking away as she neared forty. In response to her question I answered, "Deciding not to have children has been a long, hard decision for me. I've tried to be responsible in making this decision because I was always away flying. I wouldn't want someone else to see my child take a first step or say a first word, then have to hear about it later."

"I know what you mean. It was really a difficult decision to make. I feel it's more than a decision, it's a defining decision."

"Well, at least we have a choice. Our mothers didn't have the luxury. In those days if a woman was married and able, she probably had children." Speaking with another woman who understood this weighty decision was a salve to my lonesome heart. Nancy and I continued visiting on this subject through the years until one day when we began never mentioning having children again.

When crew scheduling called one morning over the Marine Band, Nancy and I jumped into Butch and flew from near Castle

Rock. It took only a few minutes to get to the Page Airport, parking next to a rose and pearl colored E-90 King Air, a birthday present from John. We hopped in and prepared to fly to SLC. Nancy elected to fly home early to complete a project. I planned to return to pick everyone up Sunday evening.

"Seems like a nice way to go. How long have you had your plane?"

"For several months; when we first got it, I had fun redoing the bright canary yellow over in my favorite colors. On our days off, we flew to Mena, Arkansas, about a hundred miles north of Dallas. The Rose Aviation family owns a 5500 foot asphalt strip with a number of big hangars along it situated just back from the parallel taxiway. One hangar housed an engine repair shop, another, avionics, another, a paint shop. Each accommodates some aspect of airplane repair, retrofit, or refurbishment."

"So you got the works?"

"Yes, and my favorite was the Interiors Hangar. Bolts and bolts of material extended ceiling to floor. The first day I walked in, my eye went immediately to one bolt in particular." A wave-like pattern of color moved across the material in warm hues of amethyst, burnt umber and taupe appliquéd with cotton batting. "I *knew* I had to have this for the couch; in fact, it was so unusual and beautiful that I decorated the rest of the airplane around it."

"It looks wonderful! especially the mauve leather seats."

"You think so? At first I thought it might be a little over the top." The pilot seats were amethyst hopsacking but the headliner was pearl-colored suede. "Umm, I'm glad you like it." We watched reflections in the polished engine cowls and silver spinners as the propellers started to turn.

"Things seem to be going good for you."

"Thank you, it feels like they are," though I always had a niggling feeling there were things going on at work I had no control over. I backed out of our parking spot, which always made me smile, by putting the props in reverse, and an hour later we're landing at Salt Lake International.

✈

In the spring of 1990, a year after checking out as First Officer, I flew several rotations on the L 1011, model 10, to Hawaii with Captain Bill Lake. He was another Western pilot who made it through 1011 school. We were both on reserve. The L 1011 flying category out of SLC was small and I expected to fly with him a lot. When crew scheduling called to let me know I'd be flying with him, I looked forward to it. It would be a chance to catch up on the years since our last flights on the DC-10.

Once en route, I was surprised to notice he wasn't alert. He was sleepy and snoozed not only on my legs but his. Basically, I had to fly all the legs. Was he still flying for Aviation Methods in California as he used to back in our dating days? When he was awake, we made polite conversation. I let him know of my marriage. He said he and Penny were living in Park City with their two little children. He invited us over for cocktails one evening.

We met at their home after skiing Park City all day. With us were John's 25-year old twins, visiting from California. These young men were good athletes and avidly skied through the very last run of the day. It was a cold, dark evening as we rang Lake's doorbell. Waiting for someone to answer, I recalled waiting at his door another time and my mind's eye wandered back to that time.

Bill Lake opened the door. He greeted us cordially, inviting us in. We made our introductions and sat down to visit. I noticed the ceilings in his townhouse were high and the sitting room had a view of a rather steep hill covered with snowy pine trees.

Their little girl had a fistful of chocolate chip cookies, melting in her hands. She grabbed hold of her father's slacks to hug his leg. He fumed, removing her hands and holding them out: "Penny, come get your daughter. Clean up her messy hands." This scene was reminiscent of an earlier time I remembered when Penny cooked dinner for a party celebrating their first adoption. I sadly wondered if Lake thought of Penny now as he did then: "A sloppy, sloppy girl." I hoped he thought of her as a lovely wife and mother.

John tried to visit with Lake but he was unresponsive almost to the point of rudeness. I couldn't understand why. Perhaps my expansive husband was an uncomfortable contrast. John turned his attention to Lake's five-year-old boy, who took to him right away. During their interaction, observing her son's glee, Penny lowered her voice and candidly said: "Bill is terribly bored and desperately needs something more to do. He's on reserve and sits by the phone waiting for it to ring. He studies his manuals all day as if he's at an office."

I said nothing but felt a little guilty about my exciting life. I gave her a wistful but understanding smile. She was such a lovely woman. My heart went out to her. It couldn't be easy living with such a difficult personality. Though I found him quite pleasant in the past, perhaps I just hadn't known him well. Lake sat in his corner and didn't join in the conversation. He was either bored with the whole scene or brooding, I couldn't tell which. He hardly spoke, nursing his drink as John played beautifully with his little son. I counted my blessings that my husband was such an upbeat, optimistic man who loved children.

Finally, Lake asked John what we did for entertainment. When John told him a little about the fun we were having, I realized Lake wasn't happy to hear about our active lives. This brought to mind another time he wasn't happy. Several years before when the whole crew ate lunch together at a restaurant in Portland, Lake discovered he wasn't the center of attention...

One of the flight attendants asked me when I became interested in flying.

"...When I was eight years old and living in Alaska."

Another one asked, "Did you ever consider becoming an astronaut?"

"Yes, at one time I actually had a sponsor from Nellis AFB, a test pilot, Col Jack Pulliam, who encouraged me to apply for the program at Edwards AFB. They were looking for women pilots."

"Cough. Guffaw. Cough." This came from Lake.

"Having read about the difficulties the Mercury Seven had getting their program off the ground, I wasn't too anxious to pursue the career of a possible stand-in to fill some quota."

"Burrrp. Cough. Blurp." These awful sounds were coming from our captain.

"I wanted a normal life, a husband and family, so I chose not to pursue the avid, totally focused life of an astronaut..."

"Bbblluurrpp. Bblluurrpp." Captain Lake was really having a problem. Initially, we all worried he was choking. I wondered if I should continue. I tried, but my rate of speaking slowed. By now all the women were noticeably distracted and frowning at him.

"... But my acquaintance, Dr. Judy Resnick, did, and though she wasn't a pilot - she was a scientist - she spent her life after medical school devoted to the space program."

"What kind of scientist was she?" One exquisite blond asked.

"She focused on a double PhD: one in electrical engineering and the other in biomedical engineering, perhaps to the exclusion of all else in her life..."

Apparently our Captain didn't care to hear about any of it and continued clearing his throat, coughing and guffawing louder and louder. Eventually, he made so many unappetizing noises that I gave up trying to speak. Judging from their expressions, the flight attendants were quite put off by his behavior, and suddenly I wished he were sitting anywhere but at our table. I was sure the noises he was making would get louder so I stopped trying to tell the story and ate in silence. He hadn't scored any points with the crew.

✈

On our next flight together on the 1011, Captain Lake was unable to add a column of figures dealing with total elapsed times. It was simple addition in which one column should end up equaling the other. He handed the paperwork across the console for me to complete. This was not out of the ordinary - it happened often. Most calculators did not consider 60 minutes as equaling a whole - one hour - and consequently they couldn't be used for figuring time. I added the columns, checked my figures, and handed the paperwork back to him.

In preparation for departure, the pilot intending to fly the leg - PF - loaded the routing in the NAV systems while parked at the gate. When finished, the other pilot independently checked the inputs for accuracy. I was tactful in correcting his improper inputs when he mistakenly loaded general airport position instead of specific gate coordinates in the Omega Navigation System. En route, he again slept not only on my leg, but his. I didn't sleep and assumed command as he snoozed.

When he was awake, Lake usually raved about something. This time he treated the second officer and me to a diatribe saying, "When I go over the edge, I'm going to kill ATV drivers, motorcyclists, snowmobilers, and jet skiers." The second officer and I endured this raving for an hour and forty minutes on the way into LAX; and oh, joy! He was *on* for another five plus hours to Honolulu.

Now, some captains felt that because they were in command they could use the airplane as a bully pulpit. They were experts on everything, and the crew trapped in that small space had to endure their soliloquies. However, in Lake's case, I couldn't determine where all this stuff was coming from. Perhaps these machines he spoke of disturbed the tranquility of his neighborhood, awoke him from naps. He seemed taut. His behavior was inappropriate and unprofessional. We were more than surprised, the second officer and I, we were astonished.

When he left the flight deck, the second officer said: "What's eating him?"

"I don't know. His behavior is strange."

"He seems to be so uptight all the time."

On one flight we were diverted into Maui after landing in Honolulu, and he went ballistic. I thought, *He must be missing important plans in Honolulu. What's the big deal? If you're out flying and the company wants you to go to Timbuktu, go there without fanfare, if something other than the original plan comes up, so what? You're being paid to drive the bus, drive where they want you to go.*

Not Lake, he stomped off the plane, cutting in front of deplaning passengers: "I'm going to call Flight Ops. We're not going on to Maui!" An hour later, we flew into Maui as directed with Lake at the helm. I had a pleasant layover, enjoying a sunset dinner amidst tropical plants and trees on the veranda of the isolated hotel's restaurant. Lake was nowhere to be seen.

On one leg he required me to use an FMS - Flight Management System - that maintenance placarded as unusable. I thought Lake was unreasonable and incorrect to insist I use a piece of equipment that didn't work properly and needed repair. Unhappily using it en route, I questioned its accuracy and he became irate. I began to wonder, *what's eating him?*

He berated me for not knowing my position in space relative to an airborne intersection by looking outside the aircraft window. I wanted to remind him that this was the computer age and intersections represented nothing more than a five letter word in space, but he didn't give me a chance. I thought aviation had lost a most logical connection with the ground when it stopped naming intersections and fixes after towns below. It may have been beneficial to know that Chatsworth or Gorman Intersections were situated directly over towns of the same name in the event of a diversion or an inadvertent landing, because the pilot would know geographic location. All this logic seemed incidental to the real problem at the time because he seemed unapproachable, distant, and angry.

We were cleared for a descent into Los Angeles. The altitude and airspeed crossing restrictions could only be met by starting down with flight spoilers deployed. Because of traffic conflicts, ATC kept us up at high altitude too long to fly a normal high-speed descent profile. "The company doesn't allow the use of speed brakes," he lectured me.

So how does he expect me to get down, I wondered. *Throw out the landing gear and make a terrible racket? Burn lots of fuel with all that drag? If Lockheed put these devices on the airplane, why not use them?* Speed brakes are flight spoilers when airborne and speed brakes when on the ground; he misused the term, but I knew what he was trying to say anyway.

Upon returning to SLC, while putting my things away in a locker, I mulled over the difficult flight with Lake. As I did so, another first officer, Ben Martinez came up and asked if I was having any trouble flying with Captain Lake. I looked at him cautiously for a moment, "Why do you ask?"

"Because I am having a lot of trouble flying with him. I'm thinking of going to the chief pilot about it."

"Are you?" I asked. I knew I wouldn't go to the chief pilot for two reasons: I felt lucky to have this job and, I didn't trust Captain Chicago. I found out later that Martinez never went to the chief pilot and he sheepishly avoided me when trouble began.

Another captain I knew, Harold Smiley, then approached me and I turned from Martinez who continued to hover in the background. I smiled and greeted him. He and his wife had accompanied us for a week in Idaho on one of our river trips down the Middle Fork of the Salmon River. We'd spent some time getting to know each other. We visited for a moment about our river trip, then, I was surprised to hear him ask: "How do you enjoy flying with Captain Lake?"

I nearly choked. Martinez' face was a contortion of expectation. Was Smiley being facetious? I collected my thoughts, carefully choosing my words. I didn't know if Captain Smiley was a neighbor of Lake's, nor did I know the extent he and many of the pilots in Park City fraternized. Since Smiley's wife was away teaching during the business week, he may have fraternized a lot. For all I knew, he might have been Lake's closest friend. I wasn't a stranger to how fast rumors traveled around the airline, so I chose my words carefully. But he'd asked me a question and I *was* worried about Lake's behavior, maybe he could reason with the guy.

My answer was cogent: "I haven't enjoyed flying with Captain Lake. He... seems so uptight all the time." I used the second officer's phrase. I looked into Smiley's eyes, pausing between each word. I had answered honestly. Perhaps this quality I treasured for so long was not always to my benefit, but I felt compelled by my conscience to answer his question honestly, and remain true to my principles. "One minute Lake is quiet and the next he's yelling. I hope it isn't because he has to fly with me..." I smiled.

Smiley didn't say a thing, but from his wide-eyed expression, I believe he was really surprised. He must have gone to Lake with this. Few men would have done more than laugh, blow it off, but not

Captain Lake, sensitive and insecure, he reacted violently. I was soon to experience the full force of his attack.

✈

On our next flight, while walking down the jetway to the airplane an hour before departure, I heard big footsteps coming up quickly behind me. I carried yards of paperwork under my arm in addition to a heavy suitcase in my left hand and a heavier flight case in my right. Whoever was catching up to me was big and didn't slow down. I stepped aside just as Captain Lake barreled by. As he passed, the energy of his wake flattened me against the jetway wall. I felt like I'd been hit. I didn't know what would have happened had I not stepped aside. I blinked in surprise as he charged on toward the cockpit without a word. I was breathless and worried: *what would he do next?*

He ordered me to operate some items on the second officer's panel - the flight engineer's station - while the second officer was outside doing the preflight inspection. When I hesitated, it was not in my job description to operate the engineer's panel on this airplane, this was Delta Air Lines. At Western it probably wouldn't have mattered, at Delta, it did. I tried to explain I would rather not, even though in training we had begun with the flight engineer's panel. He belittled me. I said nothing, looking at him with an even gaze. I felt like belting him in the nose.

During cruise, when it is normal to engage in polite conversation once the aircraft has accelerated and the autopilot is engaged, the second officer leaned forward and asked me if I knew where he could buy an English saddle for his daughter. Before I could say anything, Lake cut my answer from the conversation by announcing in a big voice: "I hate horses, and I hate people who have horses!" Both the second officer and I stopped mid-thought, speechless. "In fact, not if, but when I go over the edge, I am going to kill people with horses, people who ride snowmobiles, people who ride ATV's and people who ride motorcycles. I'm going to figure out a way to do them all in!"

Here was this awful speech again. It was embarrassing to be present while this behavior took place. It got very quiet in the cockpit. We didn't, for the remainder of the flight, open this or any other subject for discussion, continuing in silence. Lake's behavior was inappropriate, irrational, and frightening, especially since both the S/O and I owned and loved horses.

I carefully moved over and sat near Lake on the crew bus on the way to the hotel. At first I apologized for anything I may have said that upset him. He was unresponsive and looked out the window. Amazed, I kept at him, trying to find that thread of understanding we once had. In a quiet voice only he could hear, I told him I was concerned about him, why he was acting so differently, and asked what was wrong with telling the second officer where to buy his daughter a saddle when we were secured at cruise? He turned to the window, set his jaw, and rode to the hotel without speaking. I wondered if he was afraid that if I were audacious enough to say he was uptight, would I divulge other indiscretions from his past as well?

The next morning, while riding to the HLU terminal, Captain Lake took center stage. The crew would have to listen; we were his hostages on the crew bus. "Last night I got up in the middle of the night to go to the bathroom -" I didn't think any of the nine women flight attendants on the bus wanted to hear this story – "and I made a wrong turn, accidentally going out my hotel room door. There I was, standing in the hall butt-naked wondering what to do. Someone opened a door. A guy handed me a tea towel. But it wasn't large enough to cover the offending area." Everyone on the bus groaned. "I ended up calling the front desk with the floor phone hoping security would bring a key."

This story bore a distinct similarity to another story that took place in Anchorage and became famous around the airline. The Anchorage Hilton had large white pillars that looked like they held up the ceiling of the lobby. Bill Boggs, who learned to whisper in a sawmill, apparently slept in only a tee shirt and a smile. When he made a wrong turn and found he'd locked himself out of the room, he rode the elevator to the lobby, as there was no phone on his floor. It was about midnight and as the elevator door opened, he leaped behind one of the pillars while holding his tee shirt down over the offending area. He tried in vain to get the attention of the reception desk without disturbing the rest of the lobby.

"Psssst. Psssst. *Pssst.*" The receptionists moved together in a clutch to regard the talking head sticking out from behind the pole. In his most gentlemanly Kentucky accent, Boggs explained, "I've locked myself out of my room. Would someone please be so kind to give me a key to room 626?"

Amidst stifled giggles the receptionists decided to have some fun.

"Are you registered at the hotel, sir?

"Yes."

"What was the name, sir?"

"Bill Boggs."

"I don't see it here. Are you with a company, sir?"

"First Officer, Western Airlines. I was in room 626."

"Ah, checking..." answered one of the clerks, flipping back and forth through records. "With Western Airlines, did you say?"

At that moment the elevator dinged its arrival in the lobby, and several people got off, grinning, to see Boggs' backside. Boggs wished them "Good evening," and the group looked over their shoulders laughing as they crossed the lobby. Boggs continued with the receptionist's question: "Yes, ma'am, it's Western Airlines. I'm First Officer Bill Boggs."

"Here it is."

"Do you have some identification, Mr. Boggs?"

"Only this here tee shirt and a great big smile!"

Perhaps they were concerned he might show them just how big his smile really was and so they quit goofing around. Someone stepped forward and handed him a key. With many "Thank you, thank yous," Mr. Boggs, turned from the pillar with his tee shirt still pulled down in front and mooned the entire lobby as he stepped back on the elevator.

I believed *this* story because one hot summer day a mutual friend lent me Boggs' commuter car so I could run into the city. Approaching the vehicle in a heavy downpour, I noticed all the windows were down - but the doors were locked. Boggs' stories were cute and so Boggs-like because he told them humorously, laughing at himself all the while. Somehow, the same story coming from Lake wasn't funny. I looked around at the faces of my flying partners: no one was amused. That Lake told this story with me in the audience was strange considering our past. He was unreal! Little did I know then, that his past behavior towards Greg Gertz and others who crossed him was only practice for the assault on me, which was pivotal to Lake's ambitions at Delta Air Lines.

✈

After this trip, I decided to discuss his bizarre behavior with my husband. John was laying irrigation pipe and I, fertilizing our roses. I had to dig in under the decorative bark to reach the roots. The bark seemed to be everywhere the wind had blown it. Cinders or decorative rock would certainly stay in place better.

We sat on the deck of our house eating lunch and looking out over the hayfields. Our white Piedmontese cattle with charcoal markings on their legs and around their eyes grazed nearby. One field with young horses and their tenders were sprawled out, sleeping in the sunshine. The Wasatch Mountains stretched from our valley floor at five thousand feet to nearly twelve thousand feet just a mile away.

Between bites of potato salad, John told me about his latest venture. My eyes opened wide at the seeming impossibility! "No," he assured me. "It *is* possible. We're doing it. We're transporting tertiary-cleaned sludge from Los Angeles sewage plants by truck to Yuma. We've bought and leased several hundred sections of desert and injected the sludge into the arid sand with claw-foot tractors. We'll get one less alfalfa cutting than Brazil, and Brazil gets fourteen, the most cuttings in the world. The only concern so far has been civic, over an accident causing a spill..."

"Isn't that why you run at night?"

"Yes, it is. Less traffic."

"And the produce can't be directly consumed by humans. First by cows, then by humans is all right?" I asked, concerned.

"That's right. The only problem so far is that the honeybees can't pollinate fast enough so we've had to import a different bee, a Leaf Cutter bee, comes from Canada. Looks like a cross between a bee and a fly."

"Oh. How is the leaf cutter different from regular bees?"

"They're faster. Right now we're building three-sided shelters to stand Styrofoam panels in with graphics on them. The panels have holes bored into them for the Leaf Cutter's home..."

"Why graphics on the panels?"

"Because each bee has to be able to find its particular address; they cut the alfalfa leaves and stuff them in the holes, lay their eggs, and the little ones eat the leaves. While they move around the field cutting leaves, they pollinate the crop. I think we finally have the solution to our pollination problem."

"Do the trucks run empty back to LA?" This was a daunting question.

"Yes. What are you thinking?"

"Why don't you look for a back haul? Something that's compatible..."

"With shit!" We laughed at having the same thought and saying the same thing.

"We clean the trailers after every run, but still, the back haul would have to be..."

"Insensitive to the front haul!" We were really enjoying this.

"Something like rocks or coal, maybe, certainly not lettuce or potatoes."

"How about... how about... cinders?" I thought of them in the garden rather than the light wood chips.

"What do you mean?"

"Decorative cinders, the kind people put in their gardens. Lava rocks in different colors. They're pretty expensive at the nursery. I don't think it would matter if they rode in the back of a sludge truck to LA."

"We wash the trucks out after every run, anyway. Hey, that's a good idea. I'll make some calls, maybe there's a cinder mine somewhere near Yuma."

"You could try Leroy Yellow Horse Jones on the Reservation."

"Yes..."

We sipped our ice tea thoughtfully for a few minutes.

"John, I'm really having a problem at work with Bill Lake. We're both on reserve, and we're going to fly together often."

"Oh, what's the matter?"

I outlined some of my past encounters with Lake and our recent interaction, including my comment to Harold Smiley about Lake being uptight. John was thoughtful.

"Should I go to the Chief Pilot and ask not to be scheduled with him in the future?"

"It's worth a try, if they'll listen to you. But they're going to ask why, and then you might have to tell them things about him you might not want to say."

Visiting Captain Chicago was out of the question, recalling Suzy Qs' experience. I sipped my ice tea. "I've probably made him mad by speaking honestly and being candid with Harold Smiley."

"Oh, Lake can't be that touchy and insecure, can he?"

"I don't know, he may be trying to play a hand. I never thought he was ambitious, but maybe he is. Going to management about his stability could adversely affect his future at the airline; the FAA might not take it lightly. He could lose his medical certificate. Another First Officer, Bob Martinez, witnessed the same behavior from Lake and complained about it in the pilot lounge after flying with him. He said he *might* go to management if Lake didn't straighten up..."

"Yes, but if Lake's unpredictable..."

"That would be better than me mentioning such erratic behavior. Such a thing might result in Lake losing his medical, and his job. He'd never fly again. I wouldn't want to be responsible for starting that process in motion."

"But if he's unstable... "

"I know, it's a predicament, it's like talking to authorities about someone being insane or on drugs. Let them find out for themselves how unstable he is. I don't want to be the one to tell them." Reluctantly, John nodded assent to my decision - I would *not* to go to the Chief pilot. If a *man* delivered information about Lake to management, it would most certainly be received differently than if it came from me. Let Martinez go to management. Coming from a woman, men might see themselves in my assertions, and react defensively. I was acutely aware of a double standard at the airline. We finished our ice tea and left the deck to go about our farming.

Working at pruning the rose bushes, I soon realized that my heart hurt. It ached at the injustice. "The male barrier," my father's words rang in my head. Recalling a military defense of solidarity, he'd explained that it meant simply: "Attack one, attack all." I restively thought of the glass ceiling, I was thinking of the same thing. I didn't think I would have to defend my presence after it had taken so long to get to where I was, but apparently, I would have to. My mistake had been in not seeing all the warning signs of a threatened man. His ego was now compromised by my conversation with Smiley, no telling to what extreme he would go to salve his wounds. I was so distracted by these frightening thoughts that I scratched the length of my palm with a thorn, tearing the flesh. When 'one of the boys' was attacked, would the rest form a barrier of mutual protection? Unrequited tears slid down my cheeks.

✈

CHAPTER X

AIR WARS

Fallout happened. After my comment to Harold Smiley about Lake being uptight, captains I flew with wouldn't speak to me. They answered the *Before Starting Checklist* because they wanted their responses on the voice recorder. They wouldn't operate the autoflight system or navigational computers under my direction, as was policy while I was busy hand-flying the airplane. I was solo every time it was my turn to fly. I had to fly with one hand on the control wheel and select data with the other, a somewhat difficult task, as it was a three to four- foot stretch from the control wheel to the keypads and in flight, there were no allowable parameters, only precision. Captains perched on the edge of their seats watching my every move, waiting for a mistake. If there were none, were they constrained to be inventive?

Repercussions followed. I was shut out of the loop. Captains would not communicate with me directly and turned in their seats to speak to the second officer. I had to deduct what was expected. If I asked for clarification, I was ignored even to the extent that operations were compromised. If and when my performance was directed, I was talked down to in caustic tones. Or if I was answered at all, nonsense was insinuated. Aggressive tones of voice and disgusted facial expressions openly conveyed hostility. This was so unsettling and dispiriting that I had difficulty doing my job. I noticed that Captain Harold Smiley, who was often visible in the pilot's lounge previous to my remark about Lake, went missing. Months later I saw him coming the other way. He shrunk at my approach. As I passed him in the hall, he would not look me in the eye. His gaze was averted up and to the right, body-English indicative of skullduggery.

By the fall of 1990, I was harassed, insulted, and threatened by pilots both on and off the airplane and the property. I was followed down halls, aggressed behind lockers in the pilot lounge, and accosted in the employee parking lot. I was so concerned for my physical safety that John began driving me to and from work. As we drove the distance, our conversation intensified the closer we got to the airport. I felt my alarm gathering as we approached the terminal door. My body stiffened, going nearly rigid in fearful anticipation. Sometimes John had to come around to let me out of the car; I wasn't able to turn the door handle in my grasp.

The reluctant acceptance I cultivated and gained over the past fourteen years, first as a Western pilot and then as a Delta pilot, was annulled. Hot and furious captains commanded my flights. I was careful, giving them no reason to act this way, but when they didn't follow the Operations Manuals and dictated their own agendas, my response was no less bewildering. This gave them ample reason to complain. Not only was I a woman flying their most coveted airplane, Queen of the fleet, the biggest, fastest, most highly paid flagship of the airline traveling to all the best places in the world, I was a woman who hailed from the bastard son as well: Western Airlines.

Had these pilots been provoked by Lake with visits and calls and had these offensive actions been reaffirmed by SLC pilot management? Evidently, Lake had gone to the Salt Lake Chief Pilot, Chicago, perhaps thinking he'd beat me there, not knowing that I would never go. *He* would, but I wouldn't. If I thought my reception in the chief pilot's office would be amenable, and judging from my past meeting with Demerritus it wouldn't, I might have gone early on with hat in hand, in a spirit of resolution, to try to solve these problems. But I would have to talk about Lake's instability and I didn't want to do that.

Fearfully, I waited. Captain Chicago launched a full-blown attack against me. He interviewed anyone who might know something he could use against me. He dug into my past for derogatory information. I asked myself why, when he had the power to make things right, did he choose to make things more wrong? Captain Chicago, misogynist, didn't need a reason, just an excuse.

This old Southern airline was adept at subtle repression but what I felt was anything but subtle. Disapproving facial expressions of disdain, withholding of approval, unpleasant tones of voice: all intended to intimidate and make me, the target, feel questionable, unsatisfactory, and unqualified. Delta pilot management, composed mostly of former military men educated in psychological as well as physical warfare, was well-schooled in practicing humiliation. This was apparently calculated to lead to erosion of self-esteem and loss of self-confidence in harassed individuals. I wondered if this management style was borne out of fear of losing power, the insecure response to change, or just plain *Old Thinking*. It looked like all of that and more. The *Good Old Boys Club* was alive and well at Delta Air Lines.

Future flights with Captain Lake followed the same venue. Having been portrayed as uptight really sparked his ire. He seemed more concerned about the image he presented than who he really was. Had he curried favor with the new Chief Pilot? There was no telling what unbridled ambition could do. At one point Lake backed me up against lockers in the pilot's room, hovered over me, and with spit flying in my face, told me in furious, whispered tones that my flying was "Despicable, disgusting and sloppy," words not too different from the ones he used in describing his wife. I listened to the anger behind his words and wondered what he was hiding. I looked him in the eye only inches from his wet lips drawn back in a sneer from his teeth, a response I was to come to know well. I gave him my broadest smile: "I don't need to listen to this," escaped from his looming presence, and walked away. Though I put up a brave exterior, I was acutely aware of the attention his posture gained from other pilots in the room. I felt awful.

Another time he filled the doorway of a tiny briefing room where I was doing calculations for an international flight. I looked up to see him put his hands on the top of the doorway, aggressively leaning into the opening, almost swinging on the header. He told me, "I'm going to make so much trouble for you, your job won't survive. You will never make captain with this airline!"

After some moments, during which I definitely heard what he said, I looked up with a big smile and innocently asked, "Are you speaking to me?" I rapidly collected my paperwork while he continued to vacillate in the jam; I wasn't sure what would happen next. Physical harm wasn't out of the question; we were isolated, and there were no witnesses. Surely he was smarter than that. It would be my word against his. I took indecision from him and ducked under his outstretched arm, heading for safety in the terminal upstairs.

✈

Each flight became a nightmare. There was a script a dozen out of the fifteen captains in this small SLC category seemed to follow. *The Plan* didn't include being kind to me. One captain forcefully hit my arm away from the overhead each time I dutifully reached up for a switch. Another poked me in the rib cage with his longest digit to make a point whenever I was hand-flying the aircraft. They figuratively shoved me with their flight suitcases against the jetway walls to pass ahead of me. I was excluded from all manner of conversation, whether professional or social. Their churlish behavior made performing my job next to impossible.

I listened past the hostility for necessary information, comporting myself placidly and with diplomacy. Apparently this was a different approach to handling harassment than what Lorelei Kenyon used. I heard she challenged when attacked and kept everyone uncomfortably on the defensive. I found the opposite to be true: her verbal defenses were strong and logical. They told stories about her terrible temper and how she could cut a man to ribbons with her tongue. She scared them. I didn't want to scare them; I just wanted to do my job. It was anyone's guess how long either of us could hold out.

Lorelei spoke of no one, good, bad, or indifferently, while she was spoken of in the poorest terms. A representative from the Airline Pilots Union called to ask if I'd come to Los Angeles to stand in Lorelei's corner at a meeting with their Professional Standards Committee. The meeting took place during Western's last days before acquisition in 1986. I was surprised when I was called and asked why I was invited. I was told that to make things fair, Lorelei should have the support of a friend. I wondered if I was her only friend, but there was one other brave soul, a captain, also in her corner. It wasn't something I really wanted to do as it gave the impression I was aligned with her, but the rep gave me no choice: I was to be there.

The meeting was a total embarrassment for ALPA, though the representative was incapable of comprehending this and more. The point of the gathering was not to discuss Lorelei's professionalism as one might expect from Professional Standards, rather, it was to discuss how to make her *look* more like a man.

As the evening unfolded with a half dozen people in a small room, I sat on the sidelines, listening, my head bent down because I couldn't stop laughing, though I managed to stifle the sound. I asked Lorelei only one question during the fiasco, hoping to show her propriety. I asked for information concerning a mutual friend about whom she could be candid and she responded: "I don't have anything to say about him, for him or against him, or anyone else for that matter." This comment drove home my point. Though she was the brunt of many cockpit jokes and dirty humor, she wouldn't sling mud when given the opportunity. She maintained a level of poise and professionalism above her detractors, no matter how they tried to compromise her integrity.

My admiration for her increased as the evening progressed. She handled herself beautifully. I realized those awful stories I'd been hearing were nothing more than evil gossip, seeping like poison through the airline. The one damaging story passed around most often was about breaking the towbar, not once, but twice on the same pushback maneuver. By either not depressurizing the A Hydraulic system on the Boeing 727 by leaving the pumps on, or, having a spurious electrical interruption causing the system to pressurize even if the pump switches were off, the towbar got broken. I could understand it happening once, but certainly not twice on the same flight. The duplication would be outlandish, making the story the same: outlandish.

The other destructive story about Lorelei was that she *dumped fuel overboard* to bring the tanks back into balance to appease a captain who commanded she do so *immediately*. This would also be out of the question. No one would do it. I found these stories really hard to believe and quizzed her closely. She threw back her head and laughed. Then we laughed together. Gossip distorts reality. The intent was amusement at someone's expense. The result was always the same: destructive.

The ALPA gathering proved to be hilarious. Lorelei quickly took command of the meeting without even trying. Though I was laughing on the inside, it was a serious meeting, as I gleaned the point of it was to change her, or fire her. "Can't you cut your hair?"

"Why should I cut my hair? I pull it back. It's out of my eyes. I haven't cut my hair since my little boy died and I have no desire to cut it."

"But it's so long, and so, so... golden." I laughed inside.

"I meet the criteria of appearance set forth in the company operations manual."

As I sat listening to the exchange, I was reminded that she attended the Dale Carnegie course on "How to Win Friends and Influence People." She not only completed the course but also won their national speech contest with her dissertation on how she was empowered by other people. The irony of her chosen subject stays with me to this day.

"And how about your eyelashes? Do they have to be so long?"

Lorelei was very fair-skinned. "I have no eyelashes of my own and my Ophthalmologist says my eyes need protection." Her false eyelashes were the mink kind you could shower with or wear to bed. Every question was directed to her appearance, which was impeccable, to say nothing of her beauty. She answered politely, which somehow negated the importance of their questions, in matter-of-fact tones sounding as if she'd been asked these things before. She looked like dynamite in a black suit, a below-the-knee skirt, and a cream silk blouse tied in a bow at the neck. Her hair was smoothly drawn back in a French roll. I thought I was attractively attired, also in a black suit, but I felt like a little brown wren sitting across from an elegant swan.

The man who questioned her, the rep who conducted the meeting, was an odd-looking fellow. Far from handsome, he was tall and gangly, and looked something like *Lurch* from *The Addams*

Family program on TV. He wore a wrinkled, short-sleeved shirt while other men in the room were in sports jackets. His appearance left little to recommend him, and in other circles, he might be the subject of a reprimand. Circulation of air via the air conditioning system sent *whiffs* of his perspiration across the room. Should they pass on the street, I was sure Lorelei wouldn't turn to look at him the way he'd turn to look at her. He was a forgettable character and she was not. She dominated the gathering because she had what he lacked: presence.

She was grilled for two hours, not on her proficiency, but on her appearance. I agreed to be present, though my inner voice expressed concern, asking whether I'd now be marked as she was. This affiliation could prove harmful if Lorelei lost her job, because who would be the replacement then, the butt of tasteless gossip and cockpit jokes? Who, indeed!

The conclusion of the meeting came when the ALPA representative finally realized he'd made no progress. There was a deadlock, much to his dismay. His simple intent was that she became one of the boys. Lorelei didn't want to be, nor would she ever be, *one of the boys*. It wasn't in her nature anymore than it was in mine. We wouldn't change into men. It was up to the company and ALPA to change and accept us for what we proudly were: accomplished women.

✈

Keeping my perspective lent humor to what essentially was a distasteful situation. I favored a different approach: diplomacy. I was not interested in compromising my dignity by showing emotion, so I continued to be placid no matter what came my way. And in maintaining this composure, I developed a sense of humor about these machinations, categorizing this charade as just one small aspect of my otherwise interesting and happy life.

Things would be better if management was concerned with proper operation of the airline rather than antagonism toward female pilots. They pushed me until I chose to fight back. My initial intent was not to oppose them and I withstood their offenses as bravely as I could but the slightest thing, the tiniest turn was taken to task. As always, management used flying proficiency as a hallmark for their attacks. The SLC Chief Pilot began briefing and debriefing captains and second officers, not only before but also after our flights, and without me.

The chief pilot stood at the side of the boarding area and looked at me out of the tops of his eyes while speaking in low, conspiratorial tones to the other two pilots, then ushered them to his office. I held my head high and walked erect through the terminals though I felt sick inside. There was little I could do other than to endure. For how much longer, I wasn't sure. I just flew my flights, and did my best in this adverse atmosphere.

It was but another captain who whined and yowled at everything I did. He turned in his seat to converse with the second officer, ignoring me as if I wasn't there. They met for drinks; I was not invited nor included in layover activities. No information was shared of a personal or professional nature. I was completely out of the loop. When I asked what was going on, I was assured nothing was going on. Yes, there was no conspiracy.

✈

Then I flew for a month with a cool dude from New York, who recently had been a chief pilot, there, before the Delta's acquisition of Western, and Captain Chicago's previous boss. While descending to land in San Diego after flying all night across the Pacific, our flaps malfunctioned passing through twelve thousand feet. We ran through the abnormal checklist items trying to get them extended, but they would not. We diverted into LAX, home to Delta's west coast heavy maintenance base. LAX also had a longer runway.

Everything went smoothly; we acted as a good crew. A potentially hazardous situation was handled as if it happened every day. We landed safely by approaching the runway at a higher speed, touching down on the very beginning and rolling to the extreme end. The cool dude wrote a letter to my chief pilot describing my performance as "flawless." This left the base in a frenzy. How could they hope to secure a case against me for lack of proficiency when a captain of this stature wrote a letter praising it?

✈

Pushing back from gate 22 in Honolulu, Cap blew a kiss to an attractive Asian woman coiffed in a bouffant hairdo above severely arched eyebrows. She'd been at the same place, at the same gate, standing in the windows of the departure concourse every flight this month, and I'd noticed their interaction without them noticing me. Cap's hand moved after his blown kiss in a smooth, non-stop motion to the overhead panel, turning on the rotating beacon, a signal to the ground crew that we were ready for pushback.

"Before pushback, start checklist," he ordered. Was he thinking he cleverly disguised his actions? I'd watched this pretense each time we'd flown together. How strange, he was saying goodbye to this woman in Hawaii when he'd told me he was a bishop in his church in Utah, with a wife and a dozen kids back home.

Enroute, the Southern Cross hung just over my right shoulder, slightly below the horizon. I had to stretch to see it just off Earth's atmosphere in elliptical suspension. It wasn't always visible on flights, but this evening we flew a southern course from HLU to SAN at

22 degrees north latitude. It rose slightly into view with Earth's rotation as we passed at midnight. This night the Omegas were navigationally reliable in spite of the increasing effect of solar flares. In an eleven-year cycle from peak to null, solar flares could cause radio signals to bend. We hurried, crosschecking our present position and course accuracy through triangulation. The rumble of our Rolls Royce RB424-B4 engines combined with wind displacement noise presented a comforting constant of rhythm over our five-and-a-half hour flight on this, the longest over-water leg in the world without any place to land.

As we began descent for landing west of Lindbergh Field, I maneuvered our elegant Lockheed conveyance onto a left downwind leg and configured for landing. The lights of San Diego twinkled on an hour before dawn. Fog hugged the hills like cotton batting. Clouds engulfed the building tops in downtown. The runway was a thick bar below us and to the port side of the aircraft nose. As we passed abeam on the runway numbered 27, for a westerly landing, I timed myself outbound for 30 seconds on the non-directional beacon before turning base. It was awkward to be in a visual pattern turning left while seated to the right in a cockpit so broad I could barely reach far enough to touch my flying partner on the shoulder. There was no help from the left seat except for mandatory answers to the checklists recited dutifully into the voice recorder.

We touched down smoothly, and I moved the throttles back to idle position, standing the thrust reverse levers vertically for moderate activation. A clamshell affair deployed via hydraulic pressure cupped the rearward blowing air into a forward, decelerating force. As half the runway passed below the wheels during rollout, I applied the brakes to slow for the high-speed exit in line with our gate. The ground steering tiller was located on the left sidewall of the cockpit, so I gave over control of the airplane to the captain to steer us straight in.

"Your airplane, Captain. Thank you for the landing." He took control of the airplane and approached the gate.

After landing, he called for checklists, and as we stopped at the gate, the directive parking signals on the concourse in front of the aircraft nose changed from cautionary yellow to red stoplights. In a moment or two, the jetway door swung to attach the aircraft for docking and the ground crew gave us the *chocks-in* signal of clenched fists with thumbs pointing inward. The mechanic plugged his headset into the side of the airplane. "Morning, Captain. Wheel chocks are in. How's the aircraft?"

"Morning, Earth, good ship. Parking brakes released."

As Cap swung out of his seat, he stepped right into the overflowing trash bag from our long flight which was attached to his armrest, rustled around in it, tangled with the dripping milk cartons, napkins, and plastic baggies. His ruddy face went red. What do you say to a Delta Captain with a trash bag on his foot? When he looked my way, I was careful to keep my eyes forward, not smiling, and stifling a chuckle.

He tapped the S/O on the shoulder as he went by: "Check the brakes extra careful on the walkaround. I think they may be hot after *that* landing. I'll call operations and arrange a delay."

What? I couldn't believe it! Everything about the approach and landing was normal. And my touchdowns and rollouts were consistently better than his the entire trip. Yesterday, landing in Honolulu on Runway 26 from a Localizer Directional Approach with a stiff wind from the southwest, he allowed the wind to blow us past the extended runway centerline during his turn from base to final. He hadn't started turning soon enough to compensate for the wind drift. He seemed situationally unaware. Was his mind in other places? Was he already having dinner with the Dragon Lady? The result was one of the hardest touchdowns - *ka thummpp* - I'd ever ridden through on this airplane.

Now, I fumed in my seat and said nothing as the pair disappeared downstairs. I waited, making sure they'd gone from the area, and then I got on the radio and called for the maintenance foreman. I asked him to step to the Flight Deck. Perhaps two minutes later, he appeared. He was a good guy, a mechanic I knew.

"Good morning, Ma'am."

"Good morning, Jim. Would you personally check the brakes? They may be hot and the Captain is arranging for a delay." A knowing look passed between us. Delta thought poorly of delays, especially ones created by flight crews improperly operating equipment.

"Sure. Be right back with a report."

After a visit to the first class lavatory, I accepted paperwork from the agent for our next leg, SAN to SLC, and began programming the Omegas and Flight Management System computers as much as the non-flying pilot was allowed. The next was not my leg.

I listened to and copied the Automated Terminal Information Service describing airport weather and specific airport-related departure information. I requested Clearance Delivery put our instrument clearance on request from Center, then sat back to wait for return of the crew.

Without my asking, the senior flight attendant graciously brought me a cup of coffee. I peered into the terminal at our waiting passengers and hoped the brakes weren't hot. How could they be?

Two through-passengers stopped by to gaze around the cockpit. They asked questions about the airplane and what they might see on the next leg to Salt Lake. I smiled at their curiosity, politely answered their questions, and told them we'd be passing west of beautiful Bryce Canyon. For a moment, I flashed on my late mother as she looked around the cockpit, wide-eyed, as they now did. We were going Christmas shopping in HLU; for years I'd taken her Christmas shopping somewhere in the world.

"Do you really know what all these switches and dials are?" She turned to look into my eyes as if I was still a child.

"Yes, Mother, I do know what all these switches and dials are." I guess she remembered only yesterday how young I was, and somehow, time and my maturity eluded her. How could I possibly know all this, when she didn't?

I continued to speak with the curious passengers though shortly, they were displaced to make room for the crew, and right behind them, the Maintenance Foreman, who entered and sat on the jumpseat behind Cap. "Morning, again, Captain."

"Morning. Say, the S/O and I checked the brakes on the walkaround and…"

"Brakes are fine," the maintenance foreman added before the captain could finish. "They're cool. In fact, they're cooler than usual, Captain." Cap didn't say another word about the brakes.

"Good. Then we're outta here! Before pushback, start checklist!"

When we arrived on final approach in SLC, there was a two or three-knot tailwind on the active runway, Runway 16. This was not enough tailwind for ATC to change to the opposite runway as the maximum TW component for transports was 10K. As we rounded out a bit high to flare on final before touchdown, Cap held the aircraft above the ground continuing to add back pressure on the control wheel, dissipating airspeed, dissipating airspeed, as a mile and-a-half of runway disappeared below us without our touching down. Obviously, he had miscalculated his touchdown point by not looking far enough down the runway on approach, and had flared out too high. With the runway red side lights coming into view in our peripheral vision - the S/O started to squirm about a quarter mile back - I started squirming too. There was only 2000 feet of asphalt remaining. We were too slow for a go around, and running out of landing surface. I could see we were eventually going to touch down and as the brakes were so powerful, we *would* be able to stop on the remaining runway. The captain's technique, if it can be called that, was far from a good example. Finally, the airplane landed with a huge thud! And barely rolled to the end of the pavement, our speed was so slow. I said nothing. Cap said nothing. The S/O said nothing. With all my strength, with all my willpower and self-discipline, I refrained from the irony: *Nice landing, Captain!*

A few months later, on someone else's flight, Cap discovered he burned too much fuel because ATC held him down at low altitude - where a jet burns lots of fuel - before being allowed to climb on departure from HLU. Tailwinds were not as strong as forecast, and as he approached the Equal Time Point about half way across the ocean based on winds and routing, he was advised by his S/O that they didn't have sufficient fuel to complete their trip. Wisely, Cap returned to HLU for additional fuel. From that flight on until Cap retired, a check captain accompanied him on every transoceanic flight. I wondered if the Check Captain was perceptive enough to notice the Dragon Lady in the terminal windows? My guess would be, probably not.

Soon after his retirement, Cap must have felt the prick of conscience, the need to confess, now that life didn't take him to Honolulu any longer. One Sunday, he described his long affair and asked forgiveness directly from God in front of his church congregation, which included his wife. To his astonishment, she divorced him.

To my complete surprise he showed up at my hangar in Provo to take instruction for his single engine rating. All he had ever flown and was rated in were multi-engine airplanes. Remorsefully, he relayed the events following his confession. He was miserable, living alone in a little trailer in Provo. I was awed to hear him tell the story with such detachment. If he sought forgiveness from his wife, wouldn't it have been better to tell her privately? I was amazed at his pluck, thinking he had a pipeline with The Man, and for showing up at my place in view of our past history. "How could you expect her to do other than divorce you, Cap?"

Then, when he confided that he hoped to redeem himself by teaching his sons to fly in single-engine airplanes: "I recommend you take your test with the FAA directly, rather than with me." Surely, as a pilot, he'd jump at the chance to save a hundred bucks. I didn't want to fly with him before, and I didn't want to fly with him now, though in preparation, he was welcome to hire my able instructor, Scott Jorgensen, and rent our planes. Time went by and try as he would, many flight hours later, and with nary a word from me about our past, my instructor could not recommend Cap for his single engine rating. Eventually, Cap just drifted away...

✈

As I programmed the FMS for my leg into HLU, I kept looking up through the forward windows to see if Dad, riding space available as my father, was going to get on the flight. Finally, he came across the ramp in that slow-rolling walk of his, caused by years of struggling with bad knees from football injuries. No matter how far knee-surgery technology had evolved, he prided himself on never having been in the hospital for even one night of his seventy-four years.

I breathed easier as he came slowly up the air stairs to sit in first class. After I completed loading the navigational information into the computers, since it was my leg to fly, it was the captain's turn to check the information for accuracy. I gave the clipboard with our paperwork on it to the Captain, excused myself from the flight deck, and stepped back to First Class.

Seated comfortably in his seat, Dad smiled at me as I approached. There was no one beside him so I sat for a moment. He seemed proud of me and smiled all the while. He took this event - me flying him in a Lockheed 1011 - as an opportunity to reminisce on our conversations about the airplane in my youth, and how amazing we now flew in one I was piloting.

Accustomed to riding in First Class on his forays into the corporate world, he was beautifully dressed in a suit with a diamond stickpin in his tie, I had to admit he looked pretty spiffy. The flight attendants gathered around us before the revenue passengers arrived. They wanted to be introduced to *my* dad. I'd invited him along on this Maui trip because he'd told me a number of times how lonely he was since my mother died. I felt he needed my companionship and a change of scene. My heart throbbed, thinking of his loss.

"Your dad's a real fine guy," one said as I passed her in the aisle.

"He's really cute," another confided, "Is he married?"

"No, not any more…" I kept walking toward the cockpit. I didn't want to encourage her further.

I stepped into the cockpit and was greeted with: "What have you done to the FMS!" Captain spoke sharply as I sat down in the right seat. "I can't get it to take anything. It doesn't seem to know where we are."

"Didn't I enter the true air speed?" We checked, I was correct, and thought it strange he didn't know to correlate the two. He was really angry, having spent the time of my absence trying to enter the flight plan into the computer.

"You know, you're going to have a checkride as soon as we get back to SLC!"

I disregarded this statement somewhat because why would this regular line Captain have such information? Not that it couldn't be true, it's just that this was the first *I'd* heard of it.

"I've attended a meeting where you were the subject of discussion."

The bile rose in my throat. I said nothing and continued attending to my tasks, readying the airplane for flight. We pushed back and departed to HLU for additional passengers and transoceanic fuel we could not carry out of the 7,000-foot runway at Maui. We didn't climb too high and flew an arc into HLC with the blue Pacific waves below. Flying, especially flying the Lockheed 1011, felt good on yet another glorious, tropical day.

After fueling in HLU and visiting a moment with Dad, I returned to my seat. As we departed eastbound, I was reminded of the historic moniker, Sandwich Islands, as they passed by our windows: they were the American jewels of the Pacific for certain, but I wondered how they came by their original name. There was still snow on the peaks of Mauna Loa and Mauna Kea on the big island of Hawaii. The ocean was smooth as we continued to gain altitude, climbing towards our navigational coast-out checkpoint while land was still in sight.

Arriving in SLC seven plus hours later, I packed up my flying equipment and stowed it in my flight case. I bid the crew goodbye as they marched on by me without a word. No matter. It was their problem, but I was unaware it was about to become mine. I lingered, waiting for everyone to deplane because I wanted to push Dad through the terminal in his wheel chair. As we emerged last from the jetway door, the Assistant Chief Pilot, Dirk Bullman, gave me a surprisingly firm tap on the shoulder.

"Come with me. Now!" He was oblivious to my father in the wheel chair. I pushed Dad to the side of the concourse and said I'd be back shortly, pressing my cheek to his. I left him leafing through pages of his book, looking for where he'd left off.

Bullman herded me downstairs with his hands up in the air as if he held a pistol. He moved back and forth in front of me and around behind me, as if I was his prisoner. He constantly intruded into my personal space, changing the invisible gun from hand to hand, presumably preventing my escape. I recalled Suzy Q's description of his same actions towards her. The scene was about to become a tragic comedy but for the moment I chuckled at his ludicrous maneuvers.

Embarrassed, I hoped no one in the busy terminal noticed us. He said nothing to me even though I'd known him for years. I flew with him in MSP on the 727 when he was a new captain and I was a new F/O. I'd seen him in the pilot's lounge where he was always cordial, and I'd accepted invitations to his home to have dinner with his family. All I could remember about our flying together was that he commanded the flaps-extension schedule differently than everyone else - that they be extended from zero to twenty-five degrees without stopping at the gates and waiting for green lights. Once, when I hesitated a moment to assess this command for validity and decided it would be safe to comply; he took exception to my independent thinking and challenged my compliance with his authority. Very military, but then, what else would he know?

"In here." He opened the door to an office and hovered, menacingly above me as if I'd try to escape. "Sit down."

I sat. He puffed himself up, paced, and started screaming. I was sure everyone in the secretary's office and pilots out in the lounge could hear. He behaved just like his mentor, Demerritus. I blinked at his fury. It was out of place and I couldn't decipher what on earth he was screaming about.

It was an interesting approach to a situation. I gleaned they were having some kind of problem with me. I listened for sanity in the tirade, but couldn't find any. It was laughable. "Complaints. Professionalism. Proficiency." Gibberish.

I wondered if Dad was okay. I turned in my seat and looked around the large office to see if anyone else was present. There was no one except me so I surmised this attack was meant for me. I could feel the tiniest grin of amusement on my face as he maniacally raved on and on.

"Complaints. Integrity. Woman. Fingernails. Blouse. Soft voice. Marriage. Millionaire. Kids. Airplanes."

Suddenly, he stopped. *Whew*. Dramatically, the door opened. In stepped the Chief Pilot picking his feet up just like the raven in Poe's poem. As soon as the door closed, Bullman resumed screaming. I was careful to sit as if at a ladies' tea - with my legs together even though I was in uniform slacks - a posture generally reserved for skirt attire. I regarded the length of my pale nails recalling the comment made, noting they were in need of a manicure. In short, I paid only mild attention to their embarrassing debacle. Ranting and raving went on. Looking not at the noisemaker, but at the reason for the noise - me - Captain Chicago stood, cigar in hand, quietly waiting as I did for Bullman to cease.

The SLC Chief Pilot had an air about him. He was a man who curried favor to gain power. He was designing, devious. He assessed a situation and instinctively knew how to manipulate it to his favor. He operated on another level than most men, a purely political one. While they were out actually doing something, he worked behind the scenes, a talent inherent to the true con artist. This Chief conned his way from a cargo-handling ramp-rat at nineteen to chief pilot at forty-four, without formal education, or particular flying skills. This success story bore the earmark of someone who had impressive connections and knew how to use them. He was *too* clever.

Could he be forgiven for having so much ambition? He used any and all resources to secure and assure his position. He would stop at nothing to solidify his power. It didn't matter a lick he that picked on defenseless and unsuspecting women...

He carried an oversized cigar between the knuckles of the first and second fingers on his left hand. It was too large for his diminutive size. He elevated to his toes and gestured with the cigar, drawing lines in the air. It was an extension of his persona, his prop. So large in diameter, it shaped his mouth into a round little O, and to speak, he had to take it out of his mouth. Though I'd never seen him smoke it, I knew he must because I could smell him coming. He chewed on it too, and when he did it reminded me of an old WWII glider pilot who gave me pre-solo glider lessons. He chewed cigars, too. Around the outer perimeter of his lips was a constant brownish-yellow stain so distracting I rarely heard a word originating from that discolored circle. Revolting was an understatement. Kissing? Inconceivable!

When Bullman finally quit screaming, Chicago began speaking. His was a calm, rehearsed contrast to his assistant. They must have had fun contriving this act. Did they stay after hours practicing? Did they have drinks at a private club downtown with the rest of the *good old boys* on the 1011? Did they have a good laugh about this woman who dared presume she could fly Delta's most coveted airplane?

As I listened to the allegations, Bullman blocked the door with his body, his arms spread out to either side. I could hardly believe the show. Where were the chains? Did he think I'd try to leave before this thrashing was complete? I contemplated simply excusing myself for a potty break and simply not coming back. Maybe I should ask to call the Air Line Pilots Association for representation. I waited for a chance to ask a question. I still hadn't even figured what all this was about. As I began to speak, Bullman exploded.

"How dare you interrupt the chief pilot when he's speaking!"

"I didn't interrupt. He hasn't spoken." This set off another volley from Bullman and Chicago took a drag on his cigar. It was apparent they weren't going to let me speak. I was starting to get mad. If I could move this sideshow to the lounge, other pilots might be entertained, too. They might wonder what's going on. I could take the offensive and react to them in kind. Bullman sensed I'd changed my attitude from *whatever* to *what*! and boomed out: "You'll find nothing but trouble at Delta Air Lines if you're a hard ass!" I thought this was an interesting comment, and an intimidating one.

I thought diplomacy might defuse this blast and I had used a pause to inject a question. "What complaints? Who, specifically, has been making complaints? And on what flights, dates, and…"

"You're not asking the questions here!"

"If you suddenly, after successfully flying the 1011 for a year-and-a-half, have complaints about my proficiency, my person, my integrity, I would expect you to discuss them with me so that I can, in all fairness, defend myself..." I was careful to choose a pleasant tone of voice in hopes it might smooth their ruffled feathers, diminish their mock anger. My interjection was to no avail. Bullman came unglued at my presumption and spewed forth such a litany that his spittle ejaculated into a shower felt on my face. This made me angry. I looked at Chicago. He was having difficulty hiding a smile.

"Never you mind where these complaints came from. They've been made!"

"It's unfair of you to make accusations without giving me a chance to defend myself. Hearing only one side of a story puts situations out of context..."

"How dare you speak to the Chief Pilot, presuming to tell him what's fair or unfair!"

"It's unfair if I don't have a say, Dirk."

"Do not dare call me anything but *Captain* Bullman."

"Fine." I wouldn't call him anything at all. I'd ignore him and direct my inquiry to the chief pilot: "Perhaps there is some feeling because I'm a woman..."

Simultaneously, they gulped, and both jumped to attention: Chicago, from leaning against his desk smoking his cigar, which he nearly swallowed and began coughing and choking, and Dirk, from pacing about the room. Their eyes got real big and round. Chicago repeatedly put the oversized cigar between his liver colored lips and took it out. They both clammed up. The word *woman* with its inference that everyone involved in this conspiracy was guilty of discrimination and harassment apparently stopped them *cold*. I think they'd heard of harassment, maybe read about it in company manuals, knew it was forbidden at the airline, but until now, it hadn't touched them, and they were thunderstruck! It was ironically comical that I'd be the one to enlighten them.

"Are you accusing us of discrimination?"

"You said it. I didn't. I said there might be feelings because I'm a woman and a Western woman flying Delta's largest, most prestigious airplane."

"Whatever gave you that idea?"

I exhaled in total exasperation. Bullman stood limply and without speaking in front of the door, now with his arms at this side, completely stunned. Chicago took a seat at his desk and I noticed his hands shaking ever so slightly as he proceeded with his inquisition. It seemed, in addition to everything he mentioned before, that I may have also violated some convention by getting married. The inference was, I gleaned, how could I do this job and that one at the same time? I didn't really listen to their sentences, just picking up key words, and wondered who could be responsible for giving these yahoos all this personal information. It wasn't me, because at work, I didn't talk much about my private life.

"... ranch, personal airplanes." These phrases rolled out of Chicago's mouth: "Oil business, boats... In addition to the slight shaking of his hands, did I see a trace of green around Chicago's eyes? "Four children..." Information I recognized only one person knew.

I tried reason: "I'm only trying to put some balance in my life by spending days off with a nice man. No, I don't take care of his four children. They're grown and don't live at home. Marriage doesn't detract from my performance any more than it does for male pilots. If anything, it's beneficial, stabilizing."

I felt the little smile disappear from my lips. Gone. No more smiles, no more amusement. Information about my personal life had been divulged, not as a salve for curiosity, but with harmful intent, and I always scrutinize *intent*. Information only a friend would know. It *must* be Bill Lake. It must be his blind ambition. He'd either seen an opportunity for advancement or been offered one if he corroborated with Chicago. Chicago's mean hand contrived this scenario. I wondered at the ones to come. Not that any of the information about me was bad, but the manner in which it was slanted to Delta hurt. It was an attempt to discredit me. A drama a bored chief pilot enacted knowing he could engage the entire 1011 flight department in ire. The thrust would be conspiracy, secret meetings, whispers behind hands, knowing looks with the intent of eroding my confidence and isolating me from the rest of the group. Most of the pilots would go for it but to play safe, Chicago would include them without their complicity: he would call meetings without me for other arcane reasons, such as discussing bidding or vacation time, knowing I would hear of these meetings, and fear they were about me.

"Why would you work if you didn't have to?" Chicago asked. These men construed that because I was married, I didn't have to work, and that I must be sloughing off. It was unbelievable.

"I will always work. It doesn't matter what my husband does, he does his thing and I do mine. He wouldn't like me much if I wasn't successful at what I'd chosen to do..." The moment I'd said it, I knew it was a mistake. I gave them ammunition for the future and I regretted every word.

I could feel my eyes narrow to slits. Suddenly, the odor in the room was overwhelming. It stunk. I thought of my Dad upstairs in the wheelchair. They pair continued to ask questions about my personal life I didn't answer. I looked at my watch. I'd been in this inquisition an hour and twenty minutes.

"How dare you look at the time!" Dirk was getting wound up again. "You're scheduled for an oral and a proficiency check in Atlanta in two days, if you pass, you'll fly a four-day checkride with Paul Homestead, chief line check airman on the 1011. Dismissed!"

I smiled an inappropriately broad smile because I wouldn't want them to think they got to me. Without a goodbye, I hurried through their door and went upstairs to find Dad. Suddenly, I was choking back angry tears. What a humiliating experience, and so one-sided.

✈

"That took some time," Dad said; glad to see me.

"What happened to your wheelchair?"

"Someone came along and said they needed it." He was seated in a boarding lounge near the spot where I'd left him.

"But what if you couldn't walk?" He *couldn't* walk for long distances. "I'll be right back with a chair." Exasperated, I went to an alcove where I knew wheelchairs were kept and retrieved one. As I began pushing him down the broad terminal hallway, I made a mental turn to the chief pilot's meeting.

"What happened in the chief pilot's office?" Dad asked as if reading my thoughts.

"At first I wasn't sure what it was all about because they asked such a variety of questions. But..." I clenched my teeth, blocked the tears, and managed to sum it all up: "It was a fabricated inquisition." Then the anger returned. The more I thought about the meeting downstairs, the more I realized I needed to maintain a sense of decorum until we were out of the airport, so I talked about the newest airport construction going on all around us as we headed toward the car.

Driving home, I discussed the meeting with Dad, who allowed their questioning of my ability because I "wasn't one of the boys, you're a woman, and you have to prove yourself."

"But how many times and for how many years, Dad?"

"It's the same old thing we've talked about in the past. The thing your mother was so afraid of when you pursued a career dominated by men. It's the male barrier."

Eventually, reason prevailed that day and I told myself they *could* question my proficiency if they wanted. Any extra training would only improve my skills, so I shouldn't be too alarmed. I'd always been challenged - never frightened - by taking checkrides. It wouldn't be healthy fearing tests integral to a career, and this was no time to begin feeling different. Flying in a reserve status and only once every 60-90 days, it was difficult to be perfect – I was no different from other pilots on the equipment – but unlike me, they gained experience in an atmosphere of equanimity.

Chapter XI
GOING TO SEE HENRY

aptain Chicago was aware of the power of his office, and acutely aware of his destructive power. After rotating me back through a complete and instantaneous set of orals, simulator, and checkrides with little more than two days to prepare, I knew my career and licenses were imperiled. I was additionally astonished by Chicago, this chief pilot, who then feigned not only memory loss about having assigned me these tasks, but claimed to have lost the paperwork which stated I had passed all tests with flying colors. He pretended *not to remember* I was certified proficient *again*, that I'd been through all the oral exams and checkrides *again*, and now he had every intention of putting me through the entire charade a third time!

At my wits end when Chicago said he would test me for the third time, I filed a lawsuit indicting John Does 1 through 10 in an effort to restrain Delta, primarily implicating Captain Bill Lake who had divulged confidential information to management about my personal life with the sole purpose of discrediting me and advancing himself.

Withstanding the pressure and tension, I'd somehow endured, though at the expense of my teeth. Tension caused me to grind them until nerves were exposed and it would take extensive dental work to save them. Gags are fun if you're the perpetrator, but I wasn't, and in exasperation, I began to lose one of my most valuable assets: my sense of humor.

Soon after filing the lawsuit, I was told by crew scheduling that eleven captains immediately left the base. Whether it was orders from Vice President Henry Aldridge, or of their own accord, was anyone's guess, and surprising, as it took vacancies at another base to allow transfers from SLC, and these transfers were awarded in seniority. It was true that these were some of Delta's most senior captains who could have elected and received the change, especially since a new MD-11 base was opening in Portland, but transfers and retraining took time. I deducted it was Aldridge who approved the transfers. In contacts with SLC management, I was assured over and over that: "No, there was no conspiracy," a statement of contradiction in itself, and an answer to questions they thought I might ask, but never did. Bill Showers in crew scheduling called to say he couldn't find a captain who'd fly with me. It seemed odd to me that captains had a negative preference, meaning they didn't have to fly with crewmembers of their choosing, but junior officers did have to fly, no matter if a conflict compromised safety.

At Delta Air Lines, I'd found negotiation, arbitration, and resolution non-existent in cases of employee - company conflict. I'd not been treated as a valued employee, but as a criminal. I wondered at the company agenda. I'd run out of patience with the chief pilot's office, with Chicago and Bullman. Chastised for every possible impropriety, I was guilty of nothing more than being a female pilot from the acquired airline, and choosing to fly Delta's most prestigious airplane. This opposed the male hierarchy. They hadn't, it seemed, needed a reason for their abuse, only an excuse.

No one helped me correct these problems. I wouldn't turn to the pilot's union because of past experience though it was required to represent me as one of the dues paying members of their closed shop; the fact that I was fundamentally opposed to wasting time negotiating as a part of the lowest common denominator didn't help either. The trouble started with SLC management and trickled down to poor behavior in crews. Level-headedness and fair play were non-existent. I was flying with hot and angry captains.

Assistant Chief Pilot Bullman made it very clear in the meeting which should have been between the chief pilot and me, but when Chicago didn't show, Bullman took the meeting instead, and advised me several times that I should transfer off the Lockheed 1011 and onto the 737. "The people on the L-1011 are not kind." He surprised me with this admission. Apparently, most of the 1011 pilots began commuting to the newly opened SLC base after Delta's senior L-1011 base was closed upon acquisition of Western by Delta. As spoiled and petulant as children, they wouldn't blame Delta for the inconvenience of living in one place and working in another, so they chose instead to displace their anger to Western and anything to do with Western. "They're difficult to get along with," Bullman said. I thought this an interesting assessment, considering who said it.

I would get my say some five months after filing the lawsuit. Finally, the stalemate seemed to be coming to an end when Vice President Henry Aldridge's office corresponded with my attorney in Salt Lake City, Reid Martin, requesting a meeting at corporate headquarters in Atlanta, and without lawyers. Since I was positive he'd record everything, I planned to be direct and correct. The only other person present would be my husband, whom I hoped would help negotiate peace. I looked forward to resolution. I just wanted to get on with my career and go flying!

✈

The flight across the country to Atlanta was four hours long and I sat for the duration as if I had a rod down my back. We were traveling on a positive space pass - a must ride basis - for this meeting. I was so heartsick to find myself in this situation.

Upset and feeling nauseous, my eyes tired from being open bug-wide, I couldn't seem to relax. *What would I say? What would I do?* John tried to calm me by speaking in soothing tones and help me plan my talk, but it was not he who would have to speak. The stakes were high. I had given up so much to get this far. There was no changing to another airline because I'd have to start over in seniority. I'd already lost so many years during the acquisition. To lose this job would be devastating.

John continued speaking to me in quiet, comforting tones though I hardly heard a word. I was so upset I couldn't speak. We landed in ATL and took a cab around the perimeter of the Hartsfield International Airport to Delta's brick enclave, their headquarters. Arriving on the fourth floor of the corporate offices, Henry Aldridge's immaculate and attractive secretary ushered us toward his office. Though she appeared more mature than he, it may have been her poise and sophistication that distinguished her. As she led the way, I noticed the corporate offices were dark and bunched together compared with Western's expansive headquarters that required a good stroll from the entry to the receptionist's desk. She opened his door and we suddenly found ourselves in a fair-sized room with a high ceiling. Bookcases on two walls held leather books with titles embossed in gold letters. The spaces were decorated with vases and figurines. Aldridge greeted us by rising from behind a long table used as a desk and shook our hands. He was in formal business attire but wore red and black suspenders instead of belted pants - perhaps a concession to la mode de jour - in contrast to our conservative attire. I wore a dark business suit with a long straight skirt and a salmon-colored silk blouse. Earlier, I remembered thinking how handsome

John looked dressed in beige slacks and jacket as he hailed our cab. The sun sparkled in his gold and silver hair.

I introduced him to Aldridge, whom I had met once before in Honolulu. I mentioned that John was a businessman managing 1100 people in truck stops across the country and had a good understanding of personnel and their problems. It was interesting observing Henry's dark eyes sharpen to little points as he processed this information.

We sat. His was a bright corner office with ceiling-to-floor length windows. Just the tops of broadleaf trees were visible from the fourth floor, though in February they were branches without leaves. Icy raindrops splattered against the glass. It was quiet for a moment while we settled in our chairs, collecting our thoughts.

Aldridge began by asserting, "It's good to have a discussion without lawyers." I thought this an inconsistent statement as lawyers had arranged our meeting, and it revealed either a fundamental distrust, or perhaps an honest attempt to put me at ease. I looked around for evidence of a tape recorder, certainly there was one, but I couldn't see it, and Aldridge didn't advise me we were being recorded. I took the initiative and dove right in, feeling as if my problems might keep him from something more important.

"I'm here in a spirit of resolution. I'm hoping you can help resolve our mutual problems." Aldridge rustled uncomfortably in his chair. I suppose he wasn't used to having an employee lead the discussion nor suggest the company might have problems. Continuing, I left my small red journal closed, lying in my lap, not that I would read from it, but could reference specific dates if needed. I ran through a sequential series of events for the preceding year and a half. For nearly an hour I spoke as rapidly and clearly as I could. Words rolled out of my mouth in a natural and easy way. Sentences made sense and I kept the events in order. I noticed I didn't smile or pause, and I never took my eyes from Aldridge's. He listened attentively with his head inclined toward me, our eyes riveted.

The thought occurred to me as I spoke that he might be unaccustomed to having a woman consider herself on equal footing, as he initially seemed amused I was there, and spoke in a paternal, but condescending tone. Then as I spoke portraying events as they happened, he seemed to be giving me the eye. He remained seated even while I described the humiliation of being put through checkrides I'd already passed, *again*, at Chicago's whim. He interjected that he'd known Chicago for many years and was surprised by this behavior.

When I finished, he didn't have much visible reaction to my saga. The bile rose in my throat as I sat waiting. Suddenly, I got livid. I wanted some kind of reaction, and began adding a summation of my own: "Managing by intimidation comes directly from the top!" By my statement, he knew I meant that he, Aldridge, was setting the example. He jumped to his feet and slammed his palms on the table. At least I knew he was paying attention. "You aren't accusing us of managing by intimidation are you young lady!" From his explosive reaction, I knew I'd touched a sensitive nerve. I regarded his consternation merely as a reply to getting caught. I didn't flinch because I knew my accusation was accurate. I'd spoken the unspeakable, and I felt ever so much better! It was regretful Aldridge didn't like me categorizing his management style as intimidating but I had to let him know the situation was bad. I didn't answer and kept on with my line, realizing I didn't have a job when I walked in, and might not have one when I walked out. Now I was almost lecturing him: "It isn't considered proper in western culture to treat employees as criminals and give them no chance to speak for themselves. This is predatory behavior, something expected in dictatorships or behind the Iron Curtain."

At this moment I knew I'd be happy to fly Delta's airplanes but would have difficulty with loyalty if this treatment continued.

From the look in Aldridge's eyes, I could tell his wasn't a conscious commitment to this style and form of management, but an evolution. Perhaps it was learned in the military. Power is provocative. It can be used wisely by the secure or abused by the insecure.

John interceded with: "To become competent at a job, a person needs to practice." Ever the negotiator, he defused our anger beautifully, one reason I brought him along. "And flying only once every sixty to ninety days doesn't allow a pilot on new equipment much practice."

I added to his comment. "Being left out of the loop - ignored, scolded or isolated by the rest of the crew - doesn't help, either. Captain Chicago meets both before and after my flights with the captain and second officer."

"What?" Aldridge's mouth remained in the shape of an incredulous little "O."

"Captain Chicago briefs the crew before flights and debriefs after our flights," I repeated.

"Without you?"

"Without me... After our initial meeting, where he and his assistant, Dirk Bullman, screamed a list of complaints at me, I decided to rectify as much as I could after getting put back through a whole barrage of checkrides. When I successfully completed these, I made an appointment with the chief pilot, confirmed the meeting three times, and drove sixty miles to the airport on my day off. Chicago didn't show."

"Chicago didn't show?" Aldridge's mouth remained in the "O." He was stunned.

"Captain Chicago didn't show."

Aldridge pursed his lips and moved them side-to-side. His eyes were distended in little points of anger.

"When I completed my orals, simulator and two checkrides by the line check airmen, I requested to fly with the chief pilot, Captain

Chicago. The lead line check airman, Captain Paul Homestead, said Captain Chicago would not fly with me."

Aldridge looked first at me, then at his hands.

"I trust I can believe you are telling me the truth."

"I would not do otherwise."

He was quiet for a moment, and then made it clear that "It's good Chicago is no longer chief pilot," this was new news to me as Chicago was chief pilot when I left for this meeting in ATL. Aldridge continued: "If you should ever encounter such unfair treatment, such harassment again at Delta Air Lines, I want to know about it immediately!"

I thanked him for his time, consideration, and his understanding, though I was shocked Chicago was no longer the SLC Chief Pilot. I hadn't heard of it, and it occurred to me that it was a decision Aldridge made on the spot!

We visited in pleasant tones with amiable content for a few minutes. John blew a little smoke, flattered Aldridge, noting the scope of his job commanding over sixty thousand employees. Aldridge allowed that the training department favored him during his simulator checkrides because he was the boss. I held my tongue, and tried to smile a little smile, feeling sick inside that he was passed on checkrides by the check department while other competent pilots were failed.

Before leaving, I mentioned that I was scheduled for my yearly simulator in a few weeks. "You will have no further problems of this kind at Delta Air Lines! I can assure you that you may go to the simulator and any checkrides with confidence and proceed with your job in the same spirit!" We departed shaking hands all around. I felt better about things for the moment until I looked into Aldridge's eyes. They were full of water. Could they be genuine emotion or just crocodile tears?

✈

At Aldridge's request, the Vice President of Safety, Captain Gerry Shepherd, previously a chief pilot with Western Airlines and later, a vice president with the same position as Aldridge, drove us in a company car to our flight departure on the other side of the field. We chatted about flying gliders and he spoke of missing the mountains around his hometown outside SLC. I thought chauffeuring us was simple and deprecating duty for such a heavy hitter.

✈

Once again, seated in first class, I had four-and-a-half hours to consider events of the meeting. I resolved to set aside my doubts and approach my job with at least an outward sense of confidence that Delta wanted my continued interaction in their flight programs, even though a question mark still hung in the air.

John and I visited with my attorney, Reid Martin, to discuss the outcome of our meeting with Aldridge. Reid surprised me when he concluded our mutual dealings with: "It would take a lot bigger law firm than this to successfully sue Delta Air Lines." His took up a square block of downtown Salt Lake City, housed in a building of more than twelve floors, and employed 320 lawyers.

"Why do you say that?" I asked, awed by this conclusion. I thought we'd been successful, but he was suddenly stone-faced and uncommunicative. He was optimistic before and aggressively jumped at the opportunity to spar with Delta. Somehow and for some reason he'd changed his tune.

✈

Soon after, upon successful and pleasant completion of my simulator and other yearly tests, I rolled back my lawsuit and returned to line flying with new Salt Lake based L-1011 Captains. I made a great effort to be helpful and diplomatic. From the feel of our cordial interactions, these new captains enjoyed flying with me as much as I enjoyed flying with them.

The meetings before and after each flight seemed to stop - at least they weren't apparent - and Chicago was no longer chief pilot. Replaced by his assistant, Dirk Bullman, I assumed I must be doing okay or I would have heard about it, as Bullman was as direct as Chicago had been clandestine.

I assumed the eleven captains who left the SLC base moved to either the Portland or LAX base to fly the Pacific on the L-1011, initially, and later the MD-11. Captain Chicago showed up in LAX as check pilot and on several line checks he was charming, too charming, which left me wondering what he might have up his sleeve since he was barely civil in the past.

Captain Bill Lake was one of the eleven pilots who left the SLC base for LAX. Shortly after, I was astounded to find he was promoted to chief flight instructor in the new MD-11 program. I wondered what preempted this appointment, as I knew he hadn't ever been an instructor or even a check pilot. It entered my mind that he might have been awarded this prestigious position as supplication for being named in my harassment lawsuit against the airline.

Soon after his appointment, I received a vitriolic letter from his attorney stating that I'd be sued for slander if I ever spoke to anyone about events prefacing Lake's new job. Until I received this letter, I wasn't sure if our conflict played much part in Lake's future. Judging from the vigorous assertions of the attorney's letter, it certainly had; it was a significant disclosure.

Months later, I learned that Lake refused to pay his attorney's fees. Mine were twenty thousand dollars and I struggled for a year to set aside from my salary to pay them. On a flight with one of

Lake's cohorts, I learned that, in keeping with Lake's character, he had refused to pay his attorney fees, so Delta paid them!

Appalled by this discovery, I felt completely betrayed! For days and many nights the bile rose in my throat. I couldn't sleep. The only way I could quiet my fears was to tell myself that Delta was just taking care of one of its boys. Oh, and of course, there was no conspiracy!

Chapter XII

FAIR SKIES

My flying partners were congenial and professional for the next three of the four-and-a-half years I spent flying the Pacific. There was no harassment on the line or from management. I took care to treat everyone as I would like to be treated and flights were pleasant. But I found Lake had done his work well. With every pilot in his confidence, humbled by his powerful new position, he spread news of my "ridiculous" lawsuit that had caused eleven captains to leave the base. Via whisper and innuendo, I was gradually shunned. For my part, I did a good job and could produce opposing views that no one flew better. It didn't matter, no one asked.

Arriving in HLU each weekend to a rainbow of smiles instilled in me a happy feeling of warmth and camaraderie. My flying was textbook and I gloried in every moment in the air and on the ground. I looked forward to eating Pacific delicacies; except for sea urchin, I developed a taste for sushi and sashimi. My mouth began watering about half way across the Pacific. On the return, flight attendants served us chocolate covered macadamia nuts that seemed outrageous when we discovered they had 150 calories per small serving.

✈

241

One evening about 10:30 Honolulu time, I found myself in the employee cafeteria ordering a large tuna sandwich. Located under the aerial walkways connecting the concourses at the HLU international airport, I loved strolling by the happy gardens there, inhaling the exotic perfumes wafting on the evening breezes. As I settled into my chair with my crew seated also at the table, I heard a familiar voice coming from the other side of the large room. There were few people in the cafeteria this time of night, and I quickly recognized the voice as belonging to Raul Chogge, an old flame. Fortunately, my crew was engaged in some subject and not listening, as I was, to the conversation across the room.

"Eleven captains left the SLC base because of her!" Raul was ranting, loud enough that everyone could hear. "Blah! Blah! Blah!" My captain even commented on the loudmouth on the other side of the cafeteria, but returned to his discussion at our table.

I presumed Raul was challenging me to come over and confront him, and I considered doing so for a moment, but the little boy petulance in his voice gave him away: he didn't understand why a woman he desired left him for someone else. In his tone, I heard the heartbreak, and though I didn't want to make a scene, my first inclination was to set him straight, but I knew he was on his white horse, and if nothing else, I owed him his say. He must have felt differently about me than I did about him.

His crew shook their heads and looked in my direction. I kept my head bowed as if listening to my table's conversation. I listened to Raul rant on, hoping he would somehow feel better. Eventually, we finished our sandwiches and left him to his raving. I was more than a little embarrassed at his tirade, and thankful my crew hadn't heard my name.

I guess Raul was more serious about me than I was about him, though two dates a year hardly seemed intense. He and Lake were friends, but I don't think Raul knew of our affair. He also didn't know that after Lake, I swore to never again find my honey where I got my money.

✈

I hiked around and up and down Diamond Head every trip. I loved seeing flowers in the treetops and cascading bougenvilla clinging to garden walls. Silver water crested atop blue waves that rolled in from the horizon with the regularity of breathing in, breathing out. I amused myself on layovers by taking violin lessons from Hiroko Primrose and dressage lessons from Terri Tugman. Friends weren't too sympathetic when I mentioned I had to work weekends because they knew I flew to Hawaii. It was a pleasure escaping to sunshine, blue sky, and bone-warming weather while Utah was buried under snow.

At our home ranch in Utah County between Spanish Fork and Salem towns, I applied athletic and artistic skills to riding, and contracted first with Judge Sally O'Connor - mother of Olympian and USEF President David O'Connor - and then Pete Costello to build a three-day event course, beginner to intermediate, limited to Horse Trials. After several trips to Europe to walk the courses of the royals in Holland and England, we returned with volumes of pictures to begin building for Zephyr Ranch Horse Trials. Eventually, the event became nationally recognized. It continues to this day, hosted by the Mountain Paradise Pony Club, at home on our ranch. That those children had facilities and instruction available for riding filled my heart with smiles. Not having the luck to bear children of my own, I was happy to share one of my life's treasures, Zephyr Ranch, with them.

John concentrated on his business as he passed age fifty. He worked not only during the week but also on the weekends while I flew. My seniority was so junior on the 1011 that I couldn't hold anything but weekend schedules. Eventually he transferred his offices to Phoenix, building a reclamation plant north of Quartzite where the Williams Pipeline crossed the desert. The Arizona California Railroad transported the mixed fuels - transmix - by rail into his yard where he recycled the general array back to and sold the specific.

We were so busy with our separate lives that sometimes three weeks passed before we got together. He either flew his Solitaire home with his construction guys from Utah, or I flew to Phoenix and drove to see him at the plant in Parker. I was left to run our ranch in Utah, alone.

Deciding I'd love to see the other side of the world, I investigated a transfer to ATL. I'd be able to visit all the major cities in Europe and Russia *and* have greater seniority. Besides, I'd get to fly the wonderful Lockheed 1011-500, a newer and more powerful extended-range version of the dash 10's I was flying in the Pacific. Those years of French I took to learn the international language used by Air Traffic Control - which soon changed to English in the early 1960's - might come in handy. Though European Air Traffic Controllers speak English, it was with accents. It was helpful to know just enough French – French accented English - to decipher their instructions. Other than the long commute from Utah to Georgia, and the long trip flights, I couldn't see a reason to not transfer, although when we first married, John asked that I not fly long-range international. Since we were now sometimes apart for weeks working at our respective careers, long-range international trips seemed viable.

✈

One evening in SLC as I waited in the boarding lounge, Gurley Cameron and her husband, John Boehm, came to sit beside me. Her in-laws stood beside their granddaughter's stroller nearby. Gurley was as sweet and beautiful as ever but her sad eyes were filled with tears as she spoke to me.

"What? What is it?" I asked.

"I found myself in a 409 checkride with the FAA because I sided with the pilot's union after Continental's takeover of Eastern. What else could I do? I had to stand up and count for something." I loved her for being so candid and committed. When Frank Lorenzo of Continental bought Eastern Airlines, he forced the union out and implemented "B" salary scales for his, the largest of airlines. Many pilots quit, abandoning their precious seniority, and went elsewhere rather than cross the picket lines and become "scabs."

"I was a check pilot on the 727 for Eastern." She haltingly spoke the next few words. I suddenly felt fearful and wondered what was coming. "Continental gave me that awful 409 checkride and...and they took my airline transport license. Without it, I lost my job." The effects of Frank Lorenzo's management style were far-reaching, even into the bias of check departments and the FAA.

My heart ached that she suffered such trauma. "Oh, you poor thing." I took her hand and put my other arm around her shoulders. She began to cry. This made me cry on the inside, too.

Her family remained attentive but reverently quiet on the sidelines peering out the terminal windows at snow falling on the Wasatch Front. Her eyes closed then, brimming over, and tears slid down her cheeks. As if losing her job wasn't bad enough, they took away her coveted license so she couldn't find any flying job because the 409 checkride was a checkride establishing mental competency.

"They built up to the checkride by harassing and intimidating me. They called me on the carpet for the tiniest infraction, the smallest, most ridiculous thing. Suddenly, I couldn't do anything right after being completely right for so long. I was in the chief pilot's office for all the wrong reasons, their disciplinary reasons. Pilots who weren't in on the conspiracy but heard about me from management began to doubt me. I was poison and no one wanted me around. I lost my support system, all my friends."

"You've been through a lot - terrible pressure for a long time before Continental gave you this checkride. I'm so sorry this happened to you."

"As if the 409 checkride wasn't bad enough, when I returned to the FAA to requalify, somehow the inspector and I got distracted and landed gear up in my Seneca on the final landing. So of course they wouldn't return my license."

Listening to this story, I was shaken. I thought of the pilot licenses in my pocket. They were among my most important possessions. Without them, a pilot had no legal way to earn a living. I recalled a narrow escape of my own.

Some aviation publications include stories submitted by pilots who learned some noteworthy lessons about aviation from surviving bad experiences. Accidents frequently happen as a result of a chain of mishaps leading to an almost foregone conclusion. By sharing the stories, the publication's intent is to enlighten pilots and steer them from harm. As an Accident Prevention Counselor appointed by the FAA, I was aware of some of the pitfalls and how important it was to recognize and break a chain of bad events.

The air was crystal at 2500 feet above the ground as we flew south from Provo toward Bullhead City, Arizona. We were hurrying to check in for the start of the All Women's Transcontinental Air Race, successor to the Powder Puff Derby. The derby was changed to a more specific race after a man entered - an example of women's lib being men's lib, too. Sponsored by Sam's Club, the course made a "U" with mandatory stops around the country.

My student, Valola Crandall, rode co-pilot in the front seat of the open-cockpit Waco with only an altimeter, a throttle and a compass for reference, while I flew from the back with engine instruments and a partial panel of flight instruments, including a communications radio, a transponder and a VOR receiver. We stopped for an hour in windy Cedar City and met our husbands for lunch. They accompanied us with an on-board weather station and flight-planning resources. Planning of and familiarization with each leg of the race would have to be done in advance because once airborne, there was no autopilot: this was hands-on flying. I planned to fly pressure patterns, taking advantage of winds circulating around highs and lows. It was fair to say that either the fastest or the slowest craft could win given the handicaps, and my Waco was the slowest airplane in the race.

The Waco was a new 1991 version of the 1934 biplane and had just arrived with a few modifications for safety. This included beefing up the brakes and changing from heel application to toe brakes. We'd also had our mechanic, Clyde Fredricksen, install a 22-gallon auxiliary fuel tank, which moved the center of gravity of the airplane to its forward limit. It took longer for this modification and approvals by the race committee than we'd anticipated, limiting my practice in the airplane to the two days remaining before the race.

As we circled overhead the old Bullhead City Airport, I could see where the competitor's airplanes were impounded at the start. The entrants were checking in at a table by the taxiway, visiting and eating what I imagined were gourmet sandwiches with a full view of runway operations. The runway in use was paved, several thousand feet long, and parallel to the Colorado River. It sloped downhill to the south, ending at the base of a rocky cliff.

I looked at the windsock. It stood straight out and snapped at the end. Airport information said the direction was NW at 22knots with gusts to 28, temperature 113 F. There was no tower but if there had been one, traffic would have been changed to the opposite runway so we'd land *into* the wind, not with it, a tricky maneuver and ill-advised in any airplane.

I weighed my alternatives. I had to choose between waiting until every plane in the pattern landed so I could turn traffic around and land on the other runway into the wind, making us late and disqualified to enter the race, or chance ground-looping the airplane by landing in the most hazardous of conditions for a taildragger, a strong, gusty, quartering tailwind. I chose to land immediately.

I completed my single, overhead circle of the airport, reminded myself of my considerable flying ability - that landing downwind was no hill for this stepper - and headed for the entry leg of the airport traffic pattern.

As I circled the visual checkpoint marking the entry for the pattern, I looked over to see a Mooney aircraft about a mile southwest of our position. I completed the turn and headed for the downwind leg. Suddenly a voice from the past came over the radio. It sounded familiar but I couldn't quite place it during that first transmission. "Red biplane over the checkpoint, we *were* ahead of you!"

How could they be? They weren't to the visual checkpoint yet, still southwest. I didn't answer and continued toward the airport, limiting my radio transmissions to professionally reporting my position with intentions of entering the traffic pattern, as I was busy flying.

The Mooney flew in behind me, faster and overtaking us. I dove slightly to get to the traffic pattern altitude and gain speed beyond my 95 knots.

"Red biplane, you cut us out of the pattern!" That voice suddenly jogged my memory with its gruffness. Sure, it was Billy Blue, long gone from the Grand Canyon. I remembered her distinctive tone; she still sounded raspy.

I could have answered, probably should have answered, but I could wait and talk to her on the ground, besides, wind noise in the microphone would make my voice distorted, indistinguishable, and she probably wouldn't have remembered me from our days at Scenic. I was intent on arriving before the close of the race or we'd have gone to all these preparations for nothing. I followed the traffic ahead, sequencing our arrival ahead of the Mooney.

Valola remained silent over the interphone. She was aware of the conditions existing at the airport because it had been hot and turbulent aloft. As we descended over the irregular terrain, our ride got rougher. I was sure she'd assessed the conflicts and come to the same conclusions. Since she didn't voice a complaint, I took it to be concurrence, and I continued inbound. Billy, on the other hand, had to slow down to land, complained bitterly all the way around the pattern that I'd "cut her out." I was busy handling the airplane in turbulence and ignored her barrage and continued the approach with only minutes 'til closing of the race. I didn't have time to let her go ahead!

During the flare, I corrected for the wind by inclining the stick sideways and full back to hold the tailwheel on the ground. We touched softly one-third of the way down the runway, allowing for the down slope of the asphalt and terrain clearance on the approach, and the tailwind extending the distance to touchdown. Once in contact with the ground, we began rolling toward the end of the runway. Suddenly, the Mooney screamed in my earphones: "Clear the runway! Clear the runway immediately!" with such urgency I thought there must be something terribly wrong. We weren't able to "go around" because of the cliff looming ahead. I waited two beats for the airspeed to slow below 50 knots before applying moderate then fairly heavy braking to exit at the taxiway just ahead rather than at the end of the runway. I could feel that Mooney chewing up my tailfeathers!

Suddenly, as if in slow motion, our tail flew back up into the air of its own accord. I struggled to get it back on the ground with full back stick. But the elevator didn't have any effect! To my utter astonishment, the tail was flying again! The wind had got under it, and though try though I may with rapid control inputs and a burst of power to arrest the inevitable, we began a somersault in what seemed a slow, agonizing revolution with ever-increasing brake pressure as my feet were pressed firmly, immovably, into the pedals.

I remembered looking over at the ladies as we rotated upside down. Their conversation froze in mid-sentence; gourmet sandwiches poised in front of open mouths as they stared at the spectacle. Then all went black for a moment with the increasing g's. When I saw light again, I came to hanging from my seat belts over the white centerline of the runway looking at the "G" meter, which registered slightly more than eight forces of gravity, and hearing our ELT *whoop-whooping*. I smelled for gas – there was none – but I turned the valve off anyway. Furious, I reached for the seatbelt lock, pulled it, and on purpose, dropped the three feet to the pavement onto my head. Crumpled, I stretched up with an aching head and turned off all the switches and silenced the ELT.

"Valola, I screwed up... Let me help you out of the airplane."

"Ww..hh.aa.tt happened? It was such a good landing." She was dazed.

"Come on. You need to get out and away." I felt terrible that I'd put her, my student, a new private pilot, through this. She'd trusted me so. She stiffened in pain from the impact of the "G" forces as I undid the belts, put my arms around her, and lowered her gently to the ground. We went to sit in the shade of a high winged Cessna. I perched on the tire of an airplane parked near the scene when the Mooney roared by with Billy in the right window. There was a look of disbelief on her face.

Thanks, Billy.

Soon John arrived with Ray. They'd landed before us in the King Air and saw everything. Hurrying to the Waco in a hastily borrowed pickup truck, John immediately went for the airplane. Ray came to see us. They didn't know about the Mooney.

"It was such a good landing. I saw it, and in that wind! What happened?" Ray said bending down under the wing. "Are you all right?"

"I have a bad headache but I'm okay. Angry, but okay." We'd missed the race entry deadline and crashed the airplane. We couldn't enter the race.

An EMT and some air race ladies inquired about our welfare as the men turned the sweet Waco, its tail all wrinkled and crushed on the top, back over onto its main gear. The words of a friend who owned a crop dusting service and operated a few biplanes, some intact and others not, sounded in my ears as I watched them turn the biplane over: "What do you think that upper wing is for anyway?" I guessed now I knew. My heart beat hard. This was the first time I'd ever bent an airplane. Fortunately, with the airlines, bending *little* airplanes didn't even count, or I'd have jeopardized my airline job, too.

The men tore the competition number from the empennage. John held the Waco's damaged tail feathers while standing in the bed of the pickup while Ray drove pulling the plane backwards from the flight line. I apologized to the racing committee and hastily departed to avoid the press which suddenly began arriving on the scene.

In speaking with the National Transportation Safety Board investigators, the finding in the accident report revealed the brakes were too powerful for the weight of the airplane, and existing and subsequent models were rapidly modified back to the original braking pressure at the factory.

So many things happened before and during the flight that I recognized the chain of events leading to the accident: I felt compelled to continue the flight, maneuvering to turn things to my favor with incisive action, but disaster was only a heartbeat away. Luck ran out on me when the Mooney appeared.

I felt I didn't deserve my position as Accident Prevention Counselor because I'd caused an accident, so I resigned as soon as I got home. Instead, I thought I deserved the infamous Darwin Award in aviation. I learned about flying from that!

✈

". . But he wouldn't intentionally allow you to land gear up because he'd look bad, too..." I said to Gurley.

"I know, but we did." Then in a tiny voice she added, "I think he was distracted by flying with me."

Ah, the old "her beauty was a distraction" excuse. I hesitated with this thought then searched for the words that hopefully would make her feel better. "Gurley, you have a husband and family who love you. Stay home with them awhile and heal. Try the checkride again when you're feeling better. Things have a way of working out, really they do, and for the best. Because you were setup by Continental and the outcome unjustified, everything you've tried has been adversely affected. I know in my heart, that if you have faith in yourself, give yourself a chance, that eventually things will come right." We smiled through tears and hugged each other tightly, parting to board our commute flights.

✈

The patchwork quilt of Europe as we flew at 35,000 feet - plus or minus four thousand according to our weight, traffic, and a flight plan which took advantage of most favorable winds - looked for all the world like the maps in my colorful sixth grade geography book, or what we saw watching the Weather Channel overviews. Listening to news commentaries on the BBC at hotels in Europe, the U.S. was somehow portrayed in a different light. We weren't the center of the universe; rather we were viewed by British newscasters as the somewhat still-errant colonies.

As airline crews, we hurried through customs and were transported to elegant hotels via large, comfortable Mercedes buses. Sitting high above traffic, our views were expansive as we rolled through the English countryside, adorned by blue fields of rapeseed – an unlikely moniker for such a lovely plant. Or in Germany, by fields of sunflowers whose heads tracked the sun. In morning, the sunflowers faced east and in the evenings, the same flowers faced west, taking advantage of every moment of sunshine. In England, all the farm animals grazed outdoors - horses even wore raincoats, water-repellent blankets -whereas in Germany, animals were unseen, kept in barns. Fields were groomed right up to the pavement of highways and country roads with not even an inch to spare. Windows in houses were meticulously clean – a seeming impossibility given the inclement weather, but when the sun shone, hausfraus were out scrubbing away. Every house neatly adhered to the same attractive, preconceived Bavarian-style and color code: white with dark trim of exposed timbers, and orange roofs. On one corner of each house there was an alcove with a statue of the family's patron saint painted in gold leaf and bright, basic colors.

I was lucky to be scheduled into St. Petersburg in 1993 at the beginning of the Goodwill Games. Lowering of the Iron Curtain and the subsequent dissolution of the Cold War were events I thought I'd never witness in my lifetime. I'd grown up in this pervasive shadow by having a father whose U.S. Army career spanned a generation of communism. Though an uneasy peace existed between the Socialists and the free world, this divisiveness became known as the Cold War. I was thrilled to venture to places I studied in Russian History classes taken at UC Berkeley from Dr. Martin Malia, a professor of Russian descent. In the truly abrasive fashion of his time period and the experiences he contended with before his arrival at the university, he unjustly failed me in his class because *he* lost my final examination Blue Book test booklet comprising the complete grade for his class. After 16 years appealing to him in writing to reverse my grade, he retired and left for Paris with all the honors and pensions due a full professor. His magnificent lectures notwithstanding, when I heard of his forthcoming retirement, I wrote to principals at the University explaining my situation. They contacted him, implored him to reconsider, and said they could do nothing more. He wouldn't relent.

Shortly after my letters to the Chancellor and the President, CBS reported on student problems with UCB administration on *60 Minutes*. Film clips of students chasing professors across campus attempting to gain professorial approval required for class entry were tragically humorous as professors hid behind hedges and students ran with papers in hand begging for approbation by signature. But the injustice of my "F" went deeper than that. I, who spent all my leisure time and money on colleges and universities, some thirteen years of effort to maintain a straight A average, turned an emotional corner.

Remembering the pain and subsequent resolve, I set course across the Atlantic and headed north toward the Arctic Circle and Russia.

Passing the last point of land before the Atlantic Ocean known navigationally as *coast-out* just north of the city of Moncton, Nova Scotia, we received our oceanic clearance from Canadian Air Traffic Control: a specific named-track, altitude assignments for different portions, and communications frequencies to report our arrival times over points on our high frequency radios designed for communicating our position and information relative to flight over great circumferential distances anywhere in the world.

As we passed over the isolated city lights of Moncton, I recalled a childhood trip there with my father, who planned our vacations around scientific objects and such events as the Moncton Bore. The phenomenal tides that come and go each day in a valley-like channel, a distance of seventy-five miles from the ocean to the city, creates what is the world's highest tidal bore. At more than 40 miles per hour and fifty feet deep engulfing all within its path, it roars up and down the channel. As we flew on by toward the ocean - it was so dark over the water it was like flying into a void - my thoughts turned to our flight plan. I became absorbed in our continuing pageant.

Later, we approached Greenland, a continent of ubiquitous ice and snow, pleasantly named by the Danes as *Greenland* in hopes that adventurous settlers would travel there and make it home. It rises out of the North Atlantic Ocean more abruptly than a ship out of the sea. Having mountain peaks with heights of 15,000 feet at the center, we were constrained to carry additional oxygen beyond the norm for our passengers. On routing for northern latitudes like our destinations of Finland and Russia, addressing the possibility of depressurization became more complex. Because of the higher terrain, we couldn't descend to lower than 15,000 feet, where when decompressed, the cabin's air would be inadequately thin for breathing. Should we have to fly across the width of the continent at this altitude without the additional oxygen, hypoxia - oxygen deprivation - might occur. So we carried ample oxygen for all passengers aboard on flights at these altitudes. This meant a compromise in other loading considerations because of the additional weight.

We stopped in Helsinki. It was spring and our Finnish flight attendants with spectacular white-tufted hair insisted the best time to visit Finland was at Christmas: when they cross-country skied with their families through silent fairylands of snow-laden trees and across frozen lakes. We left our Finnish flight attendants in Helsinki and picked up our Russian flight attendants, both inherited with

Delta's acquisition of Pan Am. We carried a mechanic on the cockpit jumpseat going into St. Petersburg, as we had no maintenance there. The Russian Controllers were difficult to understand and we asked for clarification many times and in several ways to assure we understood their instructions. The altitude assignments were in hectopascals. We converted feet to meters to hectopascals and back again. Positive control was dubious with the possibility of misunderstanding controllers's pronunciation and we were relieved there was little other air traffic during our approach and landing.

St. Petersburg ramps had grasses growing from cracks and we passed many parked Russian Tupilev transports while taxiing towards the International Arrivals Area. I was amazed at how similar in appearance they were to our Boeing 727's, though they were narrower, giving the appearance of greater delicacy.

We were barely noticed by our customs agent, who was quite taken with his lovely assistant, which created a problem later in the trip. To find our assigned agent so disinterested seemed out of character as I recalled how difficult it was to get a Russian visa. An additional passport photo exposing a facial profile of bone structure and one complete ear had been required.

Our ride from town was fast and comfortable in an automobile of indescribable manufacture driven by a very tall man in his thirties. He was dressed in a suit and knew no English at all. Similar to autos in 40's newsreels, the car's appearance was not unlike a Rolls Royce. After growing up with unflattering pictures in *Life Magazine* of Russian women looking like Khrushchev wearing babushkas, I was surprised and pleased to find the opposite. The women were slim, fashion-conscious, and vibrant. Many were fair with white-blond hair. Others had darker complexions and high Asian cheekbones. But mostly their hair colors were auburn in shades ranging from light to dark. Accompanied by almond shaped eyes slanting up and away, they were most attractive and feminine women. Russian men were unusually tall and broad shouldered with strong, prominent noses. Generally they had dark hair.

In long overcoats that swayed with their steps, crowds of people strolled along in the golden spring afternoon along broad sidewalks on the perimeter of boulevards in downtown St. Petersburg. When they reached the end, I noticed they turned around and strolled back again. Historic statuary adorned bridges that crisscrossed rivers downtown. Buildings in French style were painted in pastel colors with wrought iron balconies. Except for the shuffling rhythm of feet, there were few other sounds. Only a few cars passed by of a large, gray sedan type not recognizable to me. Couples turned to each other in occasional but spare conversation. For the most part, everyone just walked. With little food on grocery shelves, they had trim figures.

During the layover, I spent some time sitting in a city park. Dressed somberly in dark colors and without jewelry, I wore little makeup so as not to attract attention. I thought I fit in. There were numerous statues without titles and though there were gardens, they were bare and uncared for. Benches and places to sit were ample. Crowds of people gathered in the park. Groups of girlfriends clustered without conversation or laughter. Children sat unmoving beside their parents. No one spoke. It was so quiet I could hear the birds in the trees. As if a signal to depart, a cold breeze suddenly rustled last year's dry leaves.

Passing Parisian building facades while walking back to the elegant Nvjesky Hotel, I felt a bit chagrined that I reclined in near opulence while the crowds outside might not have a place to live.

The Station Manager from the airport graciously offered any services for our pleasure; we asked for a guide. A tall, young woman named Natasha, fluent in English with a heavy accent, conducted us to various points around the city. We were sure she received recompense from the merchants for escorting us here and there, but she had a lot of pride and the good taste not to encourage us to buy anything.

We arrived at the Hermitage, winter palace of Catherine the Great. It seemed larger than the Louvre and held lost treasures from the past thought destroyed. Uncarpeted gold inlay floors mirrored the ceilings; it felt criminal to walk on them.

The next day, our little band of three crewmembers - our flight attendants had returned to Helsinki - convened for our ride to the airport. The Captain was bruised and battered. "What *happened* to you?" I asked, alarmed at his appearance.

"I know I'm not supposed to be out exploring alone, but I woke up early and took a walk. On a beautiful street with large houses and trees, I suddenly found myself surrounded by about thirty kids ten to sixteen years old. They jumped me. I grabbed the biggest one by the waist and swung him around like a windmill, keeping the other kids away. Somehow, they didn't get my wallet with my medical and flying licenses. Two women sweeping the streets ran over and hit them as hard as they could with their brooms. As quickly as they appeared, the kids disappeared. I think they were gypsies. The women patted me and brushed me off, clucking and making soft sounds, shaking their heads. I tried to thank them the best I could. Then I hurried back to the hotel." The two of us listened to this story in silence. It portrayed what we were warned about from other crews flying into the area. But for the one incident with the gypsies, we had had no other problems. My visit was enlightening; nothing was what I'd envisioned.

Once inside the vacuous terminal, while we cleared Russian Customs, the agent noticed I carried a violin, not posted as an item on the inbound list. How could it have been? The inbound customs agent was more interested in his attractive intern than making notes of our possessions, and simply waved us through. In broken English difficult to understand, the Agent thought I'd purchased an expensive Stradivarius violin sold in desperation, and he hesitated to let me leave the country with an *Objet d'Art*. I was detained while the rest of the crew passed through. Frowning, they strode toward the plane, pulling their wheeled suitcases and looking back at me over their shoulders.

I couldn't say I was afraid, but I was concerned. It was terribly difficult to communicate with this Agent, and though he knew English, his accent was heavy. I could barely discern his words, but his intent was clear. Conceivably, I might be held somewhere until the violin problem was resolved. And should I delay the flight, I'd find little consolation from Delta.

I showed the Agent my sheet music. "Would a person buying a violin be carrying sheet music?" I opened the case and held the violin up for him to look inside. "Please look at the sticker. My violin was made in Italy by Caesarius."

After some consternation, he let me and my violin pass to security where he was also in charge. I put the violin onto the scanning machine conveyor along with my luggage and other small purchases. He was so embarrassed when the ancient machinery broke open my box of glass caviar containers, smashing two in the roller assembly, that he threw his hands into the air over his head and stomped away without further inspection.

I quickly gathered my things and hurried across the vast and vacant ramp to Delta's waiting airplane. All doors and bins were buttoned up for departure and I could hear the APU running. I looked up at the waiting air machine and smiled at the crew. I glanced at my watch; there were several minutes left before departure.

I read the captain's lips: "Here she comes and she has her violin." I ran up the steep, rickety, see-through stairs to the cockpit with my flight case, suitcase, and purchases in hand; my violin was in a blue case hung by a strap across my shoulders. We started the engines as soon as I settled in my seat. I copied our clearance and carefully read it back to the Russian Controller. As we began our long taxi for take off from a distant runway, I apologized to the crew for any concern they may have felt. They said nothing. In the future I regretfully left my violin at home. I missed my layover companion, muted and played softly in my room.

In the fall of the same year I was scheduled again into St. Petersburg at the conclusion of the Goodwill Games. There was a biting nip in the air. It was early November and the trees had lost their leaves, dark sentinels vying for sunshine on the Arctic Circle. In the winds, their branches tapped roofs of apartment-like buildings whose pastel facades lent the only visual note of gaiety. However, something had changed. The people behaved differently. They spoke to each other, wore beautiful furs, and walked large, wolf-like dogs so gray they looked blue. Cats patrolled sidewalks where none walked before and shops were as open as the smiling faces I passed on the avenues.

CHAPTER XIII

TIP OF THE ICEBERG

The captain who sat beside me looked as pudgy as the Pillsbury®
Dough Boy. His eyes were circled with ridges of fat. Specks of
perspiration flew into his hair, wetting the wisps that wiggled
above his forehead as he spoke. Pale and miserable, he looked like
he'd lost his best friend. I seldom flew with a pilot so far out of
good physical condition. Most pilots these days were fit: Captain
Clearance was not. Gone were the days when a potbelly profile
alluded to prosperity; robust, trim physiques were the trend in 1993.
My eyes dropped to his ring finger as he gestured, and I noticed
there was a white circle where a wedding band used to be. My heart
went out to him; it must be difficult for him to cope, and lines etched
on his face had become inherent in his expression.

This was the first time I'd ever flown with Captain Clearance, not
an unusual situation, as I was new at the ATL base and the category
was large; seldom did I fly with the same crew twice. "In order to
maintain my international currency, I need to fly an occasional
international trip," he told us. This was why he was present instead
of the scheduled captain.

En route to Manchester, England, Clearance began what became
a North Atlantic crossing dissertation on a Mrs. Renee Flowers. I'd

never heard of her, but she was apparently employed as a dispatcher with Delta. Dispatchers work in flight operations and by design, share equal responsibility with captains for the planning of each flight. Dispatchers sign the Flight Release jointly with captain. Dispatchers often are not pilots but have arrived at this vocation via a fascination for meteorology, calculation, and planning, whereas most pilots live to be among the clouds.

Captain Clearance's introductory comments about Mrs. Flowers were rather global, and initially, I didn't pay much attention as this speech-making was the norm: give a captain a platform and he'd make a speech about something; this time it happened to be about Renee Flowers. It was interesting he chose to talk about a professional woman now that he had another one at his side. Did this include me? Was I to be held accountable because I was one, also? I groaned inside and waited for what followed.

"She doesn't know what she's doing."

What a broad statement, I thought, and since I didn't know him, regarded it as having little credence and paid only casual attention to his lecture, choosing instead to gaze out the window at the countryside, drifting along absorbed in my own thoughts.

"She misses key items such as wind effect in her planning." This was an important item to miss! Now he had my attention.

"Then she flight plans inappropriately *using* winds."

Was this a contradiction of his previous statement? Or that she'd not considered wind in the first case but had in the second? If these statements about Flowers' ability as dispatcher were true and she consistently miscalculated winds, it would be difficult for pilots to function. Accurate calculation of winds is instrumental because wind either speeds or slows a craft depending upon direction relative to the flight path; the consummate effect is time spent aloft and provision for fuel.

If Mrs. Flowers didn't consider tailwinds, her flights would proceed to their destination arriving too heavy to land, as each aircraft has a maximum landing weight for structural integrity which is less than the maximum weight possible for take-off. Or, if she didn't consider the effect of headwinds, the flight would slow, taking extra time and burning more fuel than planned, necessitating a landing short of the destination. In either case, disregarding these items was unlikely as flight planning, including wind calculations, is what a dispatcher *does*.

This dissertation left a question in my mind: Was she *our* dispatcher? Our paperwork was readily available to the flight crew, folded and placed on the center console. While listening to Captain Clearance, I picked it up, fingered and smoothed the pages from their tri-fold, and looked for the dispatcher's name. It was not Renee Flowers. So why would Captain Clearance talk about her?

Captain Clearance's tone and the content of his monologue were not flattering. Ultimately, he said other things not specifically related to Mrs. Flowers' dispatching abilities, but his comments were generally unpleasant and left me with several questions: Why would Captain Clearance single out Flowers, a professional woman, with disparaging remarks, who had nothing to do with our flight? Could he be making some connection between Flowers and me because we both worked at jobs traditionally held by men? Or was the point of his talking just that, talking? "Blah, blah, blah..."

He gestured, speaking to the air outside his window as if he was an omnipotent being, and people 35,000 feet below on earth were his subjects. But his only audience was his captive flight crew, and neither of us chose to comment. Embarrassed that he'd speak about a dispatcher, a company professional, so unkindly, I wanted to plug my ears as Captain Clearance went on dishing Flowers. I hoped he'd finish his tirade and allow peace and quiet to return to our small space.

When Captain Clearance left the cockpit on a break, the S/O and I established that neither of us knew of Renee Flowers, but it didn't matter, as by dawn, approaching the Irish coastline, we felt we did. The Mrs. Flowers portrayed by Captain Clearance was not someone we wanted to know, or have plan our next flight.

From the beginning of the trip I wondered, *did his wife leave him?* Was he translating his unhappy feelings about women to Mrs. Flowers? If he wasn't bashing her, would he choose some other woman? Captain Clearance vented about Flowers nearly the entire oceanic portion of the trip to Manchester until we got busy with arrival duties at top of descent. I found the old adage true that flying was hours and hours of boredom occasionally shot through with moments of sheer terror. These moments were still to come...

Once on the ground in Manchester, Captain Clearance joined the entire crew of nine flight attendants, the engineer, and me for an Italian dinner at Coco's Too. He generously bought the many carafes of wine consumed outside the duty envelope.

Proceeding westbound on the second day of our trip, Clearance acted as just another vanilla captain until Greenland loomed on the horizon in the front and starboard windscreens. Glaciers traveled to the water's edge and calved icebergs that tumbled along in blue offshore currents close to the continent, while distant water resumed its oceanic green. The safety of our ship aloft was poignant compared with those on the sea whose fate was sealed by proximity. Carried by currents curving around the continent, the bergs visible above and below the water confirmed the anecdote only the 'tip of the iceberg' as much more mass below the surface was clearly visible from the air. I inhaled deeply with the phenomenal, stark beauty of it all.

Suddenly, as if Captain Clearance felt he was alone in the world rather than flying through the air in a thin bubble of glass and metal with a captive audience, harsh words began rolling from his mouth. The diatribe expelled from his bulbous, wet lips assumed the character of an arrogant ritual. He couldn't spit the words out fast enough. I wondered, how much more there could be - how much more below the surface? He began with an interesting statement and pontificated without pause. Except for the occasional question, my intent was to diffuse this blast, the S/O asked again and again for clarification. This tirade lasted from Greenland nearly to the US/Canadian border - hours!

"You know, I'm known as the Terminator," he quipped smiling at his own cleverness. My eyebrows rose in surprise. If true, shouldn't we know him by reputation? "I am the Chief Instructor on the Lockheed 1011 for Delta Airlines." *Now* I connected his face with a name given me by several line check airmen. Chief Instructors normally were approached with respect and some amount of fear. One check pilot, Captain Charley Hunt, candidly called Captain Clearance the *hatchet man*. This declaration was just one of several I received while paired with line check airmen who disclosed that Delta used its check airman like weapons against its line pilots to intimidate them, remind them of the company's liability, *and* its power. "*I* decide who'll fly Delta's most prestigious airplane. *I* decide who passes or fails."

I held my breath, waiting for more. It took only a moment, a click: the gravity of his vent was not so much in the content as in the revelation. He was the end point, *the man*, and he was more than anxious to let us know, but why now, and in present company? Had the fierce beauty of Greenland incited this speech? Or, should I be fearful there was something foreboding in the future for me? I searched my repertoire of past flights since I'd arrived at the base, and found nothing. This somewhat eased my mind.

It looked like our return flight would be a duplicate of the previous one. I didn't know one captain from another, having only recently transferred into the Atlanta base. I treated everyone the same, from ship cleaners to president of the company, with respect and diplomacy. Certainly my comportment didn't invite this foray. Both the second officer and I listened because we had no other choice, captive in the small space aptly named the cockpit, suggesting the gender of egos residing there.

Captain Clearance proceeded to name a list of Western captains he fired, whom I'd known, among them, Captain Rick Weeds, past president of the Air Line Pilots Union, and Captain Gary Fillmore. Prior to acquiring Western, Delta pilots had no union. There were no unions representing any employee group at Delta Air Lines, instead, Delta embraced the idea of a "family," asserting unions were unnecessary.

"Fired?" I asked for clarification. "Don't you mean retired?"

"I mean fired. Fired!"

I was surprised and troubled. I was sure he meant fired from the program and not from the airline, but when I pressed him on this detail, he wouldn't expound and fell ominously quiet. "What about their families and all the years they've already spent flying, Captain?" I lowered my voice, attempting to carry the adrenaline to my brain and not to my mouth. I couldn't help asking *why* in their defense. Their lives were so inextricably aligned with flying, their egos so entwined, that failing invited disaster. I recalled listening with concern to stories of former Western captains who failed checking out on Delta's Lockheed 1011, though they'd successfully checked out on other planes. During those stories, I'd wondered at the agenda. Western pilots who were initially *overjoyed* with the acquisition - they'd described it as a good marriage – soon discovered intimidation and professional humiliation. They were nothing more than bastard sons, like Gary Fillmore.

✈

I remembered him as very tall, dark-haired, and quiet. He may have been a native Alaskan, perhaps descended from the handsome Tlinquit Indians, whose physical beauty rivaled that of the Cherokees. He came to Delta through Western when Pacific Northern Airlines was acquired in 1968. With routes in the Pacific Northwest and Alaska, PNA pilots were based in Seattle until Delta gave up these routes in the middle '90's, closing the base. Several times a year, my husband and I flew through Juneau to a tiny fishing hamlet in southeast Alaska called Elfin Cove. Situated up a fjord, the airport for the capital of Alaska had a challenging instrument approach. With the let-down to the tip of Admiralty Island, home to as many as seventy-five thousand Alaska Brown bears, according to Fish and Game, after the island was navigationally confirmed, the approach could be continued via a set of lead-in lights that stretched from tiny island to atoll to island, pointing the way to either the single asphalt-surfaced runway for land planes, or the parallel, fresh waterway for seaplanes. The approach was frequently clouded with low ceilings and fog, and losing sight of the lead-in lights required a missed approach. To avoid high terrain on three sides, the missed approach procedure at Juneau qualified as a mild acrobatic maneuver called a Chandelle: a maximum performance climbing turn to the reciprocal heading with the greatest possible gain in altitude. Large and small aircraft alike conducted this missed approach maneuver. Approaches and landings, or missed approaches, executed day after day, year after year, with the reliability an airline should offer its customers, entailed expertise. The pilots selected to fly in and out of Juneau were a small, select cadre experienced in difficult airport entry and Gary Fillmore was one of them.

To get to Elfin Cove, we had to first pass through Juneau, and I tried to look in the cockpit to see who was flying as captain. Usually it was Captain Fillmore. In Juneau, we boarded a floatplane for the 45 minute, scenic flight to Elfin Cove. Enroute, we were treated to glacial views and often, pods of whales. If Popeye and Olive Oyl were to live in Alaska, they'd settle in Elfin Cove. With aerial boardwalks connecting atolls in the village, it was picturesque. With inner harbor protection for the fishing boats, and an outer harbor with views of Brady Glacier across the Icy Straits, it was accessible only by sea, and home to Captain Dennis Hay's Elfin Cove Sport Fishing Lodge. To get there, we either flew aboard a Wings' De Havilland Beaver or Alaska Coastal Airline's Twin Beech on floats. Flown by owner and chief pilot, Dave Brown, affectionately known as Brownie because he resembled a Brown bear, and landing in the water in front of the lodge, friend Dennis Hay stood on the dock to greet us for a week of the most super sport fishing for salmon and halibut in southeast Alaska.

Returning to Juneau, we'd again leave Alaska via the airport at Juneau and, often as not, Gary Fillmore was our captain. I could always tell when it was his leg because his handling of the airplane was so smooth and coordinated that passengers hardly realized when he banked to initiate turns. When Captain Clearance wouldn't check him out in the Lockheed 1011, Fillmore reverted to his previous equipment, the Boeing 727, for a time. Despondent over his failure, he put a 45-caliber pistol in his mouth and shot himself at home, within hearing of his wife and four little children.

For a moment I considered bringing Fillmore's suicide to Captain Clearance's attention, but he was so avid a talker that he quickly moved to another personal profile. This time it was one I knew well, Lorelei Kenyon. From Greenland to the U.S. border, he extolled a list of her faults, real and imaginary, in a very mean-spirited way. I broke in several times to say: "I'm her friend," in hopes it would calm the storm. It didn't. The worst of it was, everything he detailed I'd heard before and recognized as second-hand information, or more. Logically, there was no way his path could cross hers. Captain Clearance flew out of a different base, and wasn't even on the same equipment, for heaven's sake.

If anything good was gleaned from this experience with Captain Clearance, it was that he gave me a window into the workings of the check department. From his rhetoric, it was apparent there was an inner department within the check department. Besides being politically handpicked, Clearance said these guys would do *anything* to advance. Apparently this inner department decided who would be the good guys and who would be the bad. This was appalling news!

"Have you ever flown with Lorelei?" I asked politely.

"No."

"How would you know if she is a good or a bad pilot?"

"Because I was told she is a bad pilot by some of the guys."

"By whom?"

"By line check airmen who've flown with her."

"Can you tell me their names?"

"I cannot." It sounded more like he *would not!* "Do you mean, Captain Clearance, you don't remember who they are?" He addressed Lorelei's lack of flying ability by substantiating his assertions with rumor. I wanted to say: *How fair is it to make judgments based on rumor?* But I decided to try another tack: "You, yourself, have never actually flown with Lorelei Kenyon?"

"No."

I chose a softer approach, aware of an invisible line of behavior over which I shouldn't step. He was, after all, today's captain *and* the chief line check airman on the Lockheed 1011, one of my bosses now that Captain Paul Homestead had surreptitiously retired, and months earlier than he'd intended, judging from our conversation on one of my early checkrides. I'd often wondered if he *had* to retire earlier because he'd passed me with good comments about my flying.

Clearance took the words of others for truth. No matter what was said, what the motivation behind the words or acts, if one check pilot made a determination, did they all, without question, espouse the same? Never mind that Lorelei had been captain on the 727 and 737 for three years!

"Passing checkrides given by these characters is like going to war," she told me.

Then Captain Clearance moved onto her person and her character. I thought, *he's really too much.*

"I protest. How can you talk about anybody like you have about Lorelei?"

His face reddened with emotion: "She's a drunk."

I gasped. It was the first time I'd ever heard this. I gathered my wits and asked, "If she is, has anyone approached her suggesting therapy?" Captain Clearance didn't answer. I hoped my question would defuse any further character assassination. I recalled many pilots who spent their days off drinking because they didn't function well when they weren't flying. Perhaps they felt a sense of isolation. Living alone in hotels, away from home too much without the comfort of a trusted relationship, and inevitably, married and divorced several times – some pilot relationships never seemed to work. Excessive drinking adversely affected everything including sexual performance - that only sent them back into the bottle. Alcohol testing for crews was imminent.

"Once, I saw the bartender at the Holiday Inn North in Atlanta, drag her out of the bar by her feet when she passed out and fell off the bar stool..."

I couldn't believe my ears. "Wait a minute. Wait a minute." This was beyond imagination that he'd even talk about someone this way. It was simply inappropriate, unreasonable, way too much. My respectful attitude towards him took a turn. I had to question Clearance, to make certain I understood him clearly. "You saw - with your own eyes - Lorelei passed out, lying on the floor, and a male bartender removing her body from the scene by dragging her across the floor by her feet?" I added the part about the bartender being male as a test, and wondered if this had occurred while Lorelei was in Atlanta for training. I fought hard to blow away the vision of Lorelei in a dress up around her ears being dragged across the floor...

"Yes. Yes, I did."

"With your own eyes?"

"With my own eyes." He said this quickly as an absolute. In fact, I knew he was lying. At the hotel in Atlanta where crews stayed over, the bartenders were women. I made a mental note to call and verify this again when I got home. I did, and they were. The hotel hadn't had male bartenders for a long time. I also called Lorelei and asked, without explaining why, what she was doing during the dates Captain Clearance said she was in Atlanta. She was in Venice on vacation with her mother, and had hotel and restaurant receipts to prove it. "Hold onto them," I said.

"Not only that, but she looks like a hooker."

Now, the real reason!

"She's so sexy and has such long blond hair that one time the guys called Security at a hotel in Minneapolis because they thought she was working the crew lounge." This story was so absurd that I had called her years before, and recounted these events. All she did was laugh and affirm the story - which she thought was funny. Ironically, the same thing that made her laugh made me want to cry.

Captain Clearance said Lorelei "Stands at the door of the cockpit," and says goodbye to passengers as instructed by management for good public relations. "Everyone tells her: 'Nice flight. Good landing.' She says 'thank you' and thinks she did a good job - is a good pilot. But she isn't. She's a terrible pilot. She doesn't have a clue."

Wasn't this the same line – she doesn't have a clue – he had used in reference to Renee Flowers? I wondered, didn't the passengers arrive safely? It was so unprofessional to comment on a pilot's flying skills and pretty unsettling to hear that a person who devoted all her adult life to her flying career was a bad pilot. She'd passed her checkrides for 17 years at the airlines, and under such terrible circumstances that I knew of no one who could withstand such pressure. I knew I couldn't. She didn't have a husband or family, or outside interests beyond entertainment until it was time to fly again. She was devoted to and concentrated on her career at Delta Air Lines.

"She's so mean that she'll rip a man to shreds with her words. She's full of so much hatred it's impossible to carry on a conversation with her. She has the most vicious tongue I've ever heard."

"You've had conversations with her where this happened?"

"Yes, on several occasions, when we tried to reprimand her. She'd rip us to shreds."

This was all very new to me. I didn't know Lorelei as mean, or articulate in a vicious way, though I was sure she was able to defend herself when attacked. I wondered how Captain Clearance knew of Lorelei. Did the *check department* have conferences on pilots? Could they be aimed at something other than constructive resolution of training problems? If this was true, wasn't this a repressive, predatory style?

Had Captain Ray Clearance been present during the proceeding, or was his information second-hand or worse? There was no reason he, a Lockheed pilot, would ever come into contact with Captain Lorelei Kenyon, a Boeing 727 and 737 pilot, yet Lorelei was the brunt of his antagonism. Pilots, who traded in dark stories because they had nothing more interesting to say, attempted to damage her. I always, immediately, told anyone who began to criticize her that she was my friend. It seemed the only defense to make them stop talking. I thought Lorelei was treated more unfairly than anyone I'd ever known. The only reason I could glean was that she was her own person, not guided by convention, and an attractive woman who somehow didn't fit some preconceived profile. Her individuality added to her mystery. Her detractors wouldn't dream of such creative élan.

✈

Months later, I met *the* Mrs. Flowers when she rode as an observing dispatcher on the jumpseat of my flight to Germany. She prepared a personalized dispatch for our flight, something special for a flight crew. It was a gesture thanking us for tolerating her presence in the cockpit during the long flight. I was neutral, but interested, recalling Captain Clearance's disparaging remarks. In the end, her text was clear, her thinking logical, and her figures involving flight planning and winds were correct. Her humorous ditties illustrating a dispatcher's life were charming.

During our layover in Old Town, Mainz, while visiting the colorful open air market on the Dome Platz, I looked up to see Renee Flowers strolling by the produce, coming my way. She smiled and waved. "Hello, wonderful day," smiling, radiantly competing with the rare sunshine that brightened the scene. We visited for a few minutes amidst the gondolas of exotic fruits, commenting that we'd not seen them before, and noting they were grown in Africa. She invited me to dinner that evening with her husband and another dispatcher.

Over veal shanks served in a wondrous sauce at *Margo's*, she and her husband told us about adopting three abused children, adding to their brood of seven. Very pretty and full of life, I found her warmth endearing. When the subject turned to why she was in Germany, she said she was proud to be invited to Frankfurt to attend a council of international dispatchers. As I listened to the enthusiasm in her voice, I thought about Captain Clearance's unkind remarks and wondered why he'd attack her? My impression of Renee Flowers was that of a professional woman working diligently in her chosen field. She was interested in her work, and professional enough to be invited to attend international meetings as a representative of the United States where dispatching policy was established for the world. I asked myself, *Is she not a dispatcher among dispatchers?*

✈

For several weeks following the trip with Captain Clearance, I paced the deck that wrapped around my house in Utah. At dawn, Admiral, an Indian Runner duck whose vertical profile made him different from the squatty Mallards, rounded up our 26 other ducks. Strange and different, he was their leader. He strutted up and down the gathering, his white figure standing out among the rest, quacking at them until they stood one behind the other. Then he led the undulating Congo line from pond to barn at sunrise, and back again at sunset. Like clockwork, this activity took place twice a day. I knew that elusive red fox had missed again: there were still twenty-six figures in a rolling cakewalk across the ranch.

Autumn colors brightened, and then dimmed. Leaves blew around in swirls like miniature tornadoes. John was busy building his reclamation plant in Arizona and hadn't been home much. Snow began to fall with fair accumulation on the valley floor. Looking upward into the void, I felt the icy flakes on my face and in my eyes. Catching them on my sleeve, I admired their uniqueness recalling a passage I'd read written by the naturalist John Muir: "It's not the wind, rain and erosion which creates the shapes of landscape, but the generations of the tiny snowflake."

My Newfoundland dog we named Bear, because he looked like one, walked to and fro on the deck as my shadow. After a few strolls, little dog, Ladybug, joined us. A young ewe showed up at the ranch one day, whom I'd named Mary; she must have come from some ways away as no one around kept sheep. She fell in love with Bear and followed him everywhere; her tiny hooves tapped a quick rhythm in contrast to his quiet footfalls. Bear was somewhat impatient with her. A nosy person said she was witness to Bear's infatuation, but I'd never seen him act this way.

In the hush of this isolating snowfall, I found I was lonely for John's company. In the evenings around eight, I walked the thousand feet to the covered arena to sit on my young gray Oldenburg, Beau. Barn activity was over and during this quiet time, he focused on me. Not accustomed to having weight on his back, we posed, a silhouette illuminated by a single overhead light high above our heads. For perhaps thirty minutes each evening, I imagined myself an old master sitting on young horses. The old master might be reading the paper and smoking a cigar, while I wasn't able to think of much more than that fateful flight from Manchester.

Captain Clearance had allowed me a peek into the workings of the check department at Delta Air Lines. What would Delta pilots do if they knew there was a plan to keep them off the airline's most prestigious airplane? Would a grievance be filed with the union? Or would there be a revolt, a class action lawsuit? There was already a lawsuit filed by a group of Western pilots for a loss of seniority after the acquisition. For a few moments, I was distracted from the original problem by another: my loss of seniority, perhaps as few as eight years and as many as thirteen. Though I elected not to join the Western lawsuit against Delta over seniority, I was aware this loss would result in my being constrained to fly smaller equipment as captain, resulting in less pay, overall, for the duration of my career. I would be late to fly captain anyway, because of this loss of seniority. One of the many reasons I chose to check out on the L-1011 as first officer was because the RD in the left seat of my previous equipment, the 727, was often ten years younger than me. Western pilots were spaced along the acquiring airline seniority list in *relative position*, not the customary *date of hire*. In airline history, seniority determined when a pilot might advance in equipment and get to the higher pay. The greater number of seats aboard the airplane, generally, the larger the paycheck. As the scale was based on revenue passenger miles as well as seat liability, a twenty-five year Captain on Delta's largest equipment, flying international on a regular eighty hour per month schedule had the "A" scale salary potential of a quarter million dollars per year by the year 2000. Add the benefits of travel, insurance, and retirement pensions, to time off and prestige, and the job became a plum, a ripe plum. It was probably one of the best paying white-collar jobs in the country.

I was concerned as any stockholder about company revenues being spent on lawsuits, and Delta already had a legal department equal to its concerns. Being privy to information that adversely affected the futures of pilots... possibly harboring information with destructive potential, not only for individuals but for the company... What were the ethics? What should I do? Go to the union? I hadn't attended a union meeting since 1977 in SFO when two pilots seated on either side of me began a shouting match that nearly ended in fisticuffs. I was caught dangerously in the middle and couldn't forget that uncomfortable feeling. I never attended another shouting match, er' meeting. No, I couldn't go to the union. It was too public. I'd handle this information quietly and take it to someone who had power. Chief pilot? No. Not strong enough. Vice president, Henry Aldridge. He seemed like a fair man... yes!

This information was too hot to put into writing. Should I just call him? Somehow, calling didn't seem appropriate; I wouldn't want him to think I felt I had a pipeline to his ear. But I remember his admonition three years ago that if I ever found anything so unfair again at Delta Air Lines, I should contact him immediately. Well, here it was.

I had to write, but what about? I couldn't prove any of the firings - those men were gone. Then the light came on. I'd write about Lorelei. It would alert Aldridge to the potential of a sexual harassment lawsuit and open a line of communication through which I could let him know later, eye to eye, of the other problem: arbitrary failure and subsequent firing of pilots. If Aldridge didn't do anything, and I thought he was the right person to go to first, should I take these issues to the board of directors?

Returning to the house, I peeled off layers of winter clothes as the dogs settled in for a snooze. Mary's head was peeking through the glass looking for Bear. I fired up the computer and opened a new document: Letter to Henry Aldridge.

November 30, 1994

Dear Captain Aldridge,

This week I flew a rotation to Manchester with Captain Ray Clearance, L-1011 Check Pilot. He was generous to buy the entire crew dinner.

During the return flight, I was astonished by his sudden vitiation of fellow woman pilot, Captain Lorelei Kenyon, Dallas-Ft. Worth based; a person he has seen, has heard about, but by his own admission, does not know. The text of his denouncement was stunning, and extended from Greenland nearly to the United States border. Early on, I let him know that I was her friend, hoping it might soften the forthcoming diatribe. It didn't. It appears that "they" were unable to flunk her out, and so have resorted to character assassination. The things Captain Ray Clearance had to say were unforgivable. I would never say to my worst enemy or best friend the things he said to the second officer and me about Lorelei. Captain Ray Clearance's depiction of her was destructive.

I did not want to endure the lecture any longer than necessary, or I would have related to him that over the last twenty years, Lorelei had stood up against all odds. For example, a chief pilot, Denton Gribbons, at Western Airlines, was fired from his position, and died shortly thereafter of a heart attack, and check pilot, Jack Mark, suffered the same, in their missions to discredit her ability and character. When they could not do it reasonably, they did it unreasonably, and were found wrong and unfair by their peers.

I'm not completely sure why some men are so offended by Lorelei, but they are. She does not mince words and is cogently correct. She does not allow convention to guide her. Most of us women pilots are quiet, brown haired women, who, like our male counterparts, slip on by, happily unnoticed, for the most part.

Not Lorelei. She is a regal battleship who sails into their midst armed for war, capable and ready to use her weapons. She is accustomed to the role of flack jacket and lightning rod. She acknowledges power, but is confident of her own, and so does not tremble when her adversaries appear. This seems to generally infuriate men as their egos are abashed. She gives evidence that her ego is every bit as big and important, certainly blasphemy coming from a mere woman.

Captain Ray Clearance says she is not a good pilot, but he has never flown with her. He evidently obtains his information and opinions second hand or more, and from those who have the same agenda. Captain Kenyon has completed everything the check department has thrown at her. When she went down for captain's training in ATL, notes were received from pilots demanding that she not be checked out. Can you imagine the impact such advance billing would bring? Fortunately, her instructors were fair and their own men, a tribute to Delta Air Lines.

They wonder about crew management resources. Now it seems, according to Captain Ray Clearance, that because she does not acknowledge the harassment but continues to do her job, the check department imagines she will not heed the words of her crew. This is absurd. Could it be true that pilots are briefed before and after her flights? Why don't they just let her do her job and provide the support available to the rest of the boys? I do not think I could stand up to the pressure and stress she has endured during the previous twenty years.

Now, Captain Ray Clearance et al, have sided against her in all ways, it seems. They need to look at the past. She has survived and her detractors have not. They are gone. How many times does she have to prove she can do the job, pass the checkrides, fly into weather, handle the emergencies, and administrate the flight? I offered to talk to Lorelei after listening to Captain Ray Clearance. He commented that she had legal counsel and pending suits, and that it would probably not do any good. I agreed, but felt something had to be done... perhaps a negative preference option would help to combine crews without personality conflicts. This might work compatibly in her case if the check department hasn't poisoned everyone with rumors.

Captain Ray Clearance will be surprised that I have written to you, sir. I feel this is too important an issue to pass over. In reflection, I know you are the only one who can put a stop to this as you once did for me. Lorelei will not give up, and they won't give *it* up. Captain Kenyon needs someone to be on her side. I am, and her friends are, but we're not enough. Would you consider this problem please, the implications, the safety aspects, and come to her defense?

She may not thank you, but I will. Thank you for your efforts on Captain Lorelei Kenyon's behalf.

Sincerely,

Bliss Knight, first Officer, L-1011

✈

CHAPTER XIV

THE GAUNTLET

I waited for a reply to my letter. Winter came with grayed skies and barrage after barrage of storms. The countryside lay quiet beneath heavy snows. Still I waited.

The last night in December, we drove into Salt Lake City in a Wasatch blizzard to attend a New Year's Eve party. The drive took about an hour longer than normal because of the reduced visibility and snow accumulation. The highway shoulders were randomly littered with cars damaged in harmless fender-benders. The asphalt surface was a treacherous combination of snowmelt from the traffic and black ice formation from the dropping temperatures. Thankful for an El Dorado with front wheel drive, John skillfully negotiated the sliders and accidents to meet our friends Captain Herb and Jean Riley downtown. When our foursome finally arrived at the party, we discovered it was unlike any we'd ever attended.

The party took place in an uptown penthouse with a stunning view of the city. The quarters rustled with the movements of guests and shone with holiday décor. Lilting music from a stringed quartet wafted through the hallways. An ice carving of a seahorse drew our attention to a huge plate of salmon-shaped mousse. Greg and Hooper stood in the entry greeting their guests. Ruffled shirts complimented their tuxedos. With them was our mutual girlfriend, Cory, dressed as they were. An impressive woman, she was beautiful and large, every bit as tall as Greg and Hooper. The three of them stood shoulder to shoulder making a handsome trio. I looked around at the other guests, realizing there were only but a few women.

Greg and Hooper excelled in the cleaning and laundry business and had just opened a new facility in Park City. Greg had been a successful oil buyer for my husband for more than twenty years. Were his persuasive powers and subsequent understanding of human nature instrumental in his ability to read people well? I thought so. My thoughts were interrupted as Cory began one of her stories. Greg and Hooper knew what was coming as they just smiled and smiled. Certainly they'd heard this story before and knew Cory was a kick - why we loved having her around!

She ran the restaurant in a mental institution for years. It was the kind of story one might see in a movie, never expecting it to really happen, which made it all the more intriguing. We were a captive audience and she got right to the point. "I was behind the counter of the Ice Cream Shoppe giving head to one of the inmates." Immediately, we all gasped, and then started laughing. "He perched on the sideboard with his pants down." I was quite taken aback that Cory would do such a thing with an inmate of a mental institution even though I knew she had trouble keeping her clothes on. Gasping for breath, laughing, I tried to let her know I was astonished by her actions.

She answered by directing her line straight at me: "Long ago, I discovered it was tough to get sex since I was big, over forty, and not married. So I had to take it where I found it." She turned back to the group. "Suddenly, the Director appeared in the doorway. Real fast, I jumped up in front of the guy. I didn't think the Director could see him because I'm real big and Peter was real little. But I was worried. The Director didn't say anything. I wondered, what's *he* doing here?

I asked if there was something I could do for him. His stare and silence drove me crazy. I smiled and tried to look charming, though I was scared. All the while, I'm thinking about what I'd say to people and how it'd look if I got fired for this. What'd I put on my resume? I couldn't just leave the job out. Somehow I'd have to explain... Then, he asked me for an ice cream cone."

While I gazed out at the sparkling view and sampled the elegant salmon banquet, unexpectedly, I found friend Nancy Morris from Lake Powell and her husband, Dick, at my side. She was dressed in a velvet cowgirl suit with a ruby red western hat to match. She looked regal but frightfully thin. As we visited, I wondered if something was wrong with her health, finally commenting on her weight loss with polite dismay.

Though she smiled, she was not lighthearted, and delivered a summation of her career end as Superintendent of Schools for Utah in a few words: "Ben Rack, a pilot from your airline, who was not even involved, took up the gauntlet."

I recalled hearing newscasts about Nancy and her Park City fiasco where she suspended an errant principal who refused to follow policy she'd set for the district. Suddenly, there were news reports that Utah's first lady Principal in the history of the State and, now, Superintendent of Schools, plagiarized her thesis for her doctorate. I recognized that this unrelated, mean spirited piece of misinformation was probably contrived by Rack. Using it as a smokescreen to cloud the real issues at hand, it was just another example of his underhanded tactics. Win at any cost. His intention was to blindside the central issue: a principal would be suspended if he did not follow the superintendent's policies. The fact that a woman held a higher office than the principal should have nothing whatever to do with the case, but unseating such a queen apparently was entertaining to Rack.

The fight started by slinging mud. Knowing Nancy as honorable, these things could not be true, but the scandal aired on the radio for days, heard by many Utahans, creating doubt and dismay in citizen's minds. How could the Superintendent of Schools have plagiarized a thesis? How could *she* be Superintendent of Schools?

"Realizing I was going to lose no matter what the outcome, I resigned after twenty-two years in education in the state of Utah. I wasn't going to play their game. I would not dignify their accusations by even answering. I headed for upper management in the corporate world, Stephen Covey Institute, as Vice President of Innovation."

All I could think of while she was speaking were the babies she'd wanted and never had because of her professional dedication. Now it was too late. My heart bled for her.

✈

Rack may have left the battlefield, but the battlefield was where he lived. A warrior, he was not alive unless engaged. It was an addiction of the very worst kind. To feed it required victims. It wouldn't be out of character to suggest it was strategy to carry candy bars for North Vietnamese children in the speed brake stowage of his fighter. Making an initial pass over villages, dumping the candy bars to attract the children, and then on the second pass...

As the sights and sounds of the war dimmed with time, it was not easy to find altercations suitable to the magnitude of his craving. What happened when Nancy quit the battle early? Did he go home and put his fist through a wall? For relief and away from prying eyes, did he ejaculate in the shower? Was he not orgasmic unless he got a chance at the kill? When yearning became fretting, violence followed close behind. Desperate, any conflict would do, even one involving a very fine woman...

✈

One month, two months, three months went by. I'd heard nothing from Delta Air Lines. A question mark hung in the air. Didn't Aldridge care about Delta's liability? Four months later I noticed, posted on bulletin boards, that Captain Ray Clearance was still the Chief Line Check Airman on the Lockheed 1011... Five months passed with no response to my letter; not a reply of any kind. I was dismayed. Nothing *seemed* to have happened, but in the ominous silence I knew all too well the earmarks of tragedy.

I hadn't written to Lorelei – the interaction with Clearance was too embarrassing to let her know. Sadly, I assumed the worst: Aldridge was not only in concert with Delta's policies of professional humiliation and intimidation, but he was most likely, the architect...

✈

One spring day while I was in the ATL pilots' lounge before a trip, Captain Jeff Ricketts, international chief pilot, and my current boss, directed me to his office. He didn't sit or invite me to sit as he had in the past. Instead, he nervously leaned against his credenza. I remained standing in the middle of the room. While I was composed and waited for him to begin speaking, he fidgeted with his ear, shuffled his feet, and generally surprised me, as I knew he was a high-ranking officer in the Marine Corps and his mannerisms were not the typical behavior I expected from *some good men*. As I waited for him to begin, I realized the point of this audience was probably my letter to Aldridge. I was surprised it would be *my* chief pilot who addressed the issues with me.

"Your letter of November, 1994, has been passed down from Henry Aldridge to Prichard Dolby to Randy Gaff and finally to me." Instead of getting a response directly from Senior Vice President Henry Aldridge, the letter trickled down through the different layers of management to end up on the desk of my chief pilot, Jeff Ricketts. I'd bet the letter never went *up* to Gerald Grinstein and the board of directors.

The essence of this meeting and his communication was "...to assure you that as long as I am the chief pilot, you will have the support of this office!" I was surprised by this statement. To maintain this position would certainly place him in an awkward and precarious position though, frankly, he didn't seem to realize it at the time. *You can always tell a marine, but you can't tell him much!* Surely, he wouldn't go against management to champion me, and for him to even think he could, meant he was as naive and idealistic as I had been about the inner workings at Delta Air Lines.

"We had to find the second officer, who was on vacation and not a bit happy about being interviewed, to verify the allegations you made about Captain Clearance in your letter. You are correct. Clearance gains his information second hand and has been spoken to. As long as I am the international chief pilot, you will have the support of this office," he said again.

I felt a rush of adulation followed immediately by feeling sorry for him. He didn't realize how precarious his attitude must be to management, how it endangered his career. I wondered how long it would take him to reverse his position, leaving his ideals behind.

I managed a thank you while composing a response. He'd caught me by surprise with this meeting. So much time had gone by; I figured management had chosen to blow me off. I searched for a way to ask if there would be an audience with Aldridge. I decided not to talk around the serious issue of firing Western captains. It was shocking that Captain Clearance, a man with such little substance, was entrusted with an important position, and allowed to make decisions that terminated career pilots. I circled around the issue, addressing only my letter, and concerns about Captain Lorelei Kenyon.

"Will they be able to help Lorelei?"

"They're looking into it, now."

I pursued this issue to see if any suggestion of her fate would materialize: "I don't know why Lorelei has such problems with men, but she does. Maybe it's because she's so beautiful."

Captain Ricketts quit talking. He wouldn't speak further; instead, he stood stiffly and uncomfortably in the middle of the room looking at the floor. In the long and pregnant silence that followed were the answers to my concerns. Management had no intention of supporting Lorelei, or changing the predatory manner in which they dealt with pilots. By the silence which followed my appeal, I knew Lorelei was not the only one who needed to fear for her career.

✈

A month later, when I concluded that the matter was closed, I wrote to Lorelei with a copy of my letter to Aldridge. In return, I got a Fed Ex package from her almost immediately, and preceded by a letter asking, "Are you a crazy lady or something? Questioning management about their indiscretions *and* sticking up for me?"

"I didn't stick up for you, Lorelei, I advised them you were very good at sticking up for yourself," I wrote in my return letter. "Unless they want litigation, they should correct the check department, and right the wrongs." She didn't know my conscience had left me no choice.

✈

Months later, I flew another trip from Frankfurt to ATL with Captain Ray Clearance, whom I didn't at first recognize as one 55-year old international captain looked pretty much like the others: glasses, heavy, graying. "Good morning, Captain, my name is Bliss Knight. I'm first officer on the FRA to ATL flight."

"I know you, Bliss Knight," he looked up with what seemed uncontrived pleasantness. I was certain I didn't know him. It was not until the paperwork arrived that I noted his name on the flight release: Captain Ray Clearance. I was surprised at the change in his appearance. He was a slimmed down version of his former self and looked sharp. A bright, shiny gold wedding band was on his ring finger. One could say he almost looked content, even happy.

I was sure that during Ray Clearance's inquisitions by Aldridge, Vice President, Prichard Dolby, Executive Vice President, and Randy Gaff, Director of Operations; Captain Clearance verbalized the content of his discussions across the Atlantic to include not only Lorelei, but Renee Flowers and firings of Western Captains as well. That he would reveal information I never mentioned in my communiqué was predictable given his capricious vent for non-stop talking.

In reflection, after all that had happened, I asked myself if I was sorry I wrote the letter to Aldridge. The answer was always the same: No. But I wasn't deaf or blind and knew I'd have to be very clever to survive. I asked myself if I even wanted to try. I suspected my days at the airline were numbered because I'd been allowed a peek, nay, more, a guided tour inside the workings of the check department at Delta Air Lines by one of its very finest, and couldn't believe the conspiratorial skullduggery that went on there.

I never went to the board of directors about these issues though I was tempted. If their eventual pick for president, Henry Aldridge, was architect of these policies, perhaps the tone, itself, was gleaned from the board. However, the board was privy to Henry's methods if they chose to investigate. That someone of Gerald Grinstein's stature would tolerate such impropriety was unthinkable. Additionally, the risk of being sued for harassment by Lorelei, and other employees, seemed like a misuse of company time and money. Perhaps Mr. Grinstein chose not to regard the manner in which execution of policy took place, only that results occurred. As a student of history, I was aware this was not the first time entrusted power was abused.

✈

CHAPTER XV

THE STALKER

ritchard Dolby needed to be a fighter pilot. At seventeen, the top of his head touched the measuring stick at sixty-and-one-half inches. He would not grow any taller, barely attaining the height of his mother rather than matching that of his six-foot father. Why his hands were little more than the size of a child's by the time he was fourteen years old was at first a mystery, but he wasn't slow on the uptake. It became painfully clear he would never be more than petite. He perceived himself so slighted by Mother Nature that his diminutive size became secondary only to the intensity of his anger.

Women would never be of consequence to him because he would never be anything to them. Most women were bigger, like his sisters who taunted him, and he despised them. An inner fury of such magnitude seethed inside him that to hold it in check required all his willpower and more than the understanding of intelligent, loving parents. Pritchard required a vent.

When he went down to find out about becoming a fighter pilot he was told he was too small to reach around the cockpit. His blood pressure shot to an extreme as he stood at the interview table. He did not hear encouragement from the kindly recruiter and nor did he speak or acknowledge him in any way. The interview was over.

Ignoring the outstretched hand, Pritchard stomped through the door. It was true! He really was too small. Something clicked in his head then, and from that time on he wasn't given to, for even one second, considering normal methods for accomplishing his ends. Standard formulas simply would not work. He had proof.

He calculated a meeting with his uncle, William Dolby, as he drove into the parking lot. He parked beside the Director's car and was given entry by the guard and access to his uncle who came forward to the lobby to meet him.

Pritchard had a plan to get what he wanted. Exploiting his knowledge of potentially harmful information, he wasted no time in availing his uncle of the opportunity to help. He told him what his goals were and what he planned to do if not mollified. Uncle Bill felt coerced and frightened, an interesting twist for someone in his position. Pritchard not only got his fighter pilot seat, but entrance to the Academy. It was an outlet providing him with an education, an officer's commission, and several years of salvation.

Later, files were made available. Pritchard freely used this advantage to intimidate and exploit. Though he still had to do the work, he seemed to roar past the competition. Pritchard rapidly became part of the power team that ultimately took control of the airline. He became the powerful vice president of flight operations for Delta Air Lines.

✈

Journal entry: January 1995 Atlanta Training
Transoceanic Ground School final exam: 100%
Lockheed 1011 Systems Ground School final exam: 95%

On Line Oriented Flight Training day (LOFT), a small man sat in on the simulator flight briefing. He didn't wear required identification which was immediately a red flag. When I asked to be introduced, he gave his name as "Jerry" and said he was giving Jim Fincher, our instructor, a company checkride. Somehow, neither seemed true.

Making small talk before the testing began, smiling all the while, I commented in a manner I thought acceptable, trying to set my mind at ease by finding out who the interloper was: "I didn't think you were with the FAA because you're dressed so handsomely."

He was wearing a pale green suit with a paler lavender shirt and tie. It was tasteful but out of character for pilot checkrides. Suddenly, Jerry vehemently snarled with his lips drawn back from his teeth: "If the fourth floor came over and saw your blue suit, they might send you home!" This explosive reaction silenced the room.

It positively was an overreaction, and to what? - an attempt to find out who was monitoring my checkride, a principal part of the yearly set of hurdles to continue employment as an airline pilot. I thought it would be good to know this man and why he was present on this very important day.

He immediately jumped up and escorted the instructor from the room. They were gone for perhaps ten minutes while we three crewmembers sat in silence, wondering and speechless. I felt a terrible knot clenched in my stomach; what if these fellows were compromised by my comments? My throat closed. I eased my fear by reminding myself that his response was inappropriate, an excuse to become angry at nothing, assert authority, a common tactic used to terrify employees by management at Delta Air Lines.

When the two returned, the effect of the incident hung heavily in the air. I ran through a list of possibilities. Was this backlash from my letter to Aldridge? Was this what I could expect from the check department every time I appeared for testing?

Suddenly, the instructor was asking me a question ending with my middle name. I'd seen my paperwork and it listed only my middle initial of "B." How interesting he would know my middle name,

Bliss. Perplexed by this, the small man's presence, and vehemence, I didn't hear the instructor's question.

"What is the max flaps extension speed for fuel dumping capability at flaps 4 to 22?" I dared not ask him to repeat it. I knew the answer was V2+20 knots, but somehow couldn't make myself say it. I was ominously silent, a response not so much to the question but to the situation.

Missing the answer precipitated a blast from the instructor about knowing limitations on the airplane before the oral exam scheduled for the following day. I nearly walked out, but I wasn't ready to throw in the towel, yet.

✈

The Lockheed 1011 simulator was unstable in pitch and roll, just as it was in my previous checkrides, making it difficult for the instructors to know if the instability was caused by the machine or pilot technique. This anomaly was frequently taken into consideration, counted on by the airline, and used to advantage. I figured since the captain flew the majority of the time and dealt with this problem as I did, the instructors wouldn't be able to pin bad pilot technique on me. In the end, reluctantly, Instructor Fincher admitted our LOFT was not just good, but *very good*. I felt somewhat redeemed, but from what, their attempt at humiliation? At the conclusion of the LOFT syllabus, practice for the proficiency check was difficult because of the sim's instability, with the result that a lot of maneuvers were best accomplished by hand flying.

The captain got to practice over and over. I got to make one, one-engine out take-off. The instructor reluctantly granted my request for a second one – this was supposed to be practice for the proficiency check - audibly sighing his exasperation, and one VOR/DME approach to Runway 27L at Atlanta, and a missed approach single engine out. That was it. I didn't fly for twenty minutes out of a four-hour flight session.

That night I was on edge and unhappy; unhappy at the prospect of aptly balancing presentation of my skills with the company's intimidation. I prepared as best I could, knowing we would have the same simulator the next day for our all-important proficiency check. When dawn came, I was uncharacteristically worried and tired.

During the oral, the new instructor tried to build the airplane, piecing it together like a puzzle. One piece here, one piece there. He skipped from one system to the next with little continuity. Twice, the captain asked the new instructor what exactly was he asking.

During the oral exam, I was asked all but a few of the questions. It was as if the new instructor had been instructed to do so, or, he was afraid the captain might not be able to answer. I stumbled several times because I mixed the words of my answers with the inner conversation I was having about conspiracy. Thought processing was difficult with this strain and the result was that I appeared unprepared, and the outcome of the check was nearly disastrous. I was distracted wondering what agenda had been prepared but how could I explain any of this to my captain?

The instructor concentrated mostly on the flight engineer's panel as many evaluators do even though we were pilots. Our primary concerns were with understanding and operating pilot items on the forward and overhead panels and not systems reserved for operation by the flight engineer. This evaluator loved to teach, as well as question, and he knew the airplane well.

The proficiency check went fairly well for both of us. When it was over, the instructor debriefed and excused the captain. As he sat down across the table from me, I suddenly realized that I'd stopped breathing. He began by commenting not on the fact that I'd stumbled during the oral but that the preceding day's instructor had "written terrible things in your training folder."

I was speechless. That instructor had not given me much of a chance to demonstrate anything. I wondered if he wrote the same in the captain's file. Probably not, no mention was made of it, and since we both knew the answer through our steady gaze, I didn't bother to ask the question. I listened and realized anything I said would make no difference. Somehow I'd managed to salvage the proficiency check with my performance during the oral by knowing some of the more difficult answers to questions, and relying on my considerable flying ability to pull me through the practical test. Since the instructor of the day before verbalized "very good" on the LOFT to both the captain and me, apparently a very different remark from what he put in my training file, it made me once again doubt the accuracy, and the integrity of the check department.

Crews met cordially in an area of international pilot operations before flight. Departures for Europe were typically in the afternoon, and Atlantic crossings were usually flown at night so passengers could arrive at European destinations in time to begin a new business day. Cubicles bearing destination names were areas assigned to crews for flight planning. Dressed in full uniform, I always remained standing and smiling with closed lips, introducing myself to the captain and second officer as the first officer on the flight. At the captain's invitation I took a seat to do the flight planning. We got out plotting charts - maps of either the Atlantic or Pacific Oceans as applicable - and drew course lines with headings, made notes of elapsed times between check points at calculated speeds over particular distances, then accurately estimated our fuel burn. Allowing for headwinds or tailwinds, approximately halfway across the ocean we pinpointed an *equal time point*, a place in space approximately halfway across the ocean where, if anything major were to happen before we would turn around, or after, we would continue. In conjunction with our assigned dispatcher, we determined one diversionary airport, or more if necessary. Weather and proximity were important.

We meticulously reviewed the flight plan, noting unusual weather, turbulence, and position of the North American jetstreams that followed the leading edge of the polar front. Usually we were flight-planned to take advantage of associated high speed winds but would enter these rivers of fast moving air from the southern, smooth side only if forecast to have little turbulence. This evening we were flight planned to have an increased ground speed of approximately 70 knots inside the core.

En route in the Lockheed 1011-500, we were busy with position reports, checking that our navigation was accurate by using the #1 and #2 Inertial Navigation Systems in concert for primary navigation, and the #3 INS as the check of the other two. By inserting the initial latitude and longitude of our departure gate at the terminal, we added waypoints as checks, and ended with the arrival airport position. Additional information such as forecast winds en route, temperatures, and performance criteria used by the Flight Management Computer to calculate the exact speed at which to climb, and to which desired altitude, made flight planning more efficient. When all the ingredients were complete, checked and re-checked, the flight progressed like a pageant. All that was needed to complete this plan was a clearance from FAA's Air Traffic Control to comply with this most efficient profile designed by company operations. Unless a traffic conflict existed, we were usually "Cleared as filed, flight planned route." Initially assigned altitudes progressed via step-climbs synchronized with weight reduction because of fuel burn-off. Our final cruising altitude took optimum advantage of winds.

Some of the men I flew with were gentlemen. Usually southern gentlemen, from old families, and after more than two hundred years, still tilled the family farm. These confident men were not the ones I had problems with, as they often had daughters interested that they flew with a woman. They politely asked questions. They took pride in doing a good job, and were interested that I perform well, too. Sometimes, we socialized by touring or having dinner. Our goals were mutual, and our association was built on respect.

The other men I flew with were not gentlemen, though an act of congress designated them as such when they were commissioned as officers in the military. Flying the big jets was what they did and who they were; their entire persona was wrapped up in it. They were nothing without this job and were more than chagrined to discover a woman doing the same. One frequently asked question was: "What on earth does your husband do?!" They seemed to lack substance: good breeding and manners. Sometimes, I found myself scheduled with one of the good old boys. While some captains tilled their fields on days off from flying, this group tilled their politics. They were quick to let me know their limited version, and to exercise their command. Whether they decided to collectively treat me in this manner because I was the only female they flew with on the 1011, or because they were aware of my Lorelei letter, they wouldn't converse with me except for professional exchanges. They preempted actions on my part and spoke only with the second officer in conversation, usually accompanying him to bars and other places crudely described in my presence.

One captain I endured on two different occasions was Don Stone. Each time we flew together we were scheduled for one of Delta's longest trips to Europe on the 1011: Stuttgart, Germany, with an intermediate stop in Amsterdam. The eight to nine-hour flights through the wee hours of the night, the complexity of approaches and departures at foggy Amsterdam, and the two-hour wait on the ground there, possibly ending with the NDB, non-precision approach at Stuttgart, made for a rough night. Often this last airport was in east traffic configuration during inclement weather. The approach was from near Baden-Baden, down the windy side of a cliff at the edge of the Black Forest to a landing on the 1011's shortest allowable runway of 7000 feet. Sometimes the surface was icy and gave the anti skid system a good work out. Sometimes, I held my breath when the captain was flying, as the end of the down slope runway rapidly approached.

Impressed that the company operated such a large plane as if it was a tiny Cessna, it was a couple of years before the approach procedure was changed to one with more precision and the runway lengthened by several thousand feet.

Khoutek and Hale-Bopp comets were not the only entertainment in the evening sky. Captain Don Stone had me fly the arrival and approach into Amsterdam at such high speeds that we barely made crossing restrictions of altitude, speed, and time. He constantly chided me to go faster. It took more intense concentration and effort than normal but, fortunately, I made sure I was rested before these flights, had a good grasp of the aircraft, and could fly to this extreme.

Flying all night, then stopping for two hours in Amsterdam before continuing on to Stuttgart was difficult because my body wanted to sleep after the pressure was off. After shutting down at the gate, Stone complimented my performance thumbs up, and by bobbing his head up and down. I was surprised by this concession.

I wondered what the rush was for, so I would make mistakes? Since I hadn't made one, I guessed it was for nothing. Hardened by this treatment, I didn't expect recognition of any kind. I showed a faint smile as he acknowledged my success, but then I looked away. Sadly, I remembered when I used to smile often, but now emotion connected with smiling seldom negotiated my lips. I took a deep breath and sighed over this momentary departure - thumbs up - from his loathing. Again, I became as expressionless as those who must endure patiently. Across the ocean, through the night, he allowed no breaks. I was sure he would not tolerate a snooze request permitted by the operations manual. I never bothered to ask, much less depart the cockpit for physiological reasons. While he remained turned in his seat conversing with the second officer, I stared straight ahead into the starry sky, imagining the sound a swish of a comet's tail might make.

In conversation, the captain discussed information from a clutch of 1011 captains that met Sundays at a lakeside restaurant. What indelicate forms did their camaraderie take? I shuddered to think of the topics. When it was Stone's turn to fly into Stuttgart, he didn't demand the same peak performance of himself, but then, why should he?

✈

As the summer of 1996 melted into regularity, I still commuted from SLC to Atlanta to fly international trips. The revenue passengers filled even the midnight flights, making a ride in the cockpit on the little, vertical jumpseat of the Boeing 757 an "uncomfortable must" to get to work. I was a privileged guest allowed to ride up front only because I was a Delta line pilot. Privy to their operation and conversations, I was also captive when they chose malice. Still earning "A" level salaries, it would seem they had nothing to be unhappy about but found ways to complain.

One evening the subject of conversation was Suzy Q. I was quiet but attentive in the darkened back of the 757 cockpit. Evidently, this evening's captain was the same union representative who accompanied her into the simulator the last morning I'd seen her. In company uniform of navy black and white, I hadn't recognized him. He lacked his identifying prop, the red bow tie.

"Whatever happened to Suzy Q?" Though this question was directed at the first officer on duty who shook his head, I knew it was intended for me. I'd heard from her once - she *had* passed her checkride, though her call to me had been to commiserate about the treatment she'd heard I was getting from management – but that was years ago.

He continued, "The last time I saw her was when she took her sim check. I haven't heard anything further from her or about her since. I don't know if she's even still flying."

I remained silent.

He added: "Management seemed to have an agenda for her." With this enlightening comment, I reminded myself that this captain chose to represent the tenets of ALPA in a company that had held off the pilots union for half a century. He admitted to a company agenda though I thought he was obtuse in doing so. To wave a red flag, flaunt his beliefs, seemed ill advised. The only other person I knew that had made an open allusion to a company agenda for women pilots was Bill Lake. He'd done it during his deposition where he'd perjured himself.

✈

Arriving in ATL about 5:30 AM eastern time, riding the airport train to the shuttle area, I took the bus to any of a dozen hotels that commuting pilots, at their own expense, used to rest before trips. Delta discouraged commuting, preferring that pilots live in the immediate vicinity of their home base. Commuting presented a whole list of potential hazards to arriving on time for a scheduled departure, among them, a stressful wait for a possible empty seat, with the potential of missing one or more commute flights. Crew scheduling knew the game: if a commuting pilot called in sick because he couldn't get to work, he would be visiting the chief pilot. If a cockpit jumpseat was available, it was reserved by preferential order, the commuting pilot could schedule to ride it. Designed for observation of the flight crew conduct of the flight by the FAA, the jumpseat on the 757 and 767 were miniscule tabs not designed for comfort. But base openings and closures were so common in the competitive airline world that if a person wanted any stability or financial gain from property ownership, commuting was the only answer.

If I was lucky, my reserved room was still available when I stepped up to the registration desk. Often, rooms in town were hard to find, as ATL is a popular destination, especially for conventions. Sometimes I arrived to find my reservation at crew rates had been overridden by the hotel's desire to charge "normal customers" a higher price. When this happened, no rooms were available anywhere near the airport. So I'd catch the shuttle back to the airport to catch the train to sleep in a recliner in the pilots' lounge until "show time" in the early afternoon, one-and-a-half hours before an international departure. This made for a tired start on a strenuous, through-the-night flight. The result was I lost not one, but two nights' sleep out of three.

Captain Rebo turned me into the chief pilot for momentarily dozing off. I had felt my eyelids flutter as I reached up to turn the rotating beacon on as we pushed back from the gate. I was unlucky to have him see this. I guessed he didn't have anything else to complain about and felt he shouldn't miss a lick. I advised this captain in the planning cubicle before our flight that when I arrived in Atlanta at 5:30 AM, my hotel room had been given away. He wasn't sympathetic because he lived in Atlanta. There was a convention in town, there were no more rooms available anywhere I checked, and I checked a lot, making telephone calls standing in front of the bank of hotel wall phones in the arrivals tier of the terminal.

I tried sleeping in the pilot's lounge for a few hours before departure, but it was a fitful rest due to the activity of pilots coming and going. But what could I do? I was already in Atlanta; the company knew that since I'd been authorized to ride the jumpseat.

To report myself as sick to crew scheduling, even though I was very tired, would have raised questions. I toughed it out and tried to stay awake. Time zone travel is distressing to mind, body, and spirit. Besides, I hadn't reported in sick for over five years.

When we were delayed at the gate for a fuel boost pump repair, we had to sit, ready, in our pilot seats for more than an hour. In the warm afternoon sun and comfortable, quiet surroundings, it was easy to relax. On pushback, Captain Rebo caught me struggling for a few seconds to keep my eyelids from blinking. This may have been the only time I saw both his eyes looking at the same thing at the same time, his pupils concentrated into little points. I wondered how he passed his flight physicals with those eyes. One looked here, the other there.

En route, when the flight was progressing well, I commented that I'd read all Pat Conroy's books, especially liking *The Prince of Tides* and *The Great Santini*. Conroy came from the same town the captain mentioned during introductions as his hometown. I couldn't understand why he took umbrage but he did. He bitterly retorted: "Conroy tells family secrets to sell books." During the flight, a flight attendant pulled me aside and whispered excitedly that she recognized him from her town, and that he and his brothers were legend with their many marriages. Their marital behavior was the stuff that filled pages of adventurous romance novels. No wonder he was sensitive to exposure, certainly he would be if he knew I was writing this book, but then I remembered, pilots don't, as a general rule, read. They scan magazines, trade journals, and computer readouts. They look at pictures. *The Captain's Coloring Book* at Western was a humorous allusion to this fact as the entire book depicted in pictures what could have been text. Pilots do not generally peruse anything so involved as a novel. To do so, might require a lengthy attention span, taking time to sort out a complex plot, and contemplate new ideas in a venue where they are not the center of attention.

Glaring at me with his one good eye while the wild one erratically looked everywhere else, I wondered what he'd done to get that look. A friend whose dad emphatically gestured at mealtime with a fork ended up with a dead eye. Another with a glass eye kept taking it out and losing it. He'd call asking for help in finding it and I'd tell him, "Okay, we'll keep an eye out for it."

Did Rebo have only one good eye when he started flying? Gaining commercial certification must've been a hassle. One eye bounced around while the other stared. With Rebo's wild eye, how did he get this job? To allay any concerns, and he seemed to have more than a few, he perched on the edge of his chair, watching my every move. I made sure my flying was textbook, and my comportment beyond reproach, though it was somewhat unnerving to function with him hovering, vulture-like, over my shoulder.

He, of course, did not permit me a sleep break, the power nap granted by the company. I gave him no reason to fault me, but this didn't stop him: he made a point to write me up for sleeping when all I did was take a couple long blinks, even though I let him know how tired I was at the beginning of the flight. If it had been one of the boys instead of me, I was certain Rebo would have, without question - or writing a report - assumed the other pilot's duties in addition to his own, and simply let him sleep.

It was by coincidence I even found out Rebo had turned me in to the chief pilot's office. In passing by the two men in the pilot's lounge, the chief pilot commented: "You're having a bad spring." He was looking at a report and conversing humorously with Rebo. They looked at me out of the tops of their eyes with conspiratorial grins on their faces.

The comment of my "having a bad spring" left a question mark hanging in the air, but I was able to deduct what went on between them from Rebo's smug expression. The longer he looked at me, the wilder his wild eye got. I knew immediately what had happened:

Rebo turned me in for sleeping on duty. It was foolish to think there might be recourse or even an opportunity to explain why I slipped off for a moment. In the blink of an eye, my perception of chief pilot Jeff Ricketts dramatically changed. For the chief pilot to even acknowledge such petty behavior was a good indication that he'd changed his previous stand to support me. I felt sorry for him, and my heart sank knowing that now I had no one to turn to in administration. I passed on by without speaking.

Then I had to drop a trip because my passport expired and the replacement hadn't arrived. I could have just called in sick, but I wasn't sick. My conscience wouldn't allow me to do so. When I tried to explain to the same chief pilot, Jeff Ricketts, that passport service was one day too late returning my renewed passport, though I'd planned the renewal to fall during a "window" between international trips with the speedy help of overnight Fed Ex, he became irrationally angry and lectured me that he would indeed be dropping my next trip and without pay, about $7000. I expected this might happen, but I didn't expect to also be in the doghouse for the government's slow response to my renewal.

Captain Ricketts now seemed anxious to build a case against me. Why, it was easy to guess. Something or someone had scared him, or, maybe the light in his head had come on. I'd wondered how long it would take for him to catch on that asserting support of me would be disastrous for *his* career. *You can always tell a marine, but you can't tell him much.* I certainly appreciated the gesture but worried that his loyalty would come to no good. The two small incidents noted here were hardly of any consequence, but now he was determined to make them important. I figured I was strong enough to withstand *some* criticism. The unfortunate part was that *now* he decided to hold things against me when he had the power to just ignore them. *Now* he had excuses convenient to siding with a management intolerant of me, someone who had pointed out injustice. I wondered how he dealt with his conscience. I kind of felt sorry for him. Because of his initial lapse, his declared support of me, I was sure he would be irrevocably held in suspension by the company and wouldn't progress further than his present job. That was, providing he still had a job.

I'd heard of pilots missing trips - because they got their trip dates mixed up, or flying through assigned altitudes, inattentive, or getting off-course far enough to be a hazard to and reported by other traffic. One pilot, a former Western pilot and someone I'd known for years, leaned more and more in the direction of a malcontent. He flew right on through his altitude in spite of warning chimes. Another time, he got off-course over the north Atlantic due to an incorrect entry in the navigation system. I wondered, *what's come over him?* Did he still have merger mania, as so many pilots did, allowing himself to be distracted when his full attention should have been on his flying? I'd known him and his wife, Cassie, since they were dating, and now they'd been married for years. The company hadn't fired the crew, but at one point suspended them for several months until the FAA gave back their flying licenses. What else could the company do? A pilot can't fly without a license. The inconsistency of it was that I knew the company wouldn't waste any time in firing me, and in fact let me know how alert they were for such lapses while they coped with and endured blunders from *some of the boys.* The double standard was alive and well at Delta Air Lines.

Site for the 1996 summer Olympics was Atlanta, Georgia, and John and I traveled there to specifically attend the equestrian activities, hoping to lend support to our friends in competition. We took our ranch manager from Utah, Janice Homan, with us and met our New Zealand friends there. Blyth Tait rode horses syndicated by my girlfriends, the Kiwi Belles, and hopefully he'd accept our invitation to come to Zephyr Ranch in Utah to give a three-day event clinic on our course that fall. We partied with our Kiwi friends and watched Blyth win the gold medal on a New Zealand Thoroughbred, Reddy Teddy, owned by Blyth's proud father, Bob.

Janice and I took advantage of an invitation to a wine and cheese party at the home of Linda Stolle in Social City. Rolling green hills and huge broadleaf trees were a pastoral backdrop for her farm. The horses grazed in lush pastures behind dark board fences. Linda held the party in her comfortable tack room. Amid the rich leather of saddles and bridles, we discussed the possibility of her taking one of my young horses, training it in Dressage, and selling it on the East Coast.

Linda was tall, very blond, and had the enviable long legs desirable in a Dressage rider. Her abilities were well thought of and not only in Dressage. She imported young horses from Europe, trained them, and successfully won championships. Without knowing any other language than English, she independently studied and learned German well enough to qualify as a language speaker at Delta Air Lines, graduating to international status as a flight attendant. Linda also wanted to see the world. Our mutual zest for adventure and love of horses gave us much to talk about, even between trips. The result was we flew together, socialized with the cabin crews, and frequently spoke on the telephone.

When she found I planned to attend the Olympics, she invited me to her party and we engaged in a conversation about sharing horses. I made her an offer to which she replied, " I'll talk your offer over with my husband and see what he thinks, but I'm sure he'll love the idea."

"I think it could work well for both of us," I said. It would give my breeding farm exposure on the east coast. I'll raise the horse to 3 ½ years old and then you take him from there. After subtracting the initial costs, we can split the profit 50/50. I'll be happy to write a contract for you to consider."

"I'm interested and excited." She flashed her radiant smile. "It would be great not to pay the expensive freight costs of $7000 to import young horses from Europe. It'll be a savings for us and a chance to make some good money."

Returning home to Utah after Blyth won the gold medal in the three-day event, I telephoned Linda to follow up on our earlier conversation. There had been newspaper articles about a Delta - EVA pact and I understood her husband negotiated maintenance contracts for Delta. He was presently in Taiwan.

"I'll talk it over with him as soon as he returns. I'll call you. I can hardly wait to get started."

I remembered eagerly awaiting Linda's call and our new piece of business. Weeks went by and she didn't call. Months went by. I realized she was never going to call. Why didn't Linda call when she was so excited to begin our business association? It may have been paranoia, or just intuition, but it gave me a sinking feeling. I knew her husband was in Delta management, a vice president or something. Had he checked and found something which precluded him from encouraging our relationship? I never saw or heard from Linda again.

✈

Timely verbal navigational position reports punctuated the radio silence. Expressed as a named intersection in an alphabetical sequence along our track, the report was made to AIRINC over crackling high frequency radios and forwarded to Air Traffic Control in lieu of radar coverage ashore. Aircraft performance checks and fuel burn were noted and logged. Rumbling across the oceans for hours, I came to recognize an uncomfortable feeling. I felt it most when the full moon rose. An imaginary drum roll sounded as the huge disc with the smiling face passed through the tinted atmosphere at the horizon to hang suspended in the black sky. I felt it when the aurora borealis undulated around the airplane like gold lame curtains, suddenly vanishing, chased away by a rush of geotropic winds. Inside, I felt a moaning dissonance of dark music that built suspense every time I stepped foot on Delta property.

A haunting awareness of a conspiracy became my eerie companion. While crossing the oceans, I had lots of time to consider when my troubles began. Certainly, it was when I, fulfilling a childhood dream, a former Western Airlines woman, aspired to fly Delta's coveted Lockheed 1011 internationally. Add to that, standing up for myself by threatening a lawsuit to end the harassment of repeated checkrides and loss of records verifying that I'd passed each one. The embarrassment of pilots who stumbled and bungled their depositions making them see themselves more clearly, provoking anger and future reprisals against me to salve their egos; the sudden disappearance of Captain Chicago from the chief pilot's office, and eleven 1011 captains in Salt Lake City following their depositions; the meteoric rise of ambitious Captain Bill Lake, former Western pilot and virtual unknown at Delta until our altercation on the 1011, where I stood up for myself, to MD-11 program manager in Los Angeles. My Lorelei letter asking about the ethics of the company, and other information chatty Captain Ray Clearance may have divulged in his inquisition by management but was left out of my letter. Asking about these misgivings in disbelief had not made me popular because to right these wrongs, management would have to change its tactics. I was completely at odds with an administration entrenched in predatory tactics handling company-employee relations. I debated even trying to continue my tenure at the airline as the odds were so against me. I could leave the fray and retire as 1011 first officer, forever contending with the frustrating feeling of having come this far and quitting, or I could bid a captain's position knowing I would most certainly be a target for professional humiliation.

Passing azure glaciers so dense that red light absorbed from the color spectrum reflected back as blue, my career passed before my mind's eye. In vignettes lightly imposed on the forward windows, watching them was somewhat like looking through water. I reviewed the years I'd spent in aviation, the good things in life I was lucky to have, and the things I'd never have. Occasionally, a tear escaped from the corner of my eye. Unnoticed, I smoothed it away and tightened the muscles around my stomach.

Captain Bill Lake was now appearing in the ATL pilot lounge located under the international concourse with some regularity. The MD-11 program he'd been supervising moved from the Pacific *theatre* (a term used by the military suggestive of war, which I would have immediately changed at the airline, but was offensively adopted by management to describe an area of passenger travel) with its long distance legs to the more amenably short legs of the Atlantic. When Delta purchased the aircraft from McDonnell Douglas, the range capability was *only adequate* to operate on the long, over water legs of the Pacific. Clearly, the shorter legs across the Atlantic to service the European markets were ideal for the airplane, but most senior captains preferred European flying on the L1011. This was the way the airline was set up, and many of the pilots retired as the equipment began changing.

Soon other former Western pilots I knew and had not seen for a long time began showing up in ATL. They were pilots I'd flown with on other airplanes, and we had shared a comradely friendship in the past. I was glad to see them coming down the hall or across the lounge, but as I approached I realized they were not glad to see me.

"Hello." I smiled at the first pilot, offering my hand. "I haven't seen you in awhile, how have you been?" Instead of a returned smile or the extended hand I expected, their body language showed a reluctance to even be seen speaking with me. They turned this way and that, looking concerned that someone might be watching.

What at first seemed puzzling was not a mystery for long. These men came from Bill Lake's old base in Los Angeles. I wondered why, after seven years, he even gave me a thought. It revealed the intensity of his ego. I remembered how long he'd pursued Greg Gertz. For all I knew, Lake might still be after him. It could only mean one thing; Lake was guilty of all I suspected of him and probably more. Disseminating information about me in an effort to influence, hurt, and discredit me, not only with Delta management but with my contemporaries. It didn't matter that Captain Lake blatantly perjured himself during his deposition years ago, though I was sure the report was available to management, it was astonishing that Delta would reward this behavior by promoting him to program manager on their newest airplane, the MD-11. He'd lied before; maybe Lake lied to his fellow pilots. Maybe Lake just conveniently lied.

In a surprising ambush with Pritchard Dolby leading the charge, Delta fired Lorelei for alleged abuse of sick leave. She was out with chronic knee problems. For nearly twenty years, the two airlines had been unable to fail her on checkrides. For nearly twenty years, they'd brutalized her at every turn. When they weren't able to fail her, though they really tried, the legal department found a loophole, and crawled through it.

Lorelei immediately retaliated with further legal action. She advised the Equal Employment Opportunity Commission of her plight. When they contacted me for complicity, I asked Lorelei that I not become involved in their inquiry when they wrote asking for my testimony, presumably in court. She complied with my wishes. Upon my husband's urging and advice, I wrote to Delta's legal department letting them know I was not a part of this inquiry. In retrospect, doing so was probably a mistake because it alerted them to the fact that I might be considered valuable in her case against Delta. Ultimately, I'd probably need EEOC's help, too, though at the time I hoped to salvage my career and get on with the business of flying.

I got a response from Delta's legal department. Ironically, their attorney for matters concerning harassment was a female. I wondered, if she lost the case with Lorelei, would she still have her job? It might have been a bitter pill to swallow, a lascivious travesty, and so like Delta to appoint a woman to defend against women. I was imbued with a sense, not of Delta's cleverness or humor, because there was little humor in what was to come, but of its twisted ways. The female attorney offered counseling and representation. It was an unnerving turn and a problematic one. Was I being invited to the other side?

From the day she was fired, Lorelei's lawyers, the EEOC, and ALPA representatives kept my phone busy for one complete business day and part of many others. I found myself getting irritated by all the calls because they further involved me in her problems, yet I hadn't spoken to her but twice, or laid eyes on Lorelei in more than five years. The answers I gave to their questions were perfunctory, brusque and explicit just to get them off my back. "It's too late, isn't it?" I remembered almost snarling because with all their resources,

Delta managed to find a way to finally fire her. "She has no recourse! She's been fired!" I didn't want to be an accessory. It was only jeopardy for my career.

Towards the end of a long and troubling interview with her attorney, when asked how Lorelei could possibly be so perfect, was there *anything* unfavorable they should know in preparation for her defense, I gave them cannon fodder. One was the necessity of grounding flight fundamentals that most likely were accomplished by her considerable flight experience gained through the years, and the other, was the dislike and mistrust she held for most male pilots and they, reciprocally, for her.

This response produced the effect I wanted: the law office got off my back. Shocked their client might not be perfect as they initially presumed; they reassessed their case and concluded that I was not an ally. I sorely wanted to become *uninvolved*.

Lorelei, one never to mince words or beat around the bush, let me know in person, and in no uncertain terms, that she was not happy with my comments. She couldn't comprehend that I needed defense. I felt terrible for the lonely moments of sadness and depression she must have endured over losing her career, but with her gone, I felt the guns turn on me.

Subsequent to her firing, Lorelei engaged the company in a long legal battle. Delta demanded that court take place in Atlanta when Lorelei lived in northern California. No longer entitled to pass privileges, flying her legal entourage to Atlanta for court was expensive. Accommodating them was expensive. Months into litigation, she finally settled just as she was about to lose the last of everything. In a stunning expose`, the conclusion of the court was that she was basically fired: *not* for misuse of sick leave, the initial reason given, *not* for incompetence as a pilot, per common gossip, but *by* rumor and innuendo. It was unbelievable!

Much as a family who covers abuse beneath veils of secrecy, the Delta family was - is - hysterical about protecting its public image. Lorelei agreed *never at any time* to disclose details of her settlement *or* her career. Of unflinching character and true to the end, she has kept this promise which, though I pressed her for details, even included me. I fear this final stipulation is not healthy.

✈

Returning to my base in ATL after Lorelei's surreptitious departure from the airline, I passed through the administrative offices on some colloquial matter. My chief pilot, Jeff Ricketts, sat not at his desk, but at an empty conference table. Hands folded, he wore a sad and troubled face. When he saw me, he turned to the wall. I tried to speak with him, I wanted to ask if he knew about Lorelei, but he wouldn't respond, making himself unapproachable. Realizing he postured for me to go away, I did, and never attempted to contact this man again.

Shortly after, Ricketts either left or was removed from his position as international chief pilot to work in paperwork on the fourth floor of Delta's corporate headquarters in Atlanta. Housed in a group of red brick buildings and surrounded by old, established broadleaf trees, it was affectionately dubbed Ft. Widget because of Delta's logo. I hoped Ricketts found some peace of mind. Surprisingly, Captain Jon Windham, a fine gentleman, replaced him. He was an experienced chief pilot, acquired with Delta's purchase of some of Pan Am.

✈

Initially, I thought it might be my imagination. But no, since Lorelei's departure and Lake's arrival, I was treated consistently more poorly, and decided that I wasn't imagining it. Little by little, trip-by-trip, I was being shut out and isolated. My voice was not acknowledged when I offered information of a professional nature. The responding looks scathingly told me, "What could you know?"

With attempts at pleasant conversation rebuffed, my diplomacy found no takers. If this happened only once I could ignore it, but when it occurred time after time, trip after trip, month after month, and finally, year after year, the effect was devastating. I began to recognize paranoia and defensiveness in my repertoire. Where nothing frightened me before, nearly everything frightened me now. As my confidence waned, the impression I made was diminished also.

I felt cut off, sitting alone for hours and hours in the right seat on international flights, immediately chided by captains for the slightest assertion. This chipped away at my veneer, compromised my buoyancy no matter what assurances I gave myself to the contrary. Hostility took its toll and I became passively resistant. My weight increased as my serotonin vanished even though I resorted to eating only the soup and salad and not the entrées offered from first class on international flights.

✈

Arriving back in Atlanta at the end of a trip, Delta's vice president, Pritchard Dolby, leaned against a wall as I deplaned. Recognized only by me, his stare was quite unsettling. At first I wasn't sure why he was there, and the third time this occurred, I walked up to him, smiled, and said, "Good morning." He drew his lips back exposing his teeth. Then a sound something like a growl started coming out. He looked like a cartoon character: a little bearcat with dark 1950's style glasses, an overbearing contrast to his delicate features, which I would have found humorous if I hadn't grasped his intent. I waited for him to say something, anything discernable. He continued this facial impropriety while I continued smiling. I had to let him know it wasn't working; I wasn't intimidated. Finally I asked, "Is there something I can do for you?" After a few pregnant moments while I towered over him and during which he was given ample opportunity to express himself, and didn't, I turned on my heel and left.

I came to expect his presence somewhere in the deplaning area at the end of each flight. I was seldom disappointed. I smiled, shook my head in disbelief that *I* could be so important the vice president of the company would take time to meet my flights; then I'd stride away.

✈

Recurrent training the second year following my Lorelei letter and her firing was a nightmare. It was almost that it took *them* some time to get spooled up for me as I'd expected trouble sooner. Completing the necessary ground subjects of security, crew resource management and L-1011 aircraft systems successfully, I moved on to two simulator sessions. The first one was a LOFT. This half-day session was to be flown with a full crew as specified in the company operations manual. Simulating actual flight experience of particular issues worth review, a scenario was built into a training session that addressed particular concerns or reflected perplexing situations encountered while flying the line. The LOFT allowed the training pilot some practice in flying the simulator after a year away because simulators can either accurately or inaccurately replicate the live control response present in the airplane. A pilot friend once told me that an airline job entailed flying two very different machines: the airplane and the simulator. In preparation for my Proficiency Check the following day, I looked forward to the LOFT and wondered what interesting scenario would be selected.

I arrived to find the new program manager for the L-1011 as my instructor for the LOFT. An engineer was provided for the first part of the session but there were aggressive exchanges between him and his younger, militaristic instructor that were both distracting and troubling. The applicant was over 60 and returning to line flying as an engineer on the 1011 after having flown as captain with Pan Am. The pair soon disappeared to another part of the building.

Then there was no crew. I wondered about this. Where was the captain? I was positive the operations manual stated that the LOFT would be flown with a full crew complement but I didn't have time to look it up as we were immediately in a full testing situation. I was the pilot in this flight scenario, flying solo on a three-pilot airplane.

In a simulated flight on the Lockheed 1011 departing from Kennedy in New York bound for Madrid, Spain, an explosion wiped out an engine and started a fire halfway across the Atlantic. Immediately, smoke filled the cockpit and cabin pressure was lost due to structural damage. Putting on reading glasses, goggles, and my oxygen mask, I declared an emergency. Departing the airway track with a ninety-degree turn to avoid traffic, I began a descent, diverting into Lajes in the Azores midway across the Atlantic. As there were no other pilots present and I got no help from the instructor, I did everything myself. Wearing this equipment and still functioning was unwieldy, especially since the goggles were elevated perhaps as much as an inch out from my cheek. To see properly, I had to lower my head much more than normal, interrupting the smooth motion needed for visual scanning of the instrument and equipment panels.

I handled the emergencies, at times flipping switches across the cockpit with a rolled-up newspaper which happened to be on the floor by the console when I arrived in the simulator. I had to execute the only approach available at the airport, an archaic, non-precision NDB approach culminating in a circle to land on a crosswind runway. Everything worked well for this scenario. I was precise and quick to handle all the duties. I got absolutely no feedback from the program manager.

During our short break the instructor was called from the room. When he returned his expression was changed. Contemplative dark shadows crisscrossed the planes of his face. I wondered at this veil. I got worried for a few moments but quickly reassured myself that his absence and expression were probably due to some issue other than mine.

Resuming my seat in the simulator, we went through the full complement of maneuvers. Between each of them, like commas separating thoughts, there were the red warning lights of wind shear alerts. Occurring with variable wind shifts in direction and velocity over very short distances, and dangerous when encountered close to the ground, these and the accompanying flight director commands of extreme recovery attitudes and power settings associated with wind shear invectives were distracting, especially as they occurred over and over in different regimes of flight. Occurring every few minutes, they lent confusion to difficult situations. One injection of wind shear would be enough to demonstrate my ability to cope with this phenomenon, but continuously repeated every couple minutes with the advent of a new maneuver seemed nothing less than stalking. When the four-hour simulator checkride and two-hour oral exam were over, I felt positive about my performance: I'd flown my ass off and under the most difficult of conditions. Then the program manager made his only comment: "You need more training."

I was speechless. Shocked. I'd never taken additional training in my 21 years with the airlines, always completing checkrides and upgrades in minimum time. No one I'd ever heard of *failed* a LOFT; it was designed to be a training experience. Not only that, I was sure the company operations manual stated that LOFTS were to be conducted with a full crew complement, but at the moment, I dared not assert this until it was verified from a company manual.

The program manager went out of the debriefing room into the hall and summoned a diminutive male. Without the courtesy of an introduction, he scheduled him to give me my proficiency check. The look, then, which passed between them was frightening. Pupils dilated, they held each other in a steady gaze. I could hear dark music from inside me, and the harpies began to moan. Nothing moved except for a growing protrusion in the program manager's groin.

✈

I went to the hotel that night, unhappy and disconcerted by events of the day, especially this last one. The first thing I did was to read from the operations manual that LOFTS were to be flown with all crewmembers present. Why would the program manager violate this policy? I thought of telling my optimistic husband in his nightly call, but he was expecting success, wouldn't understand, besides, I was in this alone, so I abandoned his compassionate resource for now. I could appeal to the pilots' union for an unbiased monitor though the thought was distasteful, and might further anger the program manager insuring reprisal. Or, I could do my best to get through this ugly state of affairs and just get back to flying.

✈

The next day I was given a training session with a different instructor in preparation for the proficiency check with the diminutive male. By his actions and demeanor, I was sure he was not in on the program manager's agenda. He was articulate and professional. My captain in the simulator was my chief pilot's stand-in while he was on vacation, Captain Phil Upland. A little scary, perhaps, but nonetheless, I pressed on, confident that I would do well. Several times during the session, both the captain and the instructor allowed as how they didn't think the program manager should be teaching. "He's too predatory," they proffered at various times. These comments made me wonder again at Delta's choice.

Captain Phil Upland motioned me to step off to the side once we left the simulator. He asked if I would stop by the chief pilot's office to let him know how my proficiency check went. I agreed I would and wondered if he had something in mind for the new program manager.

✈

Next day with the diminutive aviator, my P check oral lasted for two hours while the flight lasted for three. Concerned with the in-depth questioning, I wondered at the negative connotation of his questions. This technique seemed to confuse issues. One of the tenets of good test design is that the test-taker learns from the test. If the test is good, it gives confidence to the student in his or her ability to take information already known and apply it to the new situation with a successful outcome, the highest level of learning. It's always best if information is delivered in a positive manner.

Recalling one of the questions, I remembered thinking there was little positive to be gleaned from his questions. For example: "Explain what pressure the passenger oxygen system operates under."

"The truth is, there is no pressure which moves oxygen through the passenger oxygen system on the Lockheed 1011, rather, individual oxygen generators are activated when an arrow-like squib is fired into them as a result of a loss of cabin pressure, sensing cabin altitude above 14,000 feet. Then the oxygen begins to flow in a gaseous manner," I explained, hoping to dispel this line of questioning.

"Hmmpf," he said.

This was negative teaching because the tester asked misleading questions from the start. Recognizing most of his questions to be of the negative transfer type, trick questions, I was disappointed, and felt this venue to be unfair. Understanding and keeping track of all the different models of the airplane, and at one time there were eleven, with all their various systems was complex enough, some pilots said: second only to the human body.

Had this individual ignored the rigors of psychological test design required of FAA instructors? Perhaps he was not one. Unfortunately, a qualified pilot could instruct in commercial aviation without an instructor's rating where test design and effective teaching were the focus. Or, if he was a certified instructor, perhaps he'd been coached to do the opposite, inserting as much confusion as possible into the questions and the situation, becoming a pawn with little other than his political leanings and flight experience to recommend him.

Once again, I was alone in the simulator but for a silent instructor who occupied the left seat. He read checklists under my direction, but wasn't helpful as a crew would be. He was just a dummy in the seat. I still wondered if I was singled out for harassment, but the extra time spent in practice the day before paid dividends on the proficiency check, though the process was unnerving when I thought about what was at stake: my job.

In the end, the diminutive man passed me, justifying his actions with: "You fly such a nice airplane, I can't *not* pass you." This last passage was puzzling in itself.

I thought: W*ho wouldn't pass with all the extra training?*

"But in six months, be prepared for the oral of your life!"

This sudden outburst surprised me. Had he taken exception to my gentle repartee referencing negative teaching during the oral? "It's better if you fail me," I urged, getting hot, "because that's what you're doing. Let me take the oral and checkride over again *now* instead of in six months!"

"I can't fail you. You fly too well." He scheduled me for an oral in six months anyway.

✈

I decided to take Captain Upland up on his request right away. Pay him a call, something I'd never done, having found the chief pilots' office hostile in the past. On my next arrival in Atlanta, I asked the secretary if I might speak with the chief pilot, thinking I'd reach Captain Upland. His secretary told me he wasn't in, but that administrative superintendent Bette Ewedluvitt was available. As a brief moment of disappointment passed, I decided to speak with her.

Bette was warm and vibrant. I felt comfortable speaking with her. Sitting across from her, I thought, *Surely, she must be aware of the bias in the company,* however, I addressed only the present situation requested by the acting chief pilot. She assured me I wasn't the only person singled out for reconstruction. The new program manager had taken over since the previous one left the office vacant to return to line flying. I guessed from her statement that a new broom swept clean, but I wasn't mollified with this explanation.

"You, as a woman, must be aware of male bias in your job."

She didn't answer right away and I appreciated what was left unspoken as much as what was: "I'm not taking a man's job, so I'm not confronted with some of *your* problems." Her emphasis was on *your*. I wondered if management was coached to avoid the dirty word *harassment* as she verbally maneuvered to avoid it. I decided to give her a wake-up call and proceeded in rapid fire to tell Bette of my experience. I began with Captain Clearance and proceeded on to the mysterious appearance of the vice president at the end of each flight. I included the part about Clearance's summary firing of Western captains.

Over and over she stated, "Clearance should never have said that." She took a lot of notes and mentioned she'd get back to me in a couple of days, before my next trip, as my concerns were important and she needed time to investigate.

During my next trip, I spent hours walking around Paris. Monuments, the Eiffel Tower, and wide boulevards seen in history books and newscasts were a visual treat. The ambiance of a Paris summer night settled in and calmed me. I ate at a tiny seafood restaurant in the artist's sector not too far from Napoleon's tomb. Topping the meal with a crepe purchased from a street vendor, I savored the taste of fresh raspberries. I found the evening balmy and the long walk relaxing; it was 11:30 when I returned to the hotel.

During my walk, I remember feeling elated and with a sense of wonder that my riding instructor, Joe Sevriens, rode in expositions in Paris with the Cadre Noir. How he must have loved the time he spent at Samur! Similar to the Spanish Riding School of Vienna, which General Patton saved from Hitler and the Russians during the Second World War, the Cadre Noir travels around Europe to civic events. The only time I got to see the riders, they were in Munich at the City Hilton. They descended to the lobby, stepping off the elevator in full uniform across from where I waited for our limousine to the airport. Elegant in black uniforms with endless buttons on the jacket and high riding boots, the solitary woman in the cadre and I spoke briefly before departure from the hotel. Compact and sylphlike, she could have been a ballet dancer. Candid, she revealed she was judged by performance, but if not exemplary, she wouldn't last long. As we sped away to the airport, I gazed down the wide boulevards edged with mulberry trees and imagined the Cadre Noir on parade.

Next day, back in ATL, passing through the pilot's lounge to store my flight case, I overheard two pilots talking. One said, "Bette Eweluvitt transferred out of this department a few days ago. She's joined Jeff Ricketts on the fourth floor." This comment stopped me cold. I'd just spent portions of a twelve-hour duty day contemplating my meeting with her. What had she found out? Where would we go from here? I wondered if she'd left any messages and stepped up to a computer and accessed my file. There was nothing. I decided to find out for certain if she had transferred out of the department, so I went to the chief pilot's office, spoke with a secretary who confirmed this news, adding that our new chief pilot, Captain Jon Windham was in his office.

"He's available and you've not met him yet. Would you like to?"

Captain Windham seemed a contemplative sort as we exchanged light pleasantries. As we spoke I explained that his vacation stand-in, Captain Upland, had asked me to stop by his office after recurrent training. Captain Windham was suddenly all ears. I decided to say something about my last recurrent training experience with the program manager, explaining I was scheduled for "the oral of my life" but would have to wait six months to take it. I was sure he understood how agonizing this could be. "It would be better to take this test immediately because I've just spent the last three months preparing."

To my complete surprise he felt as I did: if I needed another oral I shouldn't have been passed on the checkride in the first place. I wondered, if he's compassionate about this proposed oral, would he be a good ear for the rest? For a fleeting moment I considered telling him what I'd told Bette. She *was* the chief pilot's administrative counterpart and now she was gone just like the former chief pilot, Ricketts. In the end, I refrained from revealing anything. I wouldn't want to suddenly find such a fine fellow gone, too!

Unexpectedly, he reached for the phone and informed the training department that my oral scheduled in six months was canceled. I was awestruck beyond words! I could hardly thank him because of the lump in my throat.

$$\twoheadrightarrow$$

I didn't hear anything further about Ray Clearance's proposed cargo company, Ray Air, he'd talked up during his enlightening harangue from Manchester. As punishment for his loose lips, had Delta withdrawn its interest? It was frightening to think I might get him for a checkride someday. And how about his buddies whom he'd promised flying jobs?

Digressing a moment while I checked my computer mailbox, happy after my meeting with Captain Windham, I again noticed that my seniority had been compromised and I had been arbitrarily docked the year I'd taken as leave. I wondered if maternity leave for the young women pilots was factored in the same way? I set this point of the pilot contract aside as I *had* taken my year of leave and perhaps this was the price I was to pay for stepping out. Mentally, I then turned to consider the scheme of pilots operating a successful business.

Few have business acumen. Performers are not usually good administrators. The two characteristics seldom occur compatibly in one person's make-up. To put a bunch of pilots who have spent their lives honing performance skills into a planning, organizing, competitive situation can and usually does result in disaster. Ray Clearance's endeavor seemed ill-fated from the start. Starting an airline was a fast way to turn a large fortune into a small one. Besides, few airlines with longevity carried their owner's names. I thought of his choice of airline name: Ray Air. There were some exceptions of course, such as Rosenbaum Aviation with the endearing call sign, Rosie, but not many.

Turning away from the bank of computers serving as liaison between the company and its employees, I noticed a growing sense of relief even though the daunting reminder of the oral was still on my sign-in screen, in fact, it remained there for another five months for anyone to see, but approaching the day of my cancelled oral, it simply disappeared.

Negotiating little clutches of passengers, I strode down the long terminal corridors. I noticed there was a little bounce in my step. I smiled as I made eye contact with people who turned to watch a woman in uniform. Relief grew to elation as I celebrated the beautiful day and how good it felt to *really* be alive!

Chapter XVI

ALARMS

The same thing that makes you laugh will also make you cry. I felt a great sense of relief and a great sense of loss that I'd soon be off the 1011. The airplane and I were facing retirement. *You're always too young, and then one day, you're too old.* The end of an era: the 1011s were about to be parked in the desert, and at 52, when they went, I considered going, too.

I'd miss flying Lockheed's elegant conveyance across the oceans to destinations I only dreamed of as a girl. I'd perpetuated the exquisite experience of pain and pleasure aboard the 1011 for nearly a decade and broadened my view of the world at the very least. The 1011 would remain among my favorite airplanes. I remember it fondly and miss it, much as one misses a friend.

By retiring early I wouldn't have finished my career; an airline career should end with a pilot flying captain. I submitted my bid for a captain's seat on airplanes I could hold because of my seniority, the Boeing 737 and 727, and eagerly awaited the award.

There were so many positive reasons for upgrading: flying different equipment meant meeting new people. I could be based in SLC, near my home. I'd been commuting nearly twenty years and laughed that I knew someday I wouldn't be able to lift my heavy international suitcase into the overhead bin. That would be the end of my commuting. By upgrading, I'd get to fly in the same territory and to the same places I'd flown all my life in general aviation: I was going home.

✈

My last flights on the 1011 were with retiring Captain Barry Wilkins, and in this final month, we flew back and forth from New York to Amsterdam and Brussels, seeing the sights on layovers. I told him I was about to begin Captain's school on the 737. He expressed concern that I had chosen this airplane and began relating a story.

His daughter was a working pilot with a regional airline in Texas, and widow of a navy pilot who died at the controls of a Grumman S2F. Unfortunately, the crash claimed the lives of innocents, and in an effort to clear his name she dedicated her time to researching the possibility of a servo failure as having been the cause. Reports blamed him for excessive use of rudder resulting in a *hardover*. Her investigations were ongoing.

Because Barry seemed so compassionate and unequivocal, I decided to discuss some of my concerns. "I know my career could be jeopardized, exposing myself to another opportunity for abuse by management. I could just retire at 53 when the 1011 retires. The alternative is contending with the program director on the 1011 in recurrent training next spring. He impressed me as a person who didn't like being thwarted and would go to any extreme for revenge. I doubted I could survive training with him. Having to contend with this sinister person was unquestionably one of the reasons I bid off the Lockheed 1011."

"It's not too far from being washed out of a program to being washed out the door," he advised. "There's no end to the havoc superiors can wreak on little worker-bees, legally getting rid of the wayward ones. The whole process is agonizing. A company might go to great extremes to legally eliminate pilots they feel are undesirable and they usually accomplish this end during training. At Delta, a pilot requiring additional training beyond what the company gives voluntarily, usually two training sessions, to pass an already failed check, usually administered again by those who failed him, the pilot is constrained to sign a letter granting one additional training opportunity. If the pilot refuses to sign, he is cast in limbo: not able to return to his previous equipment, or advance to another plane without further training."

"I've made the decision to upgrade by taking a captain's bid in SLC on the 737, and I'm happy and optimistic about it, but..." I hesitated.

He took the thoughts from my head and put them into words: "But you're wondering if there might be an alternative agenda, an ominous one in store for you. And from what you've told me, there's a good chance..."

"Yes, that possibility exists," I agreed.

"If it was me, to assure my success in the program, I would do everything in my power to absolutely affirm I was prepared and ready for any eventuality. That's what it would take for me to feel good. Eliminate any chance of being failed."

His words made an indelible impression. I decided to attend a 737 school outside the airline. I'd never airplane-schooled at my own expense but decided that I must be prepared way beyond normal to avert any professional humiliation earmarked for me. I intended to pass the course at Delta Air Lines.

I enrolled in an independent school in Miami on my friend Ed Cook's recommendation. Ed taught at the school. Past director of operations for several companies including International Air Service Company, and chief pilot for several like DHL, I'd known Ed for many years since our days teaching on the Japan Air Lines contract with IASCO in Napa.

During July 1997, I studied systems and flew the 737 simulator between international trips for Delta on the 1011. One morning while I was getting ready for class in a hotel near the Miami International Airport, Johnny Versace was shot less than a mile away. This event precipitated calls from John and Ed about my safety. I assured them I was okay.

My instructors in Miami, Fernando Ruiz and Carlos Sanchez, were past directors of operations for South American Airlines Avianca and Tacha, respectively. Versatile, they were able to teach in either Spanish or English, making the program expansive, and them, valuable as instructors. The school offered training in other transports, the 1011 among them. I filed this information away in case someday I needed it.

I recalled a classic picture of Fernando Ruiz standing beside his biplane in the earliest days of aviation. In training, I noted a vast difference between the treatment I received in Miami and the treatment I got at Delta.

My scores were high, the airplane was easy and fun to fly and I received a graduation certificate from the program. I was recommended for the same checkride I was about to attempt at Delta.

✈

Class began August 6, 1997 in Atlanta for a captain's seat on the 737. Staying with Ruth Wilson, the international chief pilot's secretary now retired from Delta, I rented a car and drove each day from her home in Murrieta to attend classes at the training center on the Hartsfield International Airport. Ruth's Bed and Breakfast was the same place we'd stayed during the 1996 Olympics with our friends from New Zealand.

I dearly hoped I'd slip through training unnoticed, but it was not to be. When I was discovered in class, voices in the training department went up an octave. It was good seeing my old friend "Deadstick" Benetta, always charming and helpful. I had an in-depth conversation with him about my misgivings. He was incredulous listening to my story, and to this day I'm not really sure he believed me. I missed having him teach our class, but he only taught the 1011.

I got a decent grade on the final exam, 94%. My aircraft systems oral lasted two hours and forty minutes while classmates' orals lasted as much as 45 minutes. However, a portion of the time on my oral exam was spent discussing the dynamics of a *hardover* on the 737. I was eager to know how to cope with this problem after my discussion with Captain Barry Wilkins because it had been identified as the cause of a number of crashes.

The rudder on the 737 models 200 and 300 was large compared with the rest of the airplane. Used for yaw control, the pilot coordinated foot pressure with aileron deflection fairing the nose of the airplane in the direction of turns. If the leading edge of the rudder redirected the oncoming air, a hardover could occur, and directional control could be lost.

One story, disseminated in ground school classes, recounted a UAL Boeing 737 that took off from DEN, destination Colorado Springs. Only a few minutes en route, the flight path was more an ellipse than the gradual trajectory associated with longer distances, and at or near the top of this ovoid, aircraft control was suddenly lost and the airplane dove to the ground. A mysterious and puzzling explanation ensued: the captain was infatuated with and ultimately rejected by his first officer. He axed her with the crash axe, blood everywhere, and then dove the aircraft straight into the ground.

I was quite shaken by this graphic story, but from the first time I'd heard it, I wrote it off as a smokescreen. The examiner had heard the same story on several occasions. We agreed it was dramatically misleading; we focused our concerns on preventing the hardover by judicious application of the rudders since the airplane was in service flying passengers.

✈

The first day I arrived in the west for completion of my captain's training, I was smiling and confident. With simulators and initial operating experience left to go, I felt reasonable in expecting a different scenario from the one that awaited me.

It was a quick commute from my house to the America West training facility at Sky Harbor in Phoenix. Summer temperatures became moderate as summer faded into fall. I was mystified by the treatment I received from my Delta instructor, formerly with Western, and became aware of an ominous undertone while training in the 737-200 simulator. At first I thought it might be paranoia or my imagination that he was so mean, so openly a misogynist, but as our sessions progressed, I realized his misbehavior was reserved for me. I observed a definite difference in treatment compared with the other pilots in my class.

Left with a sense of dissatisfaction during and after each simulator session with our instructor, Ernie Ubet, I wanted passionately to attribute it to some personality problem or difficulty in his personal life that left him impatient, obnoxious, and anything but a good teacher. But a familiar feeling - those waves of disappointment - washed over me as I struggled to hear past his anger for information pertinent to my progress.

He answered none of my questions. If I persisted and asked again in another way, he stopped dramatically, glared, then directed my inquiry to researching policy or aircraft training manuals. Discussion was out. I was not being taught; information was not delivered and only simple procedures were relayed. I found him at odds, scrappy and confrontational. His expression was a tight grimace. He got so bad during one session, my copilot, Rob, exploded: "We're doing our very best to learn and your nastiness is not helping! Please, at least give us a chance!" I guess my copilot noticed the irritability, too, and couldn't understand the reason for it either.

I turned to Rob then, smiling, thinking that was pretty gutsy of a guy still in his probationary first year. I felt sorry for him that he'd been selected as my flying partner because the way things were going, his grasp might be compromised. But Rob was a marine and I knew he'd survive.

After this outburst, the instructor backed off and things got a little better. This instructor's behavior was strange as he was previously cordial during our contacts out on the line. Why would he choose to be so objectionable now? Recalling my pleasant training in Miami, I knew he'd never have made it teaching in general aviation. No one would pay for such abuse. Having been treated so poorly through the years by some instructors, I was accustomed to listening past the abuse for information and just took this to be the standard at Delta Air Lines.

Finally, we completed the 200's syllabus and I was passed, nay, motioned with a backhanded wave from Ubet, albeit reluctantly, to proceed to the next step: 300-simulator training in SLC.

As I entered a classroom for the initial briefing, I noticed a bear of a man standing off to one side and near the front of the classroom. I nodded and said: "Good Morning."

The response was unprecedented: "If you fail your simulator checkride, those line check airmen will never pass you on your IOEs!"

I looked left and right, then behind me to see if there was anyone else in the room. Certainly this blast couldn't be my greeting! Alas, there was no one present but me. What happened to *joy* from the training department in anticipation of another new captain? It took little more than a few seconds to comprehend that the IOE's he was speaking of were the initial operating experience series of flights, supervised after completing the simulator portion of training and before being released for line duty as captain.

His comment was an interesting one because I've known several captains who initially failed training, eventually passed, and were still checked out to fly as captains on the line. Anyone could have a bad day, a sleepless night, a bout of nervousness before such a serious undertaking. This was the stuff of human nature and any reasonable outfit would not diminish the value of a person who'd spent an entire adult life getting ready for this day. Still, from the force of his delivery, I realized what he said was prophetic. Did he mean I wouldn't be given a chance? Had I been failed before I began?

For a quick moment my adrenaline rose for the fight but I suppressed a counter attack. I thought about responding with something in kind; telling him how ugly he was with his pockmarked skin and big, fat belly. He was anything but appealing in appearance *or* manner. The dark wave of disappointment returned to wash over me as I pulled out a chair. I quieted the wild beating of my heart by taking a deep breath and swallowing. I acknowledged the warnings of my inner voice, a voice I'd come to trust when things weren't going right. This same voice warned me of danger, urged evasive action, or to make changes immediately. Many times this voice has been instrumental in keeping me alive. It helped guide me through smoky mountain passes to drop retardant on forest fires. It helped me let down at night into mountain airstrips to recover critically injured people. Now this voice was telling me to be reserved, behave neutrally and carefully because I was in no less danger.

I packed it in, and in the end, decided to ignore the indelicate and inauspicious greeting by Clyde Bohr, the 737 program director. Obviously, he knew who I was and had anticipated my arrival from his surprising remark. Instantly, I knew I could look forward to a terrible struggle. Lorelei's words returned: "They've had a few years to prepare for you since me. They'll be better organized." I knew their attack would be incisive.

I continued behaving graciously, hoping I drew a contrast to his behavior but I was hardly able to restrain myself. A little voice inside told me to run, but my logical self answered: *Run? Run where? I've nowhere to go. I have to see this thing through... I'll just have to fly my way out.*

Clyde Bohr figuratively sat on my head and bullied me at every turn. He questioned my questions. He puffed-up, clenching and unclenching his fists, and spat his words out like hammers. This aggressive behavior was distracting. He tried to interfere with my ability to think, absorb, or act. I noted that a new instructor in the department who sought "a warm, fuzzy feeling" from his students eyed me with alarm and distended eyeballs whenever he was in my presence. This expression was not lost on me. I felt like Bohr was only a heartbeat away from physically attacking me though I was sure he wouldn't, but I carefully made certain I was in the presence of my copilot, or left the classroom door open behind me.

My copilot got his hair ruffled and shoulder squeezed. I got the cold shoulder and came to expect nothing more. As boss of the simulator program, Bohr asserted at one time that I had no command authority. He didn't know I'd successfully flown captain for other outfits and run companies for years. I smiled at his ignorance but I wasn't about to brag and attempt to enlighten him.

He slowed me down and impeded my progress with his aggressive behavior. With a jaw set in stone and a jerking tic to emphasize his remarks, his method of instruction greatly contrasted the excellent treatment I received just a couple months before in Miami. I felt sparks of hatred growing in my heart. In fact, I was barely able to refrain from cussing him out. Get another instructor? That would be a dead end with Delta. As for his view on the importance of my upcoming checkride, he treated me as if he didn't take my ensuing responsibility seriously. This attitude bothered me most of all. If he wasn't serious about my training, why would he go to such lengths to impede it?

What did he expect me to do? Strut around like a rooster, puffed up and blowing like he did? All that fanfare was unnecessary. Did he expect me to bark orders? Not my style. If that was his perception of command, I was offended by his version. Delta thought command ability was so important they had a seminar called *In Command,* in which prospective captains were taught the company swing, learning to follow procedures and issue orders *Delta style.* What *didn't* happen was encouragement to think independently.

Arriving for my captain's simulator checkride, I knew I had a date with fate. I stepped forward to the meeting, wary but determined. The long shadows of cottonwoods growing near the entrance to the flight training building undulated in the grass, swayed by the afternoon wind, where nature stopped and man began. As I stepped down from my truck onto the pavement, Salt Lake's mountain breezes blew a monotone of disturbing rhythms and, like harpies, were hard to ignore. But I gave only perfunctory attention to them. I felt it best to allay my concerns, but nothing had gone right since I came west to complete training. Was there an agenda designed *specifically* for me? I think if I'd remained in Atlanta I might have had better success. When I was awarded a second captain's bid on the 727 in Atlanta, momentarily I considered what it'd be like to take it. No one would know me there in that department. I would probably have more success – at least until management discovered my maneuver. I wanted to stop commuting and go home. I didn't even consider the change.

I can only surmise the tide of opinion extended not to the real source, the take-over company: Delta, because one does not bite the hand that feeds it; but to a scapegoat convenient for the target of animosity, the bastard child, Western. That cherished and familiar feeling of equanimity eluded me from the first day at Delta. I was certain my attitude was not tainted by paranoia. I was treated cheaply, my person and presence devalued. I tried to insulate myself from the anger, anger for what reason I could only ponder, but not again, and not at this time. The time had come. It was here at last: the test. I felt prepared except for the crushing feeling that something was terribly wrong. Mystery attended each of my careful footfalls on the steps leading to the second floor.

After some time, the oral examination was complete. It was interesting there appeared to be no planned flight. *But there's always a plan. This was strange. We were just going flying!*

Then Dave Pfeel, the designated examiner giving the check, dramatically announced my copilot for the check: Clyde Bohr. The harpies began singing. *Is this bad luck or just luck of the draw? No one gets the program manager for co-pilot.*

With these concerns intact and voices quieted for the moment, the examiner, my copilot, and I stepped into *the box.*

Owned and maintained by Flight Safety International, it was contracted initially by Western for training and when Western became Delta, to its chagrin, the ten year contract was binding. I hoped these hallowed halls and silent walls would remember one of its most dedicated charges. It was from this company I received nearly all my flight training in the sixties, and for whom I worked during that decade culminating in the position of chief pilot.

Darkness enveloped the simulator with an atmosphere so heavy it could only be cut with light from the overhead instrument panels. Little squares and rectangles illuminated primary colors of yellow for caution, red for hazard, blue for operating, and green for status. At different times and for variable reasons, they glowed to indicate function, unreliability, or failure. Bells and horns, whines and whirrs, clicks and clucks, noises which keyed a mental turn to a particular system operation and in a pavlovian way, invited a particular, predictable response.

Bohr and Pfeel horsed around nonstop in the simulator. They talked about their wives and kids, discussed football, and laughed about women. At one point, one called the other on the interphone and said: "Hurry up, there's a big-breasted blonde waiting outside for you." Tomfoolery, perhaps the intent was to relax, at least that would be the predictable excuse, but it served only to make me nervous because their actions were out of control and way past normal. Not only were these incidents unfair distractions, but they negated the importance of my checkride. I felt diminished, and in response, my performance was compromised. I wished I'd invited a union representative along to monitor the checkride, but it was too late, the test had begun.

Several times I interrupted their conversations to tell Bohr to listen up and focus on the task at hand. I reminded them this was my captain's checkride and to quit messing around. I told Bohr to read the checklists faster. He was too slow and there was little time between events. He didn't acknowledge my instructions or comply with the order. I was tempted to stop the checkride, but I knew that for reasons other than sickness or death, it simply was not done.

On taxi out from a simulated Los Angeles terminal to the active runway, a door light came on momentarily, then the light went out. I directed Bohr to the abnormal checklist, parked the plane on a button turnaround, and asked maintenance via company radio to drive out and check the position of the door from the outside. Once assured by maintenance the door was closed, and the "door open" light was extinguished on the panel, circuit breakers checked in, I resumed taxiing to the active runway. On take-off roll, the door light momentarily flashed on once again.

This is a redundant thing for an instructor to do. We continued the take-off, as in the briefing I'd said we would abort only for fire, catastrophe, or engine failure. The previous day my recommending instructor, who appeared much more nervous than I about my forthcoming checkride, for what reason was not clear to me, assured: "That if on departure, the weather and visibility in the simulator was at or near low take-off minimums, that this should be my clue there would be an engine failure upon rotation from the runway." I would have given this little more than casual attention except that he kept repeating and repeating it, until the scenario was played - just as he said - and on the very first take-off. I found myself anticipating an engine failure on rotation. Instead, it was the blasted door light again. It came on and went out. Then the light came on again while climbing out on the Loop Nine, standard instrument departure from Runway 25 right in LAX, heading for Las Vegas. While flying the departure, which departs the Los Angeles Airport diagonally northeast bound, it was necessary to cross the VOR navigational station, located on the airport, at or above 10,000 feet in order to arrive at the next climb segment high enough to meet chart criteria that allowed for both adequate navigational signal coverage as well as terrain clearance. Suddenly a warning horn sounded, alerting us that the cabin altitude was in concert with the airplane altitude as we passed through 13,000 feet. There was danger inherent to operating without the cabin under sufficient pressure and momentarily, automatically, the passenger oxygen masks would drop unless a level-off occurred, or a descent to a lower altitude performed. When deployed en masse, the group of oxygen masks referred to as the *orange grove* were time consuming to re stow as each had to be individually wound and stored in its own, separate compartment. Pilots donned oxygen masks. I told Bohr to declare an emergency, and maneuvered to depart the airway southeast towards lower terrain.

"Request a vector away from the mountains on a southeasterly heading." He fumbled around and was slow getting a clearance. I thought he was acting disorganized. *Could this be purposeful?* I kept telling him to hurry up and looked over to see if he was simulating oxygen deprivation as part of my test. "Check your oxygen mask and flow," I ordered, then glanced at his face to see if he was properly fitted. Assured he was, I ordered abnormal and normal checklists.

"Call the company. Ask where they want us to go." Ontario, California, was their response because the weather in Los Angeles was suddenly reported below landing minimums. We made an instrument approach and landed in Ontario.

The next set of maneuvers entailed holding patterns, steep turns, and stalls. My steep turns didn't vary in altitude even one foot because I maintained the proper pitch attitude for the angle of bank. My engine out control didn't vary one degree in heading change because I maintained the proper rudder input. This performance brought *"Hummpfs"* from both men.

Approaching three hours, I was beginning to tire of the repetition. Hadn't we done all these maneuvers several times before? Emergencies, holding patterns, instrument approaches, and missed approach after missed approach – there were so many I lost count and flown each time with an engine out, over and over. I'd aptly demonstrated all.

Then Bohr turned in his seat and stared intently at Pfeel behind us. It was such an unusual stance for someone operating in the simulator that I also turned to see what was happening. A look passed between them. It was what I'd call a *knowing look* and I didn't miss it! I knew something significant was about to happen.

I continued with the instrument approach to execute still another missed approach in bad weather. Suddenly, the ground based navigational stations failed, and no information was available to the instruments. I knew where we were a moment ago, but now we were climbing on the initial part of the missed approach, about to accelerate; we were moving fast across the ground. We were below 1000 feet. I counted: one, two, three... expecting the navigational stations to resurrect. They did not. Without the benefit of an active INS, which we were not permitted to use at this point in training, I didn't know exactly where we were unless we had the good fortune to break out of the clouds, which of course we did not. I turned to look at the accomplices: they stared straight ahead ignoring my question: "Is the sim working properly?" I repeated this several times. They continued to stare straight ahead like automatons and said absolutely nothing.

Ah, the deciding moment. More important, it was a defining moment... Instantly, I recognized the catch-22 situation. If I proceeded with the company missed approach procedure, which entailed *leveling* at 1000 feet to accelerate to a faster climb speed, then I might've hit terrain in the interim, as I didn't know *exactly where* I was because nav information continued to be missing from the instrument display. Or, if I elected to climb to the published missed approach altitude which was higher than 1000 feet *before* accelerating, I would be assured of terrain clearance, but not have followed company missed approach procedures. I could blindly follow the company procedure without the input of logic, or, climb first to the published missed approach altitude to assure terrain clearance then accelerate. I had to make a choice: they had me in a Catch-22 situation; no matter which choice I made they could say I should have done the opposite. It was the most important decision of my airline career.

Like a missed approach procedure, begun *after* the point at which it *should* begin, the published procedure was no longer applicable. I felt the Delta missed approach procedure of climbing *only* to 1000 feet then accelerating before continuing climb was inapplicable also. It may be applicable momentarily, or later, when ground based power was restored and navigation systems were back up and working, but presently, they were not. I made *the* decision: it was imperative to climb first to the missed approach altitude to assure clearance from terrain, and then accelerate.

Making this conscious decision should have been met with enthusiasm by my instructors for interpreting the situation and acting accordingly, indicative of the highest level of learning. Also knowing at this moment I was testing to see if procedures were everything at Delta Air Lines; I was once again assured they were.

What I had done was not what the examiner expected, though it was safest. I was sure that if I'd followed the airline's procedure, the opposite was what he would have wanted. It was a catch-22 situation designed to end the checkride, and end it did. I would not win on this one!

The flight examiner took the simulator, slammed the power levers to idle, extended the landing gear and flaps, and said: "It's a wrap." I blinked my eyes rapidly several times to adjust for more clarity of mental vision. I was thinking that having no positive indication of my position relative to the terrain and taking action to avoid it should be regarded as the highest form of situational awareness, in that standard company procedures didn't apply. The examiner chose to see it differently.

Reality: I'd just been failed on my initial captain's simulator checkride. In that symbolic gesture of the missed approach, everything was revealed and open to see. It was foolish to think I could pass when Bohr had forewarned me the very first day. The chasm between the airline and me deepened.

Pfeel put the simulator on the ground. Seconds ticked by and my breaths came and went. He'd just ended the checkride. I was sitting motionless at the control wheel as both pilots exited their seats without speaking. The bridge was extended from simulator to building that allowed egress. I followed, after a few moments spent reflecting, while I slowly packed my Jeppesen manuals, headset, flashlight and pen into my flight case.

As I walked into the debriefing room, flight examiner Pfeel was making out the pinkslip, my assurance that I'd been failed.

"Why are you failing me?!" I asked - no, it was too late to *ask*; I demanded to know. Suddenly my chest swelled and an angry tear escaped the corner of my squinted eye.

"Situational awareness," Pfeel said stiffly as he pulled a box of tissues from a drawer.

"What?!" My hands balled into fists.

"You're not situationally aware." This was a catchy, catchall phrase. If anything, I was *too* situationally aware. Aware of the look that passed between them; aware of their advance collusion in setting up this situation - I should have known they'd come up with something. They'd created a catch-22: damned if you do, damned if you don't.

"You didn't follow the missed approach procedure..."

"I followed the *FAA* missed approach procedure. The *company* missed approach procedure was inapplicable! It's not like I hadn't made at least ten missed approaches already! I think you could see I knew how to execute a missed approach!"

I kept at him, but Pfeel refused to hear my side. "Besides," he smiled, with a toothy grin too broad and insensitive for the sad situation I was in, "I already made out your pinkslip," as if each numbered paper must be accounted for and couldn't be torn up! I could've poked out his eyeballs and raked his face but I knew it was pointless to argue. He had the hammer. I was on the verge of physical violence and considered rushing him but I wouldn't want to dignify his malevolence with a possible security breach on my part. It was a set-up. I'd been failed on my captain's check. There was no turning back.

A chain of critical events were then set in motion.

I knew at that moment my airline career was over. I remembered Lorelei's cautionary note: "Be careful, be aware. They've had more time to devise a plan." I knew I was done. I rehashed all the *what-ifs* knowing they were now but self-flagellation, useless. After reasonable treatment in Atlanta during training, I'd been lulled with potential optimism, which I'd led myself to falsely expect would prevail throughout training. This had been a mistake. *How* could I have come, open-minded and open hearted, to such a serious check without the protection of a professional witness with an impartial eye? If I had to resort to such suspicion, was this a place I even wanted to work?

Pfeel continued making out the pink slip of failure: fail one, fail all. The list of items to be flown on the recheck went on and on. I was afraid he was going to have to start page two as he delineated each item. It was agonizing, and I could have accomplished his effort more efficiently by simply writing: *repeat entire flight test.*

I was speechless when he asked for my help. *Now, I even get to make out my own pinkslip!*

"Why don't you just put **repeat entire flight test**!" I thrust forward in exasperation.

He looked at me with a question in his eyes, but said nothing. I realized he must be a new examiner because with the FAA, knowing how to fill out paperwork was a precept for the job, rudimentary. I wondered how he could have known I'd been a flight examiner except that it was probably passed around in the check department.

Lorelei was right. They'd had more time-about three years since she'd been fired - to dream up how to *legally* get rid of me. I was correct in thinking I would be targeted for *professional humiliation.*

I subdued my growing fury while Pfeel slowly completed the paperwork. Bohr's initial greeting rang over and over in my ears: "If you don't pass your simulator checkride, none of the line check instructors will sign you off on your initial operating experience." I knew I was as good as fired.

"How does this look?" Pfeel held out the pinkslip bearing endless text for me to read. Then he stepped back to lean against the windowsill.

I looked at the paper, then past the paper to him, suddenly realizing that what I'd seen with my peripheral vision was true: he was holding his unit. I gasped. He wasn't really rubbing it, just sort of fingering the tip while he absent-mindedly gazed off into space. Was he considering some aeronautical point? It was hard to believe he could be so unconscious. I tried to ignore his mannerisms. This bizarre event was not something I cared to witness or cope with. It really was *all too fucking much*!

I folded the pinkslip and put it in my pocket, then turned on my heel and strode out the door and down the hall. Soon, I felt someone walking fast beside me on the carpet. I looked over and was stunned to see it was Pfeel. Then he was in front of me, holding the door open at the end of the hall, accompanying me down the stairs walking right beside me, and lordy, lordy! Following me right outside and over to my vehicle. I didn't say a word. I was afraid what would come out! I was a volcano about to explode.

I turned my back and inserted the key into the lock of the door. He stood behind me. "Oooohhhh," he moaned. Suddenly I felt his forehead – at least I hoped it was his forehead - on my shoulder! I gasped, recoiled, and zoomed around to face him: *What on earth is happening now!*

"I hope you don't think I had an ulterior motive in mind by failing you..."

"What?" *Don't you mean, by following me?*

"I hope you don't think I have an ulterior motive in mind by failing you..."

I was completely taken aback by the mention of an ulterior motive. *He did have an ulterior motive or why would he mention it? Had he had a change of heart? Was he feeling remorse? Why else would he follow me here?*

Quickly, I opened the door, and climbed in without a word. I started the engine and immediately backed as fast as I could out of the parking space never taking my eyes from his. I put the truck in drive and tromped the accelerator. The tires screeched as I roared away from the man standing in the parking lot looking after me.

I sped through the night to a noisy motel at the airport. Out of earshot, I began screaming a furious score: "I can't believe it! I can't believe it!" Enraged, beating the steering wheel with my fists; my heart throbbed so hard I was sure it would burst.

Trucks drove by on the freeway with predictable nighttime regularity. I had no overnight bag, no nightgown, no toothbrush, and no clean clothes for tomorrow. I showered. Standing in the torrent, I made the water hot, then hotter, and showered until the hot water ran out. Some minutes later under the covers, miserable and naked, I stirred through the contents of my purse for the little slip of paper with my husband's telephone number. He was in Bryce Canyon with his red Waco, staying at a friend's cabin. His expectations would not be met this evening. I'd insulated him over the years; he'd be as dismayed as I was. It was important that I hear the sound of his voice.

"Where in the world is that phone number?" Somehow I'd misplaced it. I moved my hand in a circular motion around the inside of my purse looking for the Post-It. In exasperation, I dumped the contents out on the sheet between my legs. No little slip of paper was revealed in the mess.

I got up and looked through the pockets of my yellow sweater and slacks. No number. I was frustrated. I decided to try another tack. Dialing information, I asked: "Do you have a Paul Fox in Bryce Canyon or Tropic, please?"

After a moment the Operator said: "Yes, here it is." A computer voice came on: "At the customer's request, the number is not available." I tried another, Classic Aviation in Bryce Canyon. The call was answered by Ruby's Inn. "Mr. Fox will be in at seven tomorrow morning. Unless it's an emergency, I cannot give out his number."

"Okay. Thank you anyway." I felt like it was an emergency. *I wish I could speak with you tonight, John.*

I looked at the phone, then at the clock. It was 12:40 AM. My heartstrings were taut. I couldn't recall ever feeling this bad. Reaching out for distraction, some ease from the pain, I turned on the television. Scanning the channels, there wasn't much to select. Network TV had nothing worth watching and there was an old western not yet colorized by Ted Turner on HBO. Turner off.

I lay back on my pillow in the darkness and tried to sleep but my anxiety and the yearning to hear John's voice made it impossible. I sucked the insides of my mouth, chewed my lip. My stomach ached like it never had before. Trucks roared by on the freeway. It was one hour and twelve minutes after midnight. I knew I was so upset that I wasn't going to get one wink. I tried distracting myself, to think about other things to calm my anxiety and soothe my feelings but there was such a large question mark hanging in the air. I couldn't shake the menacing feeling hanging over me. It was as if I had done something terribly wrong. Even though this discomfort started long before tonight, I felt as if it culminated in my being failed. I'd noticed the attitudes of pilots, some I'd known for years and others I'd only recently met, changing toward me. And how about the reception I'd gotten in training? Was it unreasonable to expect a cordial welcome as a potential new and shiny captain? Instead, I got the opposite. It was as if they'd prepped to give me the hardest time possible in the captain program with Bohr leading the charge. But these were pilots, not actors, and their charade was transparent. Bohr lost no chance to negate my previous years of flying on the 1011. It was alarming that he was so openly resentful of my world while remaining confined to his. When I gave crisp and tart orders, he took exception to my tone and I became more gracious. Then he called me under-confident and slow. I couldn't win. I'd been conscientious, prepared, and worked hard in our sessions.

Now that I'd failed on this, the most important checkride of my flying career, tomorrow would bring a day of remedial simulator in preparation for the re check. If I were sharp and alert it would be better, but I'd have to do my best given a sleepless night. Realizing I'd be fired if I failed the second check made me beyond nervous. I watched the red numbers on the motel clock flip over, advancing time towards dawn.

The next few days I tried the new instructors' patience; they were brought in to teach me and were not "regulars" in the department. I made them explain things in different ways as if their explanations were confusing and they weren't coming across. My demands exasperated them. I asked each if they were licensed instructors. Most weren't. They thought I was slow. I'd show them slow; I got so slow. I knew this was my last chance, and I was beyond furious, anyway!

New lines appeared on my face. The entire inside of my mouth was sore from sucking in on my cheeks; my teeth felt loose in their gums. My lower lip looked as if I'd been in a fight and hadn't won. A new instructor in the department, whom I'd not met, kept staring at me with eyeballs so distended they looked like little points. It was obvious I was discussed behind closed doors, but there was no conspiracy!

The poor instructor who recommended me for the original checkride, who advised me over and over to expect an engine failure if a particular set of circumstances arose, was resistant and unhappy to be chosen again by Bohr to recommend me for the recheck. If I should fail, it would be a second black mark on his record, a cruel thing to do to an instructor who lived by the outcome of his students. His mannerisms gave him away. He was fidgety and nervous. I felt sorry for him, considered drawing him aside to ask why he was so unnerved, but I didn't have the heart to inquire. I am sure he was also manipulated by Bohr, set up to be fired from the department. I couldn't decide if he was nervous about losing his job, or upset he'd witnessed a plot, and as a professional, resisted being a part of it. This poor instructor insisted over and over that if I could get "... just one additional training session, he'd feel better about recommending me again."

Following this discussion, I decided to ask for an audience with Bohr. I called from my hotel room at the Airport Hilton where I'd moved to avoid the commute from Spanish Fork and the distraction of my horses. Bohr said he was free and to come on over.

He was at his desk in his office when I stepped in to ask for the additional session, which I felt, at this point, was more for redeeming my recommending instructor than helping me. There was a Sunday paper on Bohr's desk with headlines of Princess Diana's death.

"What a shame," I commented. We both scanned the headlines for a long moment. "I can't even listen to the news right now. It's all about her life, and her life's been so sad."

"I know," he said. "I turn off all those commentaries. I can't listen to them either." For a time we were lost in our thoughts about the Princess' death before returning to the issue I'd come to discuss.

"You'll have to visit your new Chief pilot, Jon Nifty, and get his approval for the additional training." As he dialed Nifty's number, he diverted his eyes up and to the left in searching thought. His face began turning red. Following a brief conversation in which he set up a meeting for the next day, he hung up, and suddenly tears flooded his eyes. I couldn't believe this display was for me as he'd treated me so badly from the first day I arrived, bullying me at every turn. I attributed it to the story about Diana, or some personal problem. In reflection, I'm certain the tears *were* for me because he knew what the meeting with Nifty would entail.

Was Bohr having a wave of remorse, now that I'd been failed on this, the most important checkride of my career? But then, he had no reason to continue his tirade; his charade. His job was done!

As I passed through the SLC terminal headed for the meeting with Nifty the next day, I looked ahead to see a tall man in a civilian suit swaggering my way. At first, all I saw was his stature and not his face. As I got closer, I realized it was Lake. Company check personnel were allowed to wear suits and ties rather than uniforms. As we passed nearly shoulder-by-shoulder without speaking, his eyes bulged out as had an aggressor's in San Diego, and were peculiarly raised to the right at a forty-five degree angle as if hiding something. Being much taller, he saw me coming somewhat before I saw him, and had time to react to my presence with this unpleasant display. He continued this stance and stare as we passed. I wondered what he'd been up to...

I knew this angry look. I'd seen it before: eyes bulging out like eggs on a cartoon character. I saw it on the Hawaiian man who accosted me on the beach in Maui and more recently, when a man near the waterfront in San Diego chased Jean Riley and me in a car. We were there to visit a farm and look at a horse. This guy in a car flipped us off as he passed. There was no reason for his inappropriate behavior, his road rage. Had he just been fired? Did his wife leave him? Been in a losing fight? I wasn't about to let him get by with it and rose to the challenge.

His displaced anger resulted in fury. He maneuvered to throw beer cans, attempting to dent our rental car. I swerved time after time on the narrow road to avoid them. I slowed; he slowed. Soon our vacant frontage road joined a street with heavy traffic. As he bolted from his beater when we were stopped by a signal, his most distinguishing feature was his eyes: they were bulged out like eggs – and enormous. There was a lot of activity on the street, but it didn't matter because no one realized our danger. It was the kind of thing I'd seen in the movies – someone gets beaten in front of a hundred people. I couldn't let that happen.

Fortunately, he didn't have a weapon, though he carried his arms as if they held a club. At that moment I wished I had a gun. Unless I did something fast, we were about to get hurt. I waited until he was halfway to our car then aggressively maneuvered across traffic onto a sidewalk and just out of reach as he grabbed for our door handle. Accelerating, we turned the corner and disappeared towards the airport.

Lake's eyes were identical: diverted up and to the right, a telltale sign of someone purposeful and aggressive. He passed me angrily and I wondered if he'd recently tried to contact Gurley and been rebuffed? Could he have just left SLC Chief Pilot Nifty's office?

I proceeded on to Nifty's office and was somewhat less than charmed by this man who chose to sit next to me in a set of visitor's chairs rather than behind his desk. I recalled he'd tried to discourage me from transferring into his base, using new freeway construction for the forthcoming 2002 Olympics as a deterrent. "But SLC is where my home is, why should I be based somewhere else?" He had never answered. While I flew Honolulu, he had been Bullman's assistant, and the only time I ever met him was when the two of them presented me with a fifteen-year pin.

Now, he began a well-rehearsed scenario, which he delivered without emotion while holding a letter for me to sign. "One silver bullet has been fired, with only one to go. There are only two such training opportunities available at Delta Air Lines. Some airlines are not so generous. They offer only one silver bullet." He smiled at his clever analogy. I wasn't amused. I signed my career away.

The next day, my apprehensive Instructor recommended me for the re check even though he was unnerved and shattered, while I couldn't seem to fly a sick pigeon on a string. This time I decided to pay little heed to his admonitions: if this happened, do this; if that happened do that... On my way out of the training center to return to the hotel, Dave Pfeel stopped me in the hall and motioned me into a briefing room. I groaned, seethed, wondered *what the hell* and reluctantly followed him. Closing the door, I stood stiffly without breathing, on terror alert, and wondered what would happen next...

To my complete astonishment, in forty-five minutes he outlined the entire checkride he'd administer the next day. I wondered if he did this for all re checks or had his conscience gotten the best of him? When he stopped to reflect on some aeronautical point, he'd lean against the window, and again take hold of his unit. I was mystified by both his behavior in my presence and by this turn of events, though I appreciated the extra information, and told him so. He advised me that the FAA would be aboard the simulator during the re check. I gulped at this additional imposition of stress, but knew it was for the best because the FAA's presence assured a predictably dogmatic test. There would be no horseplay or tricks, we'd be all business.

My husband flew in from Phoenix the next morning. He took me to lunch - I couldn't eat a thing- and drove me around the beautiful countryside. He was aware I was beyond nervous and continuously tried comforting me, though I just couldn't be comforted. He was aware of the significance of what was about to happen and embarrassed by the extent to which the airline went to brutalize me. He left me in front of the training building smiling a resolute smile as I disappeared through the glass doors.

Eventually, the oral was over and the simulator check began. The ride proceeded as Pfeel outlined the night before. There were no traps or catch 22's. It was a good experience. My flying was smooth and professional. I didn't miss a lick. My altitude and headings never varied and I knew my flying was exemplary. I had confirmation of this when FAA Rooney made the one and only comment: "Begin your turn before reaching the radio beacon so you don't go past the station." I didn't say a word, looking at him during this singular critique. I knew if I had done as he said, he would have said to do the opposite, which was what I had done in the first place.

When the checkride was over, my husband met me in the lobby and expressed dismay at how lengthy the session had been: hours. Bohr passed by and curtly invited him to sit in on the debriefing. I could tell John was taken aback at his tone but followed us upstairs anyway.

I was happy and pleased my checkride had gone so well and I'd accomplished the 737 type rating. But Bohr interrupted my light-heartedness with the stark epithet: "You'll have another checkride in three months because you failed your first one!" John physically jerked back from the table at the force of this delivery. I felt this shot was unnecessary, and unnecessarily mean. *What if my husband didn't know I'd failed my first check?* Bohr returned to being obtuse. Now he was showing off for my husband and the FAA. The line of testers smiled, apparently enjoying every word. I was completely appalled!

CHAPTER XVII

THE IOES

My first IOE - initial operating experience, as a new captain, supervised by an instructor - was out of SLC with Captain Blarney, who had wanted to become an astronaut. "I even attended the University of Michigan where all the astronauts go." He never said why he was an airline pilot instead, but he was certainly handsome enough to be an astronaut. His personality would go over well on television during interviews. Tall and willowy with an engaging smile and upbeat personality, his only drawback was that he pre-empted my initiative by telling me, the pilot, what to do, step-by-step in advance of each maneuver, the lowest level of teaching. I knew he was not very confident as an instructor.

The beginning of our third flight day, I noticed the planes on Blarney's handsome face had changed dramatically. From the moment we engaged in the briefing room before flight, I knew something had happened. Dark shadows, grimaces and worry replaced the smiles and funny little jokes of the days before. Had Bohr let him know that I failed my initial captain's check? Of course, "Those check pilots will never pass you on your IOE's if you fail your simulator check," still rang in my ears. Had Pritchard Dolby and Bill Lake called this poor guy, too? Did Blarney really have a choice? Probably a genuinely nice guy with some integrity, he'd feel sick at their disclosure. I felt sorry for him that he should have the burden of my presence.

I gave Blarney the excuse he needed to pass me off to another instructor and he leaped at it with vigor. On a clear, VMC – visual meteorological conditions – day, when taking off from Albuquerque, I quickly looked over my left shoulder for F16 traffic advised by the tower. This happened just as I was about to begin turning at an intersection during climb out. The couple of seconds it took to turn my head then look back again at the instruments was just long enough to position the airplane a couple tenths of a mile beyond the turn point – I was late for the turn.

Blarney got excited. We were busy with the departure, I was hand flying the airplane, and he was talking. I couldn't explain that I had the traffic in sight and would be turning a little late in that I was commanding retraction of the gear, flaps in sequence and power settings at the same time.

There was no potential hazard because I wouldn't have turned into the traffic, but in that few seconds, I gave Blarney the opportunity and excuse he was looking for: inattentiveness, a by-product of situational awareness, and it went into the report.

In the debriefing, Blarney's face settled into a kind of calm, the shadows and grimace gone. When he asked for comments on his instructing, "You've been an instructor for a long time; tell me how I'm doing."

I tried to be kind but honest, telling him his constant dialogue took away from his effectiveness as an instructor. "A student may not have the chance to act independent of your instructions, and may not develop initiative." Though I didn't mention it, an instructor who talked all the time displayed nervousness and little confidence in his ability to recover from situations. If he'd been quieter, I'd have told him about the traffic in sight that delayed our turn.

✈

On the second IOE, Captain Kewin was more concerned about smooth taxi with the 737 than almost anything else. All I could think of was that he wanted to get along with the flight attendants who made his dinner or secured the cabin before take-off. He was overly brusque on the controls in flight, to the point of being ham-fisted, with abrupt turns and pitch changes with g-forces that glued passengers to their seats. I thought: *forget about the taxi, what of passenger comfort in flight?*

At the end of the second day he recommended me for my checkride with the FAA. We made out the required paperwork on layover in Reno and took the rest of the afternoon off. I drove around northern Nevada looking at my old house in the shadow of Heavenly Valley. Upon returning to my room, the message light was on, with instructions to call Kewin in his room: "Meet me in the hotel coffee shop for dinner at six."

"Okay..." It wasn't exactly what I had in mind for the evening but I relented, arrived at the restaurant before he did and looked over the menu. I decided on a shrimp salad. A few minutes later Kewin sat down without saying hello or looking at me.

"I've decided to cancel your checkride." I looked at him with a question in my eyes. *Now why would he do this after he'd already scheduled it and made out all the recommending paperwork? Bingo! Number 2, and right on schedule,* before the third day flying, first recommending me, and then without another flight, canceling the scheduled checkride. I guess I could have asked him why he changed his mind when everything had gone well. It was no mystery; *someone* had contacted him.

✈

My next IOE took place in ATL with Captain Danek and we hubbed and spoked in and out of ATL for two days on very short flights to and from neighboring cities. Danek was an RD based in ATL and I was treated well by him. He recommended me for the final check. I held my breath while he made out the paperwork. But the evening before the flight, I was contacted at my hotel by Jim in training scheduling: "The boys in SLC say that since you will be based there they want to be the ones to give you your final checkride before you're released for line flying as captain."

For a moment I considered asking for both checkrides: one in ATL, where I was sure to pass, and one in SLC where I was sure to fail. I almost confided in Jim, but *what would he know and what could he do? He only followed orders.* Explaining the contrast would only confound him and make him feel as helpless as I felt. For a few long moments I didn't speak.

He filled the void with encouraging words as he'd done during the trials of my new assignment: "Don't let these guys give you a hard time," he frequently offered, now and over the years. I'd get quiet on the other end, struggling to express my gratitude but the onset of tears and the lump in my throat wouldn't let me speak, and he'd continue with business, informing me of my next assignment. If what was happening was apparent to him, wouldn't it have been to others? There was an encouraging smile in his voice as he gave me the assignment: "*This* time your final checkride is with the SLC chief pilot on the 737, Ben Rack."

I stopped breathing. I knew my heart had stopped beating.

✈

Before the appointed day arrived, I gave much thought to and review of my notes and manuals and tried not to be so downhearted because I'd done everything I could think of to assure I was prepared. I visited the video room in SLC again to view the airport layout for several of the mountain airports we'd operate in and out of on this set of flights. I reviewed the FMS video for the Model 300 series of the Boeing 737, once again realizing the only true way to know the ins and outs of the FMS was to gain experience by using it. I studied my FMS manual, read video titles, and searched for more information about the FMS. Then, I came across an *unmarked* notebook in a bookcase with recently dated lists of pilots who were *not* eligible to operate the FMS on the 300. I wondered, *What is this book doing in here, and what's this list of ineligible pilots all about?*

I concluded that if their name appeared on this list, they were ineligible to operate the airplane on the line, which was unseemly, because how could a pilot who was supposed to be checked out in the Boeing 737 be specific-model qualified-only, when either a 200 or 300 might show up at the departure gate? It would make scheduling difficult.

I'd never heard of this notebook; it wasn't mentioned during training. Maybe the FAA allowed Delta to operate the airplane by conventional methods of calculations and navigation without using the FMS, and this was the reason for the list. I'd never known the FAA to allow something like this before, and I wondered who the powerful person(s) were that didn't know how to operate the FMS on the Boeing 300?

Setting aside these questions, I practiced the entry data and reviewed the exercises given until satisfied I could operate the FMS equipment with the same proficiency I had on the 1011. I was pleased I wouldn't have to enter my name in the notebook as Model 300 FMS *ineligible*. I made a mental note to look for names on the flight schedule in operations, appearing in this notebook, to ask how they operated/navigated their aircraft if a Model 300 showed up at the gate? They couldn't fly one airplane and not another. None of it made sense. They must be turning the FMS off and proceeding with VORs as in days of yore.

✈

CHAPTER XVIII

THE FINAL CHAPTER

On the eve of my series of flights with Ben Rack, I commuted into SLC from PHX. Riding the jumpseat of the 737 because the passenger cabin was full, I noticed both pilots were short, skinny, and odd looking. I reminisced how healthy pilots used to look and compared them to these two. Where were the muscles I used to admire on pilots' arms? There was no comparison; these guys' arms were no bigger than mine. These guys looked like computer geeks. What had aviation come to?

Once level at cruise, the pilots began conversing about a new female instructor they'd encountered in ground training. They seemed quite put off by her and I wondered if their displeasure extended to women in general. From their discussion, I gleaned they felt women were in positions gratis, not because of skill or effort. It was far from a professional exchange.

I was sure my presence on the jumpseat prompted this discussion but I wasn't invited to take part. I suppose I could have jumped in - that probably was what they hoped I'd do, but they sounded so petty and paranoid that I decided not to acknowledge any of it. Whatever happened to appreciation for hard work, and ambition, the stuff it took to take on challenge? These two characters were embittered and identified their new enemy: their female counterpart.

As I looked from behind at their pimply faces and skinny arms, I recalled when pilots were handsome he-men rather than these pasty-faced, chinless creatures whose appeal to women would be minimal at best. I kept to myself during their exchange, and noticed neither wore a wedding ring. They weren't appealing men in either looks or manner, and I thought, *It's no wonder, who would want them?* I also pretended as if I didn't hear. They continued baiting me, possibly hoping I would begin an altercation that they could spool into an incident. If I verbalized objections, if I were to be so foolish, it would result in possible loss of my jumpseat privileges. Instead, I chose to gaze at the sunlit autumn countryside and marvel at the contrast of the bright blue sky overhead.

✈

"How long have we known each other?" Rack asked me now that we were seated side by side in the tight 737 cockpit. He answered his own question because after some seconds he decided that I wouldn't: "More than twenty years?" His s'es sounded like hissing. I noted he'd given prior thought to the length of our acquaintance. I hadn't. This caveat put me on alert. Rack was known *not* for his affability, this chattiness was out of character, he was known as a keen predator. I returned his inquiry with a steady gaze.

The day before, he'd called my home. When my husband answered, he told John how much he looked forward to flying with me. When I got the message, my stomach flip-flopped hearing his name. I knew Rack was maneuvering. 'I bet he's looking forward to it! He'd eat me for dinner if he could."

John admonished me for my pessimism and trepidation, and said Rack was *charming* on the phone. I'd never known Rack to be charming; it was obviously a cover. I assured John that Ben Rack hadn't snared his job by being charming, and reminded him that Rack was responsible for the strategy attacking Nancy Moore. He'd ruined her career as an educator, ending with her resignation as Superintendent of Public Instruction for the State of Utah. John got real quiet then; he'd forgotten about Nancy.

I continued, "Captain Ben Rack is razor-sharp, a warrior in the worst sense, and unyielding in pursuit." I recalled that Rack tried his hand at business in the early eighties, owning two outlets for computer retail sales in the Twin Cities, but had quit and returned to the airline. At the time, I thought his incursion into business was out of character. He hungered for intrigue and predation not usually found in the straightforward world of computer sales. Rack's success was in intelligence work. At the airline, attributes he developed in the military he brought to management, as his strong suit. "He's been handpicked to deal with me, you can count on it!"

John's normal optimism was absent hearing this explanation. I listened behind his silence, hoping he would recall my initial IOE's and what'd happened on each. I hoped my caution and paranoia seemed justified. He was silent with my assessment. Eventually, we changed to another subject.

✈

With Rack seated beside me, I flashed back to a layover twenty years ago. A band was playing a rock and roll piece, the dancers gyrated to the beat. Rack asked me to dance. Dancing with him was like trying to ride double on a pogo stick. I wondered at the time at his lack of rhythm. *How could he possibly fly well without this innate sense?*

As I began the cockpit set up for flight, I realized I should be home. I'd developed a change-of-season cold and felt congested, run down, and unhealthy. I knew I wouldn't need a costume for

Halloween in two weeks because my neglected hair had bleached into red tufts at the ends. I was exhausted and worn out by the thrashings thus far, but to describe my upcoming flights with Rack as mere thrashings would be inaccurate - they were just his style: a relentless purge.

He told me he took a flight with Clyde Bohr just before ours. If he wasn't already aware of an agenda, he became enlightened of it then, though I was sure he made himself aware of all such dramas. I wished I could have heard the tape on their voice recorder. Since I was failed on my initial simulator, then passed, it was *someone's* policy (Bohr, Lake, Dolby?) that I not be checked out as a line captain. Yet, I could name several pilots who failed and were now flying captain.

On my flights with Rack we engaged in virulent discussions on every aspect of our tasks. I didn't permit him to assume anything about my abilities or me. I fought for every point. He tried to confuse issues, but I met him at every turn, alternately defending and advancing my actions. At wit's end, these were my last chances. My graciousness went right out the window with his first attack.

One of his techniques was waiting until a situation was well past and we were into the next event, and then he'd bring up some past action. He'd planned this to have the effect of distracting me from the task at hand in that he took opportunities to discuss these points during an approach to low minimums in bad weather, or when we were maneuvering to intercept a transition on a complex departure. I'd admonish him that we should concentrate on the present rather than questioning things long gone by, until I realized this was his modus operandi. This technique might be an effective form of harassment, an attempt at diminishing and eroding confidence if I hadn't become wise to his tactics. They were underhanded though his intent was clear, and unless he advanced another strategy, I was onto him.

At one point in the SLC terminal, former chief pilot Bullman stood with him shoulder-to-shoulder about thirty feet away. I waited for our flight paperwork to come through on the computer at our departure gate. Wearing my captain's uniform and cap with all the gold braid on it, I felt conspicuous. I noticed they were talking to each other while looking at me out of the tops of their eyes. I wondered what Bullman would have to say to Rack about me. I concentrated on his lip movements. He said, "She wasn't supposed to get this far!" I realized he was probably still angry at being deposed nearly seven years before. It must have had a profound effect on him. Bullman had changed his manner toward me to one of gentlemanly politeness. He must be smarting still.

"This hasn't been easy. She's tough," Rack returned. I realized I was the subject behind closed doors.

The day came when I was scheduled again with Inspector Jake Rooney from the FAA, who'd been present during my simulator re check. He rode the jumpseat while Rack acted as copilot for my final captain's checkride. If I passed, I would be released for line duty. I'd survived Rack so far, and he could do nothing but recommend me.

The final check was to be a turnaround to Phoenix, and compared with the mountain flying we'd done for the last three days, it would be a cakewalk. But I was not to be lulled by simplicity, because this was the moment when everything that could go wrong would go wrong. Rack's performance as terminator was sure to come to full fruition on this flight.

Rack and Rooney disappeared downstairs to do the preflight on the airplane. I could see them walking around the airplane in the reflection of the terminal windows. Rack was talking nonstop, and every so often they'd pause and speak eye to eye. When they returned, Rooney's face was scarlet; his grin was ear to ear. He'd been enjoying a terrific story, couldn't take his eyes off me with that cartoon, bulging eye gawk, which assured me I was the subject. His eyes were in the distended little points I had come to recognize so well. I wondered if their conversation began with a discussion about Rack's instructions from Dolby?

The moment we were about to close the front door and depart, the gate agent arrived with our final paperwork and a healthy change of routing in our clearance. I typed the new routing information into the FMS. The program was fixed with pre programmed departures and would not accept the new route no matter what entry variations I speedily tried.

"You must depart on time with the proper routing in the FMS," both Rack and Rooney firmly warned me. It was alarming that they said this in unison using the same words, as if it had all been rehearsed. I tried over and over to delete the preprogramming, but it wouldn't disappear from the text, nor would the computer accept the new routing. There was a navigational gap in the FMS between Salt Lake City and Bryce Canyon which I couldn't resolve in the FMS. I elected to use pilot navigation via VOR's south to Bryce Canyon, and then fly the balance of the flight via the FMS. Departure time was seconds away, and I told Rack to advise clearance delivery that we wanted pilot navigation to Bryce Canyon, then FMS flight planned routing. I called for the pushback/start checklists.

Having made this command decision, I reached up to turn on the rotating beacon, moved my legs up on the pedals to release the parking brakes so the ground crew could push us off the gate, when suddenly Rooney boomed from the jumpseat: "This airplane doesn't move until the FMS is properly programmed! You have just failed your Captain's checkride!"

I was stunned. It seemed a gross over reaction. Had I not accomplished the objectives? What else could I have possibly done to satisfy the demands of regulation *and* company objectives, which was to be off the gate on time? Judging from the force of Rooney's declaration, it must have been a sensitive issue with the FAA. Was

I to be an example? I flashed on the notebook naming the *FMS Ineligible Captains.* I sat back in my chair, absolutely crushed.

Rack then took over the FMS by leaning over the consol. His broad shoulders and big hands covered the screen. We still had to fly to Phoenix with passengers, even though we were not going to be off the gate on time. Smarting with Rack's victory and my defeat, I sat in silence, watching.

Many minutes passed as my heart wildly pumped blood to my extremities. I felt the tightness of failure in my organs and struggled to maintain control while what I felt like doing was wreaking havoc, then leaving the scene of carnage. But if I were to leave, causing a further delay for a replacement captain, I'd surely be fired on the spot. There would be no retirement, no pension, and no pass privileges. I had to control myself just a bit longer to assure that future, and prove, that marking time in this malodorous job for the last twenty years, hadn't been for naught.

Then Captain Ben Rack, my copilot, and chief pilot of the 737 program in SLC, with over ten years experience flying only the 737, tried entering the new routing in the FMS, just as I did. The computer would not accept his input any more than it would mine. *Hehe.* He began sweating. *Hehe.* His typing was fast and ardent. *Hehe.* Little balls of perspiration popped up on his forehead, then ran down his face. He rubbed his eyes. His face was aflame. The underarm of his shirt had a wet circle getting wetter. Suddenly, the pungent odor of stress permeated the air.

I realized I never expected to see Rack's name in the notebook of ineligible FMS pilots, hadn't looked for it, though it might have been there. It was obvious Rack couldn't pass the parameters he set for *my* checkride. Now, it was his turn to be at risk. He was jeopardizing his career at this moment, too, because he couldn't load the FMS to the FAA's satisfaction, either. He sweated and strained, making ardent little grunting sounds with each rejected entry, and typed with the wind. I wondered if he would lose his chief pilot position, his captain's position, his airline transport certificate, *and his job* if he couldn't successfully load *the box*. The FAA man would have no second thoughts removing Rack's qualifications, thereby ruining his career, his reputation, and his life. The outcome of this was proving to be a real cliff hanger.

As I felt my heartbeat returning to normal, I knew Delta was far too anxious to fail me. Momentarily, I looked up from the Rack's tension on the panel to realize that two images appeared in the windscreen: Pritchard Dolby and Bill Lake. Their expressions showed what I'd always observed in reference to me: Dolby's sneer with his wet lips drawn back from his little teeth, and Lake's angry, bulging eyeballs. Then I flashed again on the notebook in the video room with names of pilots not qualified to operate the FMS on the 300 but who still flew the airplane as line captains. They could, but why couldn't I?

This situation had long ago left an instructive mode and veered out of control. I was embarrassed that Rack, with his ten plus years experience on the 737, couldn't get the FMS to accept his entries. Finally, the FMS accepted some backdoor input Rooney approved of though there was so much furious typing I wasn't quite sure just what was entered. Rack's big hand covered not only the keyboard but most of the small FMS screen as well. He'd attempted so many entries that he probably didn't quite understand what worked, either. We pushed off the gate perhaps as many as eighteen minutes late. Rack had failed the parameters he'd set for my checkride.

I protested having to fly the flight and was ordered, no, threatened, if I didn't assume the duties I was scheduled for. I relented, because I didn't give a fuck. The flight to PHX proceeded professionally and well. *Downhearted* would be an understated description of my feelings. I was devastated. When we parked at the gate in PHX, I said with a little smile: "How about I get off here and go on home?

My house is seven minutes from the airport." They didn't say a word, perhaps hoping I'd leave. Then I *could* be fired. But of course it wasn't going to be that easy. First, I had to attend my funeral in the chief pilot's office back in SLC. Besides, I was one of the pilots on this crew and it *was* a revenue flight. I would be even more unpopular if I left now.

Returning to SLC, Rack flew the second leg as a normal copilot would. He was jovial and too much at ease, nearly humming, with a big smile on his face. Why not? He accomplished the mission assigned him. Following a conversation with Rooney under the wing as they again preflighted the airplane in Phoenix, I took it that Rack felt his position was secure.

After landing in SLC, as the door of the airplane was opened, a note was passed up to me: I was to have an alcohol test, immediately. Insult added to injury? It was arranged, and just part of their game.

Finally, after 45 minutes lost time associated with paperwork and peeing in a bottle, I took my seat in Captain Nifty's office with Rack and Rooney in attendance. Nifty held the alcohol report. I'd tested free.

Then each man had his turn killing my airline career. As they shifted to the formality of the last bullet, in my forty five minutes absence, I'd been dealt with, discarded, and would not be given an opportunity to utter a single word. I had to sit there like the dummy they decided I was. It was so obvious there'd been an ongoing conspiracy and now they were about to deliver the final blow.

I already decided there wasn't a set of balls in the room, took an opening, and immediately began speaking. Rack audibly gasped. He went from an orgasmic facial expression to one of complete horror. In that moment, he knew that I knew their charade to be transparent.

"Since this is the end of my airline career, I have a right to speak." Somehow I found it in me to be gracious though I could have slaughtered them all. But I wouldn't compromise myself any further, this underhanded company didn't deserve even one more second of my time.

The room got so quiet I was sure I heard their hearts pounding. Suddenly their attention was riveted on me. What a contrast to the moments before when I was summarily dismissed.

Rather than the diatribe they expected, I explained my actions leading to the failure: "I've never used the delete feature of the 737-300 FMS. I'm new to *the box*, and though I've applied the requisite practice and exercises, it's only with experience that I'd be able to work deviant problems like the one given me by ATC." I was giving them a final chance to rescind their decision. I would get to fly captain. I wouldn't write this book.

"You gave me no choice but the one I made. You demanded that I be off the gate on time *and* have the FMS programmed. That was not going to happen, so I used my command authority to depart on time, fly pilot navigation to Bryce Canyon, then pick up the FMS there, a perfectly logical approach and solution to the problem."

The room got very quiet for several long moments.

"You will rotate back onto the 1011," Nifty began in a measured, surly tone. He was not going to avail me any further opportunity. It was clear I had been a problem and he'd dealt with me, and now he wanted me gone. "Training will begin in Atlanta day after tomorrow." They'd made their decision. I was to remain failed. Commenting on the notebook containing ineligible captains would be irrelevant. Further commenting on Rack's inability to pass his own checkride would be inane. They were finished with me.

Rooney and Rack stood to leave. The men had the reddest faces I'd ever seen. I carefully reached to their outstretched hands, my chest tight. I couldn't let tears cloud my eyes. Rack pulled a business card from his wallet and handed it to me. "If you need someone to talk to tonight, if you feel suicidal, call me..."

Fuck.

My emotions veered. I felt blood rise to my face. I was furious! Then the two men were gone, leaving me alone with Nifty. He resumed his line about rotating back to the 1011. He spoke in measured phrases but I wasn't listening. I knew what I was going to do. I wasn't going to let them win. I interrupted, done with his game: "No, I'm not going back to the 1011."

"What?"

"I'm not going back to the 1011."

"You have to..."

"I don't have to do anything. I'm done with you guys. I'm retiring."

"What?"

"At this moment I retire from Delta Air Lines."

"Now let's not be too hasty. Go home. Talk to your husband. Think about it for a couple of weeks. Then give me your decision."

"You have my decision right now."

"Think about it. Don't rush."

"Where's the paper? I'll sign it immediately!"

"Sleep on it tonight. Talk to your husband."

He visibly cringed when I began talking through my teeth: I assumed the same churlish expression I'd so often encountered. "You will never see my face, or hear the sound of my voice, ever again at Delta Air Lines!" I stood, leaned across his desk, and as tough, strong, and rough as I could, I pumped his hand. "I will fax you my retirement letter in the morning. Good night."

✈

I walked rapidly from the administrative offices. The pilots' lounge was vacant as I passed through. Upstairs in the terminal, I took off my captain's hat and began loosening my tie. I strode down these worn floors for the last time, pulling my suitcase and flight bag out

369

of the Delta terminal, smelling the familiar smells that now made me nauseous.

I could probably still jumpseat home to Phoenix on a Delta flight but this would be intolerable. I headed for the Southwest concourse and bought a full fare ticket.

At the top of the B concourse, I stopped in the Ladies' room. I was alone and began stripping off my uniform. I rolled the jacket and pants into a ball and shoved them through the dirty paper slot, but when I tried my captain's hat, the brim wouldn't fit, though I tried forcing it. Then I launched it like a frisbee across the room. It rotated round and round in the air, hit the wall in a stall, and spun on the handle of a shitter. I left it there, the oak leaves dull in the gloom, and finished changing into my street clothes.

There was a considerable wait in the SWA lounge for the next flight to PHX and I was about to burst. I felt like I was about to have a heart attack, so great was the pressure of failure in my chest. I found a corner with my back to the wall, and began furiously writing, cataloging events while they were fresh in my mind. My notes turned into a letter to Lorelei, for whose support I'd paid dearly.

As soon as I deplaned in Phoenix, I called John and asked if he'd give me a ride home. I held my breath, waiting, hoping he'd say yes. Airline marriages have instantly ended with the news I delivered then. I hoped mine would stand the test.

"I'll be right there."

In the time it took me to walk to arrivals, he was there. I thought about Lorelei as I walked through the terminal, and my heart went out to her because when she was fired, she had no one to meet her and take her home.

John was waiting in my red Dodge pick-up at the arrivals curb. My dogs, the Newfie, Bear, and little Ladybug, were riding in the bed of the truck. They were standing, tails wagging, excited at my appearance in the doorway. I gave each a long hug, felt the happy beating of their hearts, and buried my face for a moment in their doggy fur.

John got out and came around the truck to where I stood. I was paralyzed by his approach and my eyes brimmed with tears ready to spill. My throat tightened and I couldn't say a word. I was sure my heart had stopped, waiting for him to speak.

He moved straight in and circled my waist with his arm. Drawing me close, he looked into my eyes with his baby blues, and covered my mouth with a passionate kiss. I drowned in his embrace. "You just have to surround yourself with people of higher caliber. Welcome home, sweetheart."

✈

EPILOGUE

There were several calls for me the next day at home in Phoenix. The first one came from Noah Blood, who identified himself as the chief pilot in Salt Lake.

What happened to Nifty? He was chief pilot less than twelve hours ago!

Blood acknowledged receipt of my one line retirement letter with some amazement: " 'Today, I retire from Delta Air Lines,' period? Period!" His tone let me know he thought I should have added eloquence. Centered in the middle of the page and signed below with my last name, first and middle initials, and followed by my employee number, I could almost hear him say, "That's all? What? No thank you?"

"You're sure you want to retire? I don't want you calling in three months begging for your job back."

I tasted bile. My blood pressure immediately shot up. I considered telling him other than what I ultimately did. I needed processing telephone numbers only he had, so I could transfer all my money out of Delta. I was quick to reply: "No chance of that ever happening!" Then I asked: "Did you answer the phone as chief pilot?"

"Yes I did."

"What happened to the chief pilot of yesterday? Was Jon Nifty his name?"

"Oh, he's gone."

"Gone? Gone where?" I wondered if he was relieved of duty because he hadn't been able to set me up for being fired. Blood didn't answer. I asked northing further.

✈

Later that morning, one of the she-men called to ask: "I heard about your checkrides. I want to know if you were prepared!"

Imagine the pluck asking me such a question! My blood pressure shot up again. I could hear and feel it pumping furiously. Through the adrenaline surge and the pressure rise, I managed to keep my voice under control. For some time I'd been aware of murmured undertones around the airline to this effect.

This question came from one of the female pilots who never held a revenue-flying job before getting hired by the airlines, an amusing fact as well as an infuriating one. At over six feet tall, her height satisfied some public relations notion of a female pilot, and that was about all there was to say about she/he.

I should have been insulted by the context of the call but quickly considered why she might be calling. I had a feeling there was a general consensus around the airline that because I was married well that I hadn't carefully prepared, wasn't concerned about the outcome, and generally blew things off. Northing could have been further from the truth and I told her so. What none of these yahoos realized, was that my husband wouldn't stay married to someone he disrespected and I was his third wife. He demanded the same quality and performance from me that he expected of himself.

I replied to her question in a quiet but strained tone. She must have suspected something had been afoot, and had to hear for herself.

To complete the exchange, I said, "Not only have I studied hard but I attended a 737 school in Miami at my own expense, I've been so concerned there was an agenda awaiting my appearance in captain's school."

She answered in a flat voice. "I was afraid something like this had happened." Then after a pregnant pause she added, "Delta is very much a man's airline."

✈

Characteristically, bad news traveled fast around the airline and good news seldom traveled at all. My next call came from Kari, my friend from outside the airline married to a Delta pilot: "Bliss, Bliss, is it true? Rich Hotcheck said you failed your captain's checkride. He was absolutely gleeful!"

"I don't know a Rich Hotcheck. I think I've heard of him though I'm not sure I ever met him." But after a few moments, I realized I might have flown with him once years before, and continued, "Unless, he's the same fellow I failed on a check years ago at Flight Safety..."

"That may have been him, but, is it true? Did you fail your captain's check?" I wondered if she wanted this newsy bit of information as gossip or if she was concerned and just being a friend. Even so, I was a bit put out that she'd called. I felt really awful having to speak on the subject so soon. I hadn't had a chance to sort things out, much less respond to rumors. "Yes, I was failed on my captain's checkride."

"What happened? What happened?" Kari asked.

"I was failed and now I've retired."

✈

Alone with Kari over dinner and wine with our husbands out of town, she called on her psychiatric nurse's training and became a good sounding board. When I told her some of what I'd been though, she eventually summed things up so innocently, so sweetly: "But just think of it! For years you got to fly all over the world as an airline pilot. Wasn't *that* something?"

I guessed it really was.

✈

After that evening, and in the following weeks, in an effort to heal, because all's well that ends well - and this had *not* ended well - I tried hard to remember, not the painful, but the positive. Two weeks later, Delta sent 1,000 business cards and a framed retirement certificate with "Captain" preceding my name.

Though I'd hung up my wings and swung shut the hangar door, I knew flying had sustained me through school, men, and marriages. It'd given me something to work on, and much, much more. It was a way to view the world, seeing big things little, and feeling bigger inside. Passing up birds and smiling. I knew things, eventually, would be okay.

✈

The booth was much smaller than I would ever have imagined. The young people working there were so different from the gray haired sophisticates normally operating Delta's ticket counters; they had to be contract labor. I turned to Delta Direct telephones adjacent to the ticket counter for employee ticketing. While I waited for an operator, I reminisced about the Seattle base, the current airline situation, and articles written recently about Delta's reorganization crediting chairman and president Gerald Grinstein with not only saving Delta from the final call, but earlier, with saving Western Airlines, as well.

These reports made me squirm because I thought they were probably written by a young journalist, one who wasn't even born then, and who simply didn't know. By arranging the acquisition of Western Airlines (WAL) by Delta Air Lines (DAL) when the choice was ostensibly, either do it or die, DAL made the decision to do because it was perceived by management that its future success was in acquiring assets to grow larger, hopefully capturing its share of the traveling market. Smaller Western Airlines was succeeding without DAL at the time, having reduced its work force to a mere shadow of its former self through furlough, the remaining employees having taken 50% pay cuts for three years until the airline returned to profitability.

Unsuspecting WAL probably didn't realize DAL was in financial review before the acquisition, and while the marriage of the two seemed viable, little did they know that with this acquisition, DAL was only staving off the inevitable. It became excruciatingly clear that Delta was in trouble when parts of Pan Am were purchased perfunctorily, without proper research.

By 1990, there was general hysteria around an airline that had never seen an unprofitable year; the #3 behemoth was staggering. It now resorted to the opposite: shrinkage of its most expensive and necessary asset, the workforce. It began snapping branches off the Delta family tree. One of the first to go was the ship cleaners, then catering. These services were contracted out to independents. Only necessary services such as crews and maintenance were retained in-house.

Remaining employees were not necessarily viewed as assets, and were dealt with reflexively: those not in complicity were termed undesirable, and often professionally humiliated, a tactic successfully used by a contemporary dictator, the late Saddam Hussein of Iraq.

At Delta, there was no psychological contract, the unwritten understanding between employee and employer which results in harmony and longevity. Employees were summarily fired, retired early, or they resigned from the company.

There are many stories to be told in the rise and fall of corporations. I've wondered, what becomes of the people tossed aside? How are they affected? And so, the contract still unaddressed is the psychological one, the unwritten one. Gerald Grinstein sat on the board at Delta at the same time he sat as chairman at BNSF. Eventually, he gave up this position to become Delta's president without pay during tenure in bankruptcy. Through Grinstein's leadership the company has reorganized. Soon, he plans to retire, I've been told by his neighbors. After four years without compensation, he deserves a rest, and to be compensated, but why doesn't he stay on to see the finish, the merger between Delta and Northwest Airlines. Will there be a bad ending? There is only a small change, a rearrangement in letters, perhaps, between the word *delta* and the word *delete*.

✈

Sidney Bay in the Broughton Islands north of Vancouver came into view. We slowed to dock. Dane Campbell met our boat and helped tie up. We'd come only for crab and shrimp but found much more. His wife, Helen Piddington, floated above us on the land, a china blue and white vision coming through her garden. I bought a book she's written called *The Inlet*. We visited about the challenges of publishing while our husbands counted out our purchases. With any luck we would soon be catching our own, but for now, with friends aboard, this would do.

As we pulled away from Sidney Bay, I wondered about Helen, watching her step back through the garden, pausing to view a plant, pushing the wide brim of her hat up from over her eyes. The grayish blue structures of her compound blended in with the trees like a collage from an artist's easel. Perched above the bay, the scene holds my gaze with its artistry, and looks to be from one of her paintings. I ask myself why such a lovely woman would choose a life of hardship, so far from civilization. Perhaps there is something in this chance meeting for me. I hurry to sit and read her book. Finishing it, I realize it is in the perspective one gains from afar, and with the passage of time: recul.

GLOSSARY

Aerodynamics – the science of air as it relates to flow

ADF – Automatic Direction Finding - used in conjunction with NDB (Non Directional Beacon) for geographical position and navigation

Aileron – a flap-like device usually mounted at the trailing edge of the wing; two are used in asymmetric combination to bank the airplane

ATS – Autothrottles

Autopilot – a device used to input pilot commands to the airplane

AFM – Airplane Flight Manual

Captain – first pilot and commander of the plane

Cheechako – newcomer to Alaska

DLC – Direct Lift Control

Elevator – a device to control the airplane pitch relative to the horizon

First Officer – co pilot or second-in-command

FAA – Federal Aviation Administration - Governing authority for aviation in the U.S.

Flight Engineer – Second Officer or third in command

FMS – Flight Management System; a device used to program the performance of the airplane and its systems

Full Panel of Flight Instruments – partial panel with supporting instruments and back up for complete complement; for flight solely by reference to instruments and visually cross checking performance

GPS – Global Positioning System – uses satellites signals for position and navigation

Hand Flying – manual manipulation of the controls without the aid of an autopilot

Honey Bucket – an Alaskan irony

ILS – Instrument Landing System – a precision approach procedure to a runway

Non-Precision Approach Procedure – an instrument approach without electronic altitude guidance to a runway

NTSB – National Transportation Safety Board responsible for aviation accident investigation

POM – Pilot's Operating Manual; airplane specific

Partial Panel – of flight instruments comprised of airspeed, altimeter, needle and ball, magnetic compass; relates to the bare minimum for aircraft controlability

Precision Approach Procedure – an instrument approach with electronic directional and altitude guidance

Reversers – part of the Reverse Thrust System; any of several types designed to decelerate the aircraft on the ground, never in the air

Rudder – device which directionally controls the nose of the airplane; trims nose in a turn

Rudder pedal – a device manipulated by the pilot with pressure from either or both feet; two pedals

Sourdough – in Alaska, an old timer

Speedbrakes – flap system designed to spoil lift when on the ground; usually deploying into the airstream

Spoilers – flap system designed to spoil lift when in the air; can be same system as speedbrakes.

Throttle(s) – thrust lever(s) used for controlling power to the engine(s)

VOR – Very high frequency Omni Range; ground-based, directional navigational station received by on-board navigational equipment

Zulu – last in the alphabet, or as it relates to time in Greenwich, England, or Universal Time

Printed in the United States
141049LV00003B/2/P